TRANSNATIONAL LEGALITY

Transnational Legality

Stateless Law and International Arbitration

THOMAS SCHULTZ

OXFORD
UNIVERSITY PRESS

Great Clarendon Street, Oxford, OX2 6DP,
United Kingdom

Oxford University Press is a department of the University of Oxford.
It furthers the University's objective of excellence in research, scholarship,
and education by publishing worldwide. Oxford is a registered trade mark of
Oxford University Press in the UK and in certain other countries

© Thomas Schultz 2014

The moral rights of the author have been asserted

First Edition published in 2014

Impression: 1

All rights reserved. No part of this publication may be reproduced, stored in
a retrieval system, or transmitted, in any form or by any means, without the
prior permission in writing of Oxford University Press, or as expressly permitted
by law, by licence or under terms agreed with the appropriate reprographics
rights organization. Enquiries concerning reproduction outside the scope of the
above should be sent to the Rights Department, Oxford University Press, at the
address above

You must not circulate this work in any other form
and you must impose this same condition on any acquirer

Crown copyright material is reproduced under Class Licence
Number C01P0000148 with the permission of OPSI
and the Queen's Printer for Scotland

Published in the United States of America by Oxford University Press
198 Madison Avenue, New York, NY 10016, United States of America

British Library Cataloguing in Publication Data
Data available

Library of Congress Control Number: 2013952038

ISBN 978-0-19-964195-6

Printed and bound in Great Britain by
CPI Group (UK) Ltd, Croydon, CR0 4YY

Links to third party websites are provided by Oxford in good faith and
for information only. Oxford disclaims any responsibility for the materials
contained in any third party website referenced in this work.

To Anne-Laure

Preface

What is international arbitration really? Is it about law? Is it about recreating a new legal order for certain business transactions? Is it about elbowing aside the laws of states? Or is it about providing another type of services to the parties? But what is law in the first place? And what does it mean to create a legal order? What does it mean to provide law to people?

This book is about these kinds of puzzles. It is about the place where the idea of law and the idea of arbitration intersect. Its purpose, though, is not to provide easy answers to the riddles. It is not a cooking recipe. It is not a manual. It is not a policy paper. Its purpose is to spur people on to think about law, and about international arbitration, and about how the two of them go together.

It is a book about thinking about law, not about doing law, and not about thinking about how to do law. Thinking about law and doing law (and thinking about the latter) are clean, separate things. That distinction is unfortunately too often forgotten in certain fields of the law. There is no shortage of books on how to do law in arbitration. Many of them are truly excellent. This book has a different aim. So do not be dispirited by the time it would take to convert ideas found in this book into things to do in practice. If that is what you are trying to do, you might mean to read a book I have not written. Do not baulk, either, at my unusual lack of systematic distinctions between commercial arbitration, investment arbitration, sports arbitration, arbitration of the quality of grain, consumer arbitration, domain-name "arbitration-like" dispute resolution, and so on. Contrasts between them are of great importance in practice. But the thoughts that need to be thought concern all of them. The conclusions, of course, may well differ, but conclusions are not the point of this book. The point of this book is to take a step back and try to think differently about arbitration in general, and to think about stateless law from a specific angle.

I once gave a talk on one of the subjects of this book. After the talk, when we were all merrily having drinks, someone came up to me and said something along these lines: "Before your talk, I thought of arbitration as I think of this glass here: just a glass with a drink in it. Now I actually discern the molecules in the drink, and recognize the glass itself is liquid." Although that overstates the point (and surely the contents of the glass were of greater interest than my talk), the metaphor captures the idea: the purpose is primarily to think about the same things differently, not necessarily to change them. Changes will come later. I am an academic lawyer. That is the core of my job.

I have endeavored to make this book as accessible as possible. Of course I try to make original contributions to the matters I discuss, and therefore have to engage with quite technical questions now and then. But my greatest hope is that the book might be read by individuals who are not overly focused on the debate whether there is such a thing as a transnational arbitral legal order. That debate is an important matter in itself, but it is used here primarily as a illustration of broader questions, such as where we should see law, how the label of law may be the product of political manipulations, what it implies to call something law, and so on. Accordingly, and as you can already tell, I have tried to keep the language as simple as possible. I probably have, on occasion, traded precision for accessibility, but I did my best to keep that to parts of the reasoning where the imprecision makes no difference for my argument.

The book was almost entirely written during a fellowship, funded by the Swiss National Science Foundation, at the Graduate Institute of International and Development Studies in Geneva. As these things go, I was quite significantly influenced by certain people at this institution. Andrea Bianchi was chief among them. What I owe him is hard to capture in a concise way. My best try is this: now I am free. I also need and want to thank all the other members of the International Law Department at the Graduate Institute, for a great time amidst the pack. Also at the Institute, but in the Political Science Department, I owe much gratitude to Cédric Dupont, for unusual support and friendliness. Beyond the Institute, my debts are primarily to François Ost at the Facultés universitaires St-Louis and to Matthew Kramer at the University of Cambridge: I owe these two Shakespeare fans a pound of flesh in the region of the heart. Many thanks also to Andrew Mitchell, at the University of Melbourne, for all manner of advice and support, to Sandy Sivakumaran, at the University of Nottingham, who gave advice nudging me in the right direction at several key junctures, to Laurence Boisson de Chazournes and Makane Mbengue, at the University of Geneva, for many discussions on the variegated colors of academia, and to my brother Johannes, at the University of Durham, for endless conversations on the sense of what we do.

Thanks also to Peer Zumbansen, at the Osgoode Hall Law School, York University in Toronto, and Ralf Michaels, at Duke Law School, for their replies to an earlier article (Peer Zumbansen, "Debating Autonomy and Procedural Justice: The Lex Mercatoria in the Context of Global Governance Debates—A Reply to Thomas Schultz" (2011) 2 *Journal of International Dispute Settlement* 427 and Ralf Michaels, "A Fuller Concept of Law Beyond the State? Thoughts on Lon Fuller's Contributions to the Jurisprudence of Transnational Dispute Resolution—A Reply to Thomas Schultz" (2011) 2 *Journal of International Dispute Settlement* 417). I had further fruitful discussions or exchanges with Jean d'Aspremont, Frédéric Bachand, Sébastien Besson, Andreas Bucher, Sylvain Bollée, Gralf-Peter Calliess, Olivier Caprasse, Vincent Chetail, Andrew Clapham, Thomas Clay, Maria de la Colina, Thomas Dietz, Zachary Douglas, Paola Gaeta, Emmanuel Gaillard, Fabien Gélinas, Tom Grant, Florian Grisel, Stephanie Hofmann, David Holloway, Jean-Michel Jacquet, Emmanuel Jolivet, Marcelo Kohen, Pierre Lalive, Sébastien Manciaux, Robert Mnookin, Sophie Nappert, William Park, Luca Pasquet, Jan Paulsson, Joost Pauwelyn, Moritz Renner, Elizabeth Tuerk, Gus Van Harten, Jorge Viñuales, Stefan Vogenauer, and Fuad Zarbiev.

Then of course nothing at all would have happened without my parents: their blind support and love made everything possible. (To be sure, all errors and omissions in this book are theirs: I had no choice but to follow the instructions in the genes.) I just hope to be able to do the same when my turn comes with my own two daughters.

And then the key to it all: I thank my wife for keeping my feet on the ground. After all, that is where the roots are.

I have published early versions of some of the core arguments in Chapters 6–8, and minor points here and there, in the following journals: *The Yearbook of Private International Law*, published by Sellier European Law Publishers; *The American Journal of Jurisprudence*, published by Oxford University Press; *The European Journal of International Law*, published by Oxford University Press; *The Yale Journal of Law and Technology*, published by the Yale Law School; and *The Journal of International Dispute Settlement*, published by Oxford University Press. I am grateful to the publishers of these journals for permission to include revised versions of my works in the present book.

I delivered as talks an early version of Chapter 2 at the University of Oxford in May 2012, parts of Chapter 7 at the University of Cambridge in May 2006, and various parts of Chapter 8 at the University of Montreal in October 2008, at McGill University in June 2009, at the United Nations Commission on International Trade Law in March 2010, at the National Chiao Tung University in Taiwan in November 2011, and at the London School of Economics in April 2012. I taught much of the contents of Chapter 1 as parts of a course at the Graduate Institute of International and Development Studies. I encountered stimulating audiences at all of these institutions, to whom I am grateful.

Contents

Introduction   1

1. Why Being Law Matters   7
    1. Does Legality Determine What is Justiciable?   9
    2. Does Legality Determine What Has Access to a Legal System's Machinery?   11
    3. Does Legality Affect Power Relations?   12
    4. Sociological Relevance   14
    5. The Field of Lawyers   15
    6. A Promise of Predictability   17
    7. The Legitimate Authority Associated with Legality   20
    8. Why it Matters that Legality Matters   31

2. Legality as Rhetorical Argument   33
    1. Better and Worse Definitions of Law   35
    2. Signals of the Label of Law   36
    3. Eight Signals   38
    4. Defining Law in Accordance with its Political and Ethical Signals   45
    5. Illustrations   46

3. Shaping Legality   49
    1. Justice Beliefs in State Law   49
    2. Some Uses of Legality for Stateless Regimes   51
    3. A Battle of Candidates for Paradigm   62
    4. The Non-scalability of Law   68

4. Analytic Obstacles in Legal Positivism to Stateless Law   73
    1. Comprehensiveness, Exclusiveness, Supremacy   74
    2. Misconceptions   75

5. Relative and Absolute Legality   81
    1. Relative Legality   82
    2. Absolute Legality   87
    3. Relations Between Relative and Absolute Legality   88

6. Why Think in Terms of Legal Systems   101
    1. Law Obtains as Systems   101
    2. Can the Lex Mercatoria Not be a System?   105

7. The External Identity of a Stateless Legal System — 119
   1. International Arbitration's Own Secondary Rules — 120
   2. A Broader Idea of Secondarity — 128
   3. Powers of Reinstitutionalization — 132
   4. Powers to Prescribe — 137
   5. Powers to Adjudicate — 143
   6. Powers to Enforce — 146

8. The Internal Identity of a Stateless Legal System — 151
   1. The School of Dijon's Eschewal of Analytic Jurisprudence — 153
   2. Legitimacy and Justice for Transnational Legality: A Laconically Selective Survey — 160
   3. The Inner Morality of Arbitration Regimes — 167

References — 185
Index — 201

Introduction

In his latest book, Robert Mnookin, one of the world's most celebrated negotiation and mediation gurus, recounts an arresting story about an arbitration he co-conducted.[1] The story includes two computer giants, golf-playing executives taking key business decisions because they like someone's face, an elevator going to secret floors not listed on its control panel and guarded around the clock ("more secure than either the Pentagon or the CIA headquarters in Langley, Virginia"[2]), huge teams of hawkish lawyers, and the concept of law without the state.

The story, in a few words, goes as follows. In the early 1980s, IBM and Fujitsu got into a fight. At that time, IBM was producing mainframe computers, and the operating system to run these big, clunky machines. It was by far the biggest player on the market. Fujitsu figured there was room for competition and entered the business of manufacturing IBM-compatible computers. That was all fine and good. But what was not fine, from IBM's point of view, was that Fujitsu had its computers run on a Fujitsu operating system, which was copied from IBM's system. The Japanese company was, in substance, seeking to avoid licensing costs for the use of the original operating system. For IBM of course, it was a copyright infringement. After a few frays, the two camps settled for battle proper: an arbitration was started.

Both sides opened their checkbooks and drummed up armies of the best lawyers they could get. Uncountable press conferences were organized on both sides. Against the background of a tense general commercial relationship between Japan and the USA, the feud between the two giants further inflamed nationalist sentiments in both countries, leading to xenophobic acts on both sides. Commercial war was raging.

At some stage in this battle, a top executive at Fujitsu took what was, in hindsight, one of the company's most felicitous decisions: the appointment of Mnookin as their arbitrator. The executive had liked his face when he came to give a talk at the company's headquarters, and thus decided that the fate of their dispute should be in the hands of this unmistakably shrewd man, and of two further arbitrators.

A few years later, the case essentially settled. The outcome was the result of an imaginative approach to blending arbitration with mediation devised by Mnookin

---

[1] Robert Mnookin, *Bargaining with the Devil: When to Negotiate, When to Fight* (Simon & Schuster 2010) 139–76.
[2] Mnookin, *"Bargaining with the Devil,"* 170.

and Jack Jones, one of the two other arbitrators. Fujitsu obtained the right to use software copied from IBM, and even to have access to more of its source code. Access to the code, however, would only take place in a specific facility, located on the top two floors of some nondescript office building in a small Japanese town. The affairs taking place on these floors were kept a tight secret. The floors could only be accessed from an elevator which displayed no buttons for these floors. (A spy movie would definitely have been a more natural habitat for such a facility.) In return, IBM would be paid a fee, whose amount was set in an adjudicative process by Mnookin and Jones. In sum, the arbitration generated a complex, multifaceted agreement between the parties, parts of which had been produced by mediation, while others resulted from adjudicated decisions. Mnookin refers to the arrangement as the "regime" or "regimen" that the arbitration created.

Crucially, a few years before the arbitration was started, IBM and Fujitsu had already reached a first agreement. It had fallen apart though, primarily because of a cultural misunderstanding: one party considered the words of the agreement to be strictly binding, while the other thought the agreement was rather a commitment to cooperate in the future in a friendly way. In other words, sheer bindingness, or *pacta sunt servanda*, was assumed on the one hand, and something in the league of moral authority was understood on the other.

But let us return to the regime created by the arbitration. In Mnookin's words, the objective was this: "The beauty of this regimen, we thought, was that it would liberate the parties from the realm of ordinary intellectual property law, which wasn't developed enough to be of much use to them in this conflict. Instead, it empowered Jones and Mnookin to create private law that would apply only to the relationship between IBM and Fujitsu."[3]

Notice these words: *private* law. This is meant not, of course, as private law as in the classical private/public law dichotomy, where the former deals with law made by states to regulate relationships between individuals and the latter relates to law made by states to govern relationships between individuals and the government. What is meant here is private as in "private-made law," law made not by the state but by private parties (the arbitrators and the companies). Private law as opposed to state law. Private law, in Mnookin's words, as opposed to "ordinary law."[4] Private law as opposed to law tout court, one may be tempted to say.

But was this really private *law*? Mnookin is not a careless writer. He is attentive to detail. And he is particularly smart—certainly one of the smartest people I have met. To be sure, it was not a slip of the tongue. What plainly transpires in his story is that the parties wanted predictability in future dealings. They wanted guideposts for future self-directed action. Mnookin speaks of "certainty" in their continuing relationship, of "clear standards" and "precise rules,"[5] and of creating a "new regime so that both companies could get on with their real business."[6] But you also get the sense from the tale that both parties, and the arbitrators, wanted to achieve something honorable, an outcome to the case that was morally

---

[3] Mnookin, "*Bargaining with the Devil*," 141.
[4] Mnookin, "*Bargaining with the Devil*," 176.
[5] Mnookin, "*Bargaining with the Devil*," 164.
[6] Mnookin, "*Bargaining with the Devil*," 169.

authoritative, something that "counts" beyond its sheer bindingness. It was definitely not meant to be some obscure deal circumventing "the law," the upshot of a war, of the use of economic force. Something much more "civilized" was evidently meant. The label of law seems intuitively fitting for that purpose.

But the label of law can also be used for darker purposes. To see the point, consider the idea of "arbitration dependents." I mean people, unlike Mnookin, whose income, social status, intellectual recognition, or professional power, depends to a large extent on arbitration, on the continued existence of arbitration as we have known it for the last few decades. For such people, arbitration must not change. They would fight tooth and nail to keep the arbitration system as it is, or similar to it, to protect it from possibly destabilizing interferences. One weapon in that fight is the label of law: the elevation of arbitration to a transnational *legal* order. A metaphor might be apposite here: the idea is to bless arbitration with the holy water of legality. Law, or legality, is indeed appealing, legitimizing, and evokes justice. Labeling arbitration as a *law*-creating institution protects it. Stamping the current arbitration regime as a transnational, stateless *legal* regime cushions it in layers of respectability and allure.[7] Using the label of law in such a way is, admittedly, a fair marketing strategy for arbitration. But a marketing strategy it is.

Now, beyond the purposes in using the label of law, *can* we in fact speak of the arbitration regime as a legal regime? To start with extremes, can we call just anything law? Can we at least call law anything that is obligatory? It certainly has been tried in the history of the concept of law. We should briefly recall an old debate in legal anthropology: Bronislaw Malinowksi, a key figure in the field, in essence considered that law should be defined by function (primarily bindingness or obligatoriness) and not form.[8] This led him to such an extensive take of legality that Sally Falk Moore, another personality in legal anthropology, argued that "the conception of law that Malinowksi propounded was so broad that it was virtually undistinguishable from a study of the obligatory aspect of all social relationships."[9] Then again, does it matter that we cannot grasp law as a distinct province of study? Put differently, does it matter that we call something law? If it matters (and it does), how should its significance influence what we should be content to call law? Put differently again, how should the consequences of calling something law shape the conception of legality we use in the first place? And if we then take these musings back to arbitration, what should we make of the idea that international arbitration is an instance of transnational legality without the state? Do arbitrators make law? To be sure, they do not make any form of domestic law—they do not make French law or English law or Brazilian law. If at least one of the parties in the case is a state, arbitrators might contribute to the making of the law that governs the behavior of

---

[7] Critics should object that there is not one international arbitration regime, but several. The point is taken, but its impact on the argument is nil.

[8] Bronislaw Malinowksi, *Crime and Custom in Savage Society* (first published 1926, Littlefield Adams 1985).

[9] Sally Falk Moore, *Law as Process. An Anthropological Approach* (first published 1970, LIT 2000) 220.

states, which is in principle made by states: I mean public international law.[10] But do they make stateless law? Do they make private law? Can they? What would it take for them to do so?

These are the type of questions I address in this book. My purpose plainly is not to close any debate. I do not intend an exhaustive treatment of any area of legal scholarship, as lawyers sometimes maladroitly think they can provide. I do not seek to supply answers that have a pretense to finality. My purpose is to open the debate on arbitration as transnational law to new territories, in the hope that it helps us better understand both the idea of arbitration and the idea of law without the state. It is the debate that matters, and that it be informed.

The debate on the legality of non-state normative systems is much less an innocent pastime for legal scholars, philosophers, and sociologists than most people assume. Attempts to define law and to define law beyond the state are not dry, technical, semantical battles. Calling something law has consequences. It is likely to determine how we think about stateless forms of socio-legal organization and regulation. It is likely to sway the way we think about arbitration for instance. Given as much, it is likely to influence the future of arbitration. The fact that the label of law has consequences contributes to making it worthwhile to think about what we should be willing to call law. Let me say that again: the consequences of calling something law should inform what we should call law. A parallel might help: when we call something a chair, one consequence is that people will take it for granted that they can sit on it. If we craft a definition of a chair that includes objects which cannot be sat on, we likely will have miscarried, unless of course our intent is to trick people into attempting to sit on something and tumble, or to illude them into buying something that we suppose would not be bought if it did not come with the label of "chair." The same idea applies to law.

Many of the questions I address are general points about law without the state. The attempts to elucidate these questions and to suggest possible answers are meant to be generally valid, much beyond international arbitration. The illustrations and examples, on the other hand, will be drawn primarily from the field of international arbitration, in the hope to contribute to both the scholarship dealing with law without territory and the state and the scholarship on the nature of arbitration.

The point of departure is this: a battle of candidates for paradigm is brewing in law. The paradigm according to which law is necessarily state law—the law produced by a state or a collectivity of states—still profoundly marks the way we usually think about law. It still largely determines what is taught in law school. It still tells lawyers what their job is about. But that paradigm is also increasingly unsatisfactory. It captures a decreasing share of reality, as powers beyond the state are getting stronger and better organized. The number of situations and the variegatedness of behavior it allows us to understand and predict is shrinking: individuals, companies, institutions, financial markets, and many other non-state

---

[10] Eric de Brabandère, "Arbitral Decisions as a Source of International Investment Law" in Tarcisio Gazzini and Eric de Brabandère (eds), *International Investment Law. The Sources of Rights and Obligations* (Martinus Nijoff 2012).

actors are directing their conduct ever more often according to norms not produced by states. During a few centuries, the relationship between law and society was satisfactorily apprehended by the proxy of the relationship between law and the state: society was primarily governed within states and it was thus acceptable to represent governance by law as governance by state law.[11] But the paradigm that law is perforce state law is less and less convincing. As a consequence, broader accounts of what law may be are being pushed. These competing accounts are candidates to become, sometime in the future, the new paradigm of what we collectively recognize and treat as law.

This development, this battle of paradigm candidates, takes place in sundry fields of the law. It has long been prevalent in the field of commercial law. It is increasingly marked in international law.[12] But the mood is perhaps most expansive in the area of international arbitration—a type of commercial law at an international level. Emmanuel Gaillard, a particularly influential practitioner and scholar in this field, has spruced up the issue a few years ago. There currently are, he says, three paradigm candidates (he speaks of "representations"[13]) to account for the legal character, or legality, or legal existence, of international arbitration. That is, the existence of international arbitration as a legal phenomenon can by explained in one of three ways: either it merely forms part of the national legal order of the seat of each arbitration; or it forms part of all the national legal orders that would recognize each arbitration's award; or international arbitration, as a set of general and individual norms forming a regime, is of a legal nature because it is a legal system in itself: a transnational, stateless, arbitral legal order.[14] Gaillard himself is a proponent of the third candidate for paradigm. My point is not so much to ponder whether he is right or wrong, to extol the virtues of his views, or to carp when he enlists the help of slogans. My point is to offer ruminations on what this question of legality is all about, on the fundamental implications of this battle of paradigms, and on the analytical soundness of some of the debate's main tenets. It is to a large extent a meta-theoretical discussion: a discussion in the realm of theories about theories on arbitration and legality. It is not for someone in search of quick truths or fashionable ideas.

Readers seeking factual descriptions of arbitration regimes, or the latest news about them, would be better served by other studies, of which there really are plenty. This is a book about ideas, about ways to think about law, law without the state, and arbitration as a device of socio-legal regulation. It probably does not provide any information that will help anyone win any case before any tribunal. But perhaps it will help certain people think differently about arbitration and about law,

---

[11] Peer Zumbansen, "Law and Legal Pluralism: Hybridity in Transnational Governance" in Poul Kjaer, Paulius Jurcys, and Ren Yatsunami (eds), *Regulatory Hybridization in the Transnational Sphere* (Brill 2013).
[12] Andrea Bianchi, "Reflexive Butterfly Catching: Insights from a Situated Catcher" in Joost Pauwelyn, Ramses Wessel, and Jan Wouters (eds), *Informal International Lawmaking* (OUP 2012).
[13] Emmanuel Gaillard, "The Representations of International Arbitration" (2010) 1 *Journal of International Dispute Settlement* 271.
[14] Emmanuel Gaillard, *Legal Theory of International Arbitration* (Martinus Nijhoff 2010) 13–66.

or allow them to better understand why they think about these things the way they do.

International arbitration, and more generally international dispute settlement, is commonly represented as a technical field, as a subject-matter that is all about procedural technicalities and black letter law intricacies. This must stop. We cannot shy away from our social responsibilities by taking refuge in the mechanics of the law. Dispute settlement, at heart, is anything but a dry, technical, mechanical field. It is about justice. It is about our fundamental human aspirations. It is about where there is law and where there is not. But of course there is also malice in this wonderland. This book seeks to do justice to this cheerful state of affairs, by attempting to make a dent in it.

1
Why Being Law Matters

On important issues that are difficult to grasp, the world is often divided into two rather strongly opposed camps. There are those who believe a free economy is our greatest achievement and those who doubt it. There are those who believe in all sorts of deities and that they will do something for us at some stage (and for the free economy) and those who doubt it. There are those who drink tea at the slightest provocation and those who look rather exasperated. There are those who understand the point of debating football and those who do not. Then there are those who warmly embrace any attempt to understand what law is, as if the highest calling of every lawyer is to pause and muse on what this thing is we invoke every day. And there are those who decry any such attempt as a rather pointless exercise in settling semantics, as if we understood law better the less we ruminate on what it actually is, as if conceptual analysis muddled our problem-solving reasoning.

Those who mistrust discussions about the nature of law are likely to be doing something else right now, I mean something else than actually reading this. So the reader and I might be tempted to think that there is no point in preaching to the converted. We might dispense with explaining why such contemplations are important and, just like those who are into football, undeviatingly plunge into the depths of the subject matter. We could simply, with no preliminaries, enjoy ourselves juggling with the elements that may make law *law* when we are not talking about the public legal system of the state. We might just proclaim our belonging to the social group of those who enjoy theoretical thinking, whose social norms allow us, even encourage us to mull over the contours of legality. After all, the question of what law is when it is not state law is sufficiently bewildered and convoluted in the literature to warrant a nearly endless flow of attempts at clarification (or of attempts to make the question even more complex, in order to eventually understand it, which then simplifies it). But we should not.

We should not forgo discussing why it is important to entertain the question, to expound why it is meaningful to dwell on just what legality is, because the reasons that make that question important inform how we discuss it, and what exactly we discuss. And in the final analysis these reasons imbue what we should consider to be law without the state. My discussions of why it is important to understand the nature of legality are undertaken not so much in the hope to tie in those in skeptical mode. They are rather made to take a step back from the efforts of our camp to elucidate the nature of law, not to question whether we should do it, but to put what is at stake more cleanly on the table. We might then, ultimately, negotiate at that table to seek an agreement about what transnational legality and stateless law may mean, or for whom it may legitimately mean what.

Let me spin this idea differently. Radically simplified, the question of why it is consequential to talk about legality may be reduced to two points. The first is that it matters to call something law: it carries weight to affix the label of law to a given regime. Being law matters. The second relates to the broader question of why analytic jurisprudence matters and what it is all about: it is not an attempt to contribute to a dictionary but an attempt to understand a social institution. I shall laconically consider these two points in turn.

Calling something law has profound consequences. These consequences should be taken into consideration when we wonder about where to affix the label of law. They should inform our reasoning when we ponder the definition of that label. For freedom is a problem here: little seems to prevent us from calling anything law, from defining law in any way we wish. A definition of law could possibly extend so far as to include every possible social norm, or be so restrictive as to regard as law only highly complex public regimes approved by thinkers of the liberal-democratic tradition. In the sand between these two rocks we shall draw a line. But where? Undoubtedly some definitions make more sense than others. To be precise, as we will discuss at many junctures in this book, they make more sense to some people in some situations. One way to understand if, how and when they make sense is by trying to expound why being law matters, what some of the consequences are of calling something law. Recall the parallel from the introduction: calling something a chair will entice people to sit on it, and that expectable behavior should inform what we call a chair. The purpose of this chapter is to lay the cornerstone of this idea by drawing a few basic distinctions about what legality is and is not. Subsequent chapters will flesh out this idea that calling something law has profound consequences, and how these consequences can and should be taken into consideration when deciding what to call law.

Now to the second point. Scott Shapiro puts it thus in a recent book called, precisely, *Legality*: "Should analytic jurisprudence matter to anyone other than philosophers and, if so, why?"[1] Analytic jurisprudence is usually opposed to normative jurisprudence. Normative jurisprudence, which in French is often equated with *philosophie du droit*, deals primarily with moral questions in law. It entertains questions such as what the writings of Shakespeare tell us about the societal *poiesis* or genesis of law,[2] what the sort of justice is that law seeks to pursue, why talion (the idea in early Babylonian, biblical, and Roman law of vengeance authorized by law, or the principle of an eye for an eye, or tit for tat) is a bad thing for society, whether we should grant animals rights, or trees and plants for that matter. Analytic jurisprudence, which in French is often equated with *théorie du droit*, is more concerned with questions such as what is law, what is a legal system, what is a norm, how can we know, how is a legal system organized (as a pyramid, or as a combination of primary and secondary rules, or as a network of tangled

---

[1] Scott J Shapiro, *Legality* (Belknap Press 2011) 4.
[2] François Ost, *Shakespeare, la comédie de la loi* (Michalon 2012).

hierarchies among legal norms, etc). It thus deals with questions of epistemology, that is the study of knowledge, as "*episteme*" means knowledge. The two forms of jurisprudence are not cleanly separate, since moral questions may enter reasonings about the nature of law, for instance, because law is sometimes considered to be morally valuable or to be creating moral reasons to obey it.

The problem with analytic jurisprudence, as Scott Shapiro explains, is that its usefulness is far from obvious to most people. It is intuitively understandable why we should reflect on moral questions in law, but inquiring about the nature of law in general? Is this not simply an effort to write an entry for an encyclopedia, that is an effort to make sure we all know what we are respectively talking about when we use the word "law"? For if defining law is just a question of convention, then surely legal philosophers are not needed. And surely the answer to the question whether stateless law is law would be negative, since the conventional use of the word has not yet extended to law without the state, except in certain circles. But no, that is not the point of analytic jurisprudence. It rather is, in the words of Scott Shapiro, "an effort to understand the nature of a social institution and its products."[3] Put somewhat differently, analytic jurisprudence is, in part, an effort to provide us with tools to decide when we can, and when we should, recognize "the state of affairs that obtains when a legal system exists and functions."[4] So the point is this: we have to understand at least some of the dimensions that make law the social institution that it is when we endeavor to decide (and I do mean *decide*) if and where to see law without the state. Understanding how a legal system is organized helps us in this task.

One way to see just how this works is to look beyond analytic legal philosophy. That is, a pregnant way to determine how we should discuss legality and what exactly we should discuss is to start from thoughtful cogitations made outside the field of analytic jurisprudence. Such cogitations sometimes mark out particularly sensible and pragmatic questions, whose analytic treatment allows us to draw a few cardinal distinctions that usefully orient our subsequent ruminations. One of the best such cogitations is provided by Joost Pauwelyn, a leading scholar in international economic law, in a book chapter entitled "Is it International Law or Not and Does it Even Matter?"[5] His treatment of that matter will set the main guideposts for this chapter. The questions he asks in his work, which are crucial for the purposes of his undertaking, lead us to distinctions and questions that are central to our endeavors.

1. Does Legality Determine What is Justiciable?

A first intuitive, and very understandable, reaction to the question whether it matters that anything is law would be to argue that it determines what is justiciable.

---

[3] Shapiro, *Legality*, 7.
[4] Matthew H Kramer, "On the Moral Status of the Rule of Law" (2003) 63 *Cambridge Law Journal* 65, 65.
[5] Joost Pauwelyn, "Is it International Law or Not and Does it Even Matter?" in Joost Pauwelyn, Ramses Wessel, and Jan Wouters (eds), *Informal International Lawmaking* (Oxford University Press 2012).

Surely if something is law, so the thinking goes, it means we can invoke it in court and have it enforced by legal institutions. But that argument, even though it seems sensible, is not accurate and calls for a first basic distinction in thinking about legality.

Joost Pauwelyn provides an excellent example of the problem. Under the heading "Criteria to Distinguish Between Law and Non-Law,"[6] he mentions the idea that "form or certain formalities or procedural steps elevate an instrument from non-law to law."[7] He refers to the examples of enactment by the legislature in domestic law and the use of a treaty to make international law. He then goes on to doubt this formalistic approach in the context of international law, arguing that "[o]ral agreements or statements can ... be binding under international law without any formality."[8] He finds evidence of the faultiness of the formalistic approach in distinguishing law from non-law in a study by Jan Klabbers. The study shows that international courts and tribunals "applied norms with a benign neglect of the type of instruments in which the norm was laid down."[9] What Pauwelyn and Klabbers do here is refer to the practice of certain officials of the legal system that international law is. That is to say, certain officials of that legal system recognize as international law certain norms on conditions that are independent of formality. What is being discussed here is not what law is, but what international law is. The argument is an attempt to define what forms part of international law, not to define law.

The question Pauwelyn in fact entertains is this: do the norms under consideration (certain types of informally created norms, which do not need to be further specified here) belong to the legal system that international law is. Because if they do, they can be applied—that is the point of justiciability—by the officials of the system whose job is to apply the norms of the system, such as international courts and tribunals. Of course the reasoning is circular: certain norms are part of international law because they are applied by international courts and tribunals; these norms can be invoked, and thus applied (they are justiciable) because they are international law. Disquieting as the circularity may seem, the argument is jurisprudentially correct, and very simply so: the officials of the legal system decide what they recognize as law, thereby exerting the powers bestowed upon them by the system's secondary rules of recognition. The empirical manifestation of that decision is to be found in the judgments of these courts. The officials of the legal system of international law do what they do and we as analysts just observe it: their views are relative to their own legal system only.

A positive answer to the question "is it international law?" means the norms can, in principle, be invoked before judicial bodies applying international law. This question pertains to an internal point of view; it is a matter of belonging to a system: are the norms under analysis part of the legal system of reference? It is the same question as asking "is it French law?" or "is it English law?" It is a question that

---

[6] Pauwelyn, "Is it International Law," 131. [7] Pauwelyn, "Is it International Law," 131.
[8] Pauwelyn, "Is it International Law," 132.
[9] Jan Klabbers, "The Undesirability of Soft Law" (1998) 67 *Nordic Journal of International Law* 381, 388–9.

can be put as: "whose rule is that?"[10] or "what is the pedigree of that rule?" Now, it is a very different thing to take an external point of view and ask "is all of this law?" It does not follow from the fact that a norm is *law* that it is justiciable, invokable, applicable before international courts and tribunals: it may be law but not be recognized by the legal system of international law. (Think of: "whose rule is that?") Conversely, it may (analytically) be "international law" but not be law: if international law is not law, if the system of international law is not law, when what that system recognizes as its own is not law either.

The question of justiciability is the question of a norm's belonging to a given normative system. If it belongs to that normative system, it is enforceable, justiciable in that system. Consequently, the question "does legality determine what is justiciable, what is legally enforceable?" yields a negative answer. Justiciability is a question of "relative legality," not "absolute legality," as Chapter 5 will argue: relative legality asks the question "what does the legal system of reference recognize as law?" or "is it law according to the legal system of reference?", not "is it law?"

2. Does Legality Determine What Has Access to a Legal System's Machinery?

The same point can be made from a different angle: if a norm is a norm of international law, as Pauwelyn points out, it benefits from the system's machinery: its rules of creation, interpretation, and change, for instance, or its enforcement mechanism.[11] Again, this is not a question of legality ("is it law?"), but a question of belonging to a system. If a norm is part of any normative system (think of the rules of the mafia), it benefits from the machinery of that normative system, for instance its enforcement mechanism (to be sure the mafia has an enforcement mechanism for its rules). It does not mean that the normative system in question is law. It does not mean that the norm in question is law.

You may now start to think that this may well be so, but for all practical purposes the questions "is it part of international law?" and "is it law?" are the same, because if a norm is part of international law, then for all practical purposes we may say that it is law. This charge of inconsequentiality leveled at the distinction is to a certain extent correct with regard to norms. If a norm is a norm of international law, or of French or English law, we may safely consider it to be a legal norm. Seen from the outside, from an external perspective, we simply observe that French law says that something is part of French law, and therefore we can take it to be law. Strictly speaking we should say that the norm is a legal norm from the perspective of the French legal system, not that it is a legal norm per se. But practically that is a difference that makes no difference.

The matter becomes trickier, and the distinction consequential, when we consider the legality—that is, the nature as law—of a normative system, not of a norm.

---

[10] Shapiro, *Legality*, 11.   [11] Pauwelyn, "Is it International Law," 147–8.

For instance, certain French authors maintain that French law considers that international arbitration is a legal system of its own.[12] But international arbitration is not a legal system according to the English legal system, for example, nor does it seem to be for most other national legal systems in the world today. This, however, has nothing to say about whether international arbitration as a normative system actually is, per se, a legal system.

The matter becomes yet a bit trickier if we consider the legality of the *lex mercatoria*. Let us assume, *ex hypothesi*, that the international arbitration normative regime recognizes the *lex mercatoria* as law. But we do not (yet) know whether the arbitration normative system itself is law. So the only analytically correct statement would be the following: the *lex mercatoria* is a legal system from the point of view of the international arbitration system, which itself is a legal system according to the French legal system.

The distinction between "what is law" and "what belongs to a given normative system" matters because the criteria to determine whether a normative system is law in the first place may be, and often are, very different from the criteria to determine whether a norm is part of a given system. The criteria to determine whether something is law are entirely open for debate: everyone can validly have a view about it. Some views will simply be better than others. However, the criteria to determine whether a norm belongs to a given system are set by the system that recognizes the norm. Only the system itself can validly have a say about what it wishes to recognize. While everyone can have a view about what a given system recognizes as law, some of these views will be correct and others will be wrong, depending on what the system actually says.

3. Does Legality Affect Power Relations?

As I said, we can distinguish between recognizing what forms part of a given legal or normative system and recognizing what a legal system is. We have seen analytical reasons for doing it. But there is a further reason, of a rather ethical nature, why we should make the distinction. It is to be found in one of the relations that law has with power.

Let us again use Pauwelyn's lucid articulation of the matter as a starting point. He asks whether "a broad definition of law defend[s] the weak or empower[s] the strong."[13] His argument is this: by recognizing who makes law, we give certain people or institutions power. By descriptively recognizing something as law, we normatively recognize the authors of that something as individuals or institutions that have the power to make things that count as law. We grant them that power through our definition of law. Pauwelyn illustrates his argument by referring to Michael Reisman when he considers that extending the concept of law to include soft law creates a "redistribution of political power in certain areas of international

---

[12] Emmanuel Gaillard, *Legal Theory of International Arbitration* (Martinus Nijhoff 2010) 188ff.
[13] Pauwelyn, "Is it International Law," 149.

lawmaking."[14] A redefinition of what forms part of international law, in other words, is a challenge to the Establishment in the field of international law.

Now to our distinction. Recognizing what forms part of international law, what forms part of the legal system that we may assume international law to be, is a way to determine who has a say in the making of international law. The same reasoning of course applies to any other legal system, beyond international law. To a certain extent, the idea may be understood by thinking of the French Revolution of 1789: the Third Estate (the commoners) were trying to have a say in the making of French law just like the First and Second Estate (the Nobility and the Clergy). Brutally simplified, it was a question of who had a right to physically sit in the house of parliament. The importance of the question in terms of power distribution is here quite obvious. In drawing this parallel, we might think of non-state actors as the Third Estate, and states as the First and Second Estate. The question of the recognition as international law of norms not made by states is a battle for the recognition of non-state actors. (To be sure, this is a rhetorically inaccurate metaphor: clearly it was morally wrong that the Third Estate, representing 97 percent of the population, had no say in the laws of France, while the First and Second Estate barely acted on behalf of constituencies other than themselves. A broader understanding of law, then, was a defense of the weak. States on the other hand, at least in theory, are acting on behalf of their population. And non-state actors are not necessarily weak institutions or individuals.)

Let us shift to the question of the recognition of what a legal system is: not what forms part of a given legal system whose legality is in principle uncontroversial, but whether a given normative system can, for itself, be considered to be law. Does legality so understood have an impact on power relations? The answer lies in the affirmative. The idea that the label of law is important because it has a bearing on the power relations of the various actors involved in a given social field may be explained by reference to law's authority.

Law demands to be respected. Instances of law are regimes of effective governance that are to a large extent autonomous and for their greatest part not hierarchically submitted to any other normative system. As Joseph Raz puts it, "[t]here can be human societies which are not governed by law at all. But if a society is subject to a legal system then that system is the most important institutionalized system to which it is subjected."[15] Law places itself above most or all other norms, trumping social and moral norms. Roughly simplified and as a matter of general principle, it is condonable to act against social or moral norms if the law forces you to do so, but it is not exculpatory when social or normal norms require you to act against the law.[16]

How does law do that? On what grounds does law claim its superiority over all other norms? One ground may be found in law's inherent claim to legitimacy,

---

[14] W Michael Reisman, "A Hard Look at Soft Law: Remarks" (1988) 82 *American Society of International Law Proceedings* 371, 376.
[15] Joseph Raz, *The Authority of Law* (2nd edn, Oxford University Press 2009) 120.
[16] This is, as I said, a generality. It has limits. See for instance Jan Klabbers and Touko Piiparinen (eds), *Normative Pluralism and International Law: Exploring Global Governance* (Cambridge University Press 2013).

because law is intimately associated with justice. To call a non-state regime (such as the international arbitration regime) law is a way to say that the normative power that this regime has should be recognized as having a legitimate claim to superiority. There is an inherent violence in characterizing a normative system as law, because it gives that normative regime a form of legitimacy in its claim not only to regulate but also to try to be superior to other norms.[17]

The salient question that emerges here in the connection between legality and power relations is this: to what extent do we want to respectively empower the state and the private sector? No one would reasonably deny that state law is law, but the further we extend the definition of law to cover instances of law without the state, the further we empower the private sector: non-state actors and communities, civil society, but also financial markets and the arbitration community.

Whether that is a matter of empowering the weak or the strong, to echo Pauwelyn's point, is a vast empirical question. Regardless of whether we deal with the question of what forms part of a given legal system or with the question of what law is and where it is thus to be found, the answer to the interrogation whether it empowers the weak or the strong is an empirical problem. The answer varies with time, geography, subject-matter, and many other factors. It is not a matter of abstract analytical investigation. So while the label of law—legality—matters because when it is applied to a regime (for instance the international arbitration regime), it empowers it and gives it a form of legitimacy, we can make no conclusive statement from an analytical, theoretical a priori perspective about whether this strengthens the weak or the strong.

We shall return to this problem of law's authority and superiority and the violence inherent in the label of law at many junctures throughout this book, starting from the final section of this chapter. But for the time being, let us shift the focus to two more basic ways in which the label of law matters.

4. Sociological Relevance

Characterizing something as law does not only accord it legitimacy in power and thus power. Affixing the label of law to a stateless normative system is also a means to bring that non-state legal system within the ambit of legal reasoning.

If you are a lawyer, or if you are otherwise interested in law, and if you attempt to map what plays a major role in regulating a given social field, you may miss a big chunk of reality if you use a too narrow understanding of law. Pauwelyn captures the idea nicely for the field of international law: "should international law give up the little formalism it has (eg thin State consent and legal capacity of actors) and embrace [a greater variety of norms] so as to stay sociologically relevant and put international law back on the map?"[18]

---

[17] Robert Cover, "Nomos and Narrative" in Martha Minow, Michael Ryan, and Austin Sarat (eds), *Narrative, Violence, and the Law: The Essays of Robert Cover* (University of Michigan Press 1993).
[18] Pauwelyn, "Is it International Law," 151.

In a different area, Lawrence Lessig has gone to great lengths in expounding the importance and fruitfulness of seeing law on the internet where legal statists would merely see social norms and real-world constraints. It is a context where the problem of the lack of sociological relevance of the dominant conceptions of law is probably even more acute. Lessig's best known, and arguably most important book focuses specifically on this question. Entitled *Code and Other Laws of Cyberspace*, the book revolves around one basic point: if you want to understand what orients behavior on the internet, for instance in order to reflect on what laws should be enacted in order to reorient that behavior, you will obtain an extremely incomplete and altogether wrong account of what matters if you work with a too narrow concept of law. If you study the legal regulation of the internet while focusing only on rules made by states, the relevance of your analysis will often be quite limited.

This problem relates of course not only to the internet, but to every social field in which there is some law. If law is taken to be, to echo Raz, the most important normative system to which a given social field is subjected, and if the scope of what counts as law is overly narrow, most examinations will fail to capture what is really going on in the field. As a consequence, the broader the definition of law is, the more types of normative systems it takes into account beyond state law, the more congruent the description of the social field will be, and arguably, the better our understanding will be of the social field. Considerations of this type led certain scholars (legal anthropologists, legal sociologists, and legal philosophers) to take an extremely broad approach to law, which we may refer to as legal ubiquity, seeing law in almost every social norm.[19] So the label of law matters because it allows us to have a better understanding of reality, to see more, really, of what regulates.

The hope to capture a greater share of the regulatory reality in the international arbitration context would undoubtedly call for a larger definition of law than state law. The question that remains, then, is the extent to which the scope of what counts as law should be thrown open, without losing its analytical purchase and without legality ending up in the wrong hands: groups and institutions that should not be empowered by recognizing their normative output as law. This is one of the question that underlies most of this book.

5. The Field of Lawyers

Extending the scope of legality to include norms and norm systems that would not have qualified as law under today's still dominant paradigm of legal statism, or classical legal positivism, does not only empower those who produce or control

---

[19] See for instance Rodolfo Sacco, "Mute Law" (1995) 43 *American Journal of Comparative Law* 455; Giorgio del Vecchio, "Sulla statualita del diritto" (1929) 9 *Rivista internazionale di filosofia del diritto* 1, 19; Leopold J Pospisil, *Anthropology of Law: A Comparative Theory* (Harper and Row 1971); Robert M Cover, "The Folktales of Justice: Tales of Jurisdiction" (1985) 14 *Capital University Law Review* 179; Emmanuel Melissaris, "The More the Merrier? A New Take on Legal Pluralism" (2004) 13 *Social & Legal Studies* 57; Jean-François Perrin, *Sociologie empirique du droit* (Helbing & Lichtenhahn 1997) 38.

these norms and norm systems. It also empowers lawyers, including academic lawyers, by extending their field. The flag of legality can indeed also be used to conquer new territories of research, for instance, to colonize further subject-matters and neighboring fields. If we cast the net of legality wider, and consider a wider array of rules and normative systems to amount to law, we haul in more material for discussion and debate. As Lon Fuller put it, "the word 'law' means the life work of the lawyer."[20] Once we are conscious to that reality, we may want to broaden our life work. More legality means an expanded academic pie to share among scholars. The label of law can be used as a tool for the self-aggrandizement of those who labor with the law.

This strategic use of legality is well known in the field of international law. Jean d'Aspremont composed the equivalent of Emile Zola's *J'accuse!* on this issue. "[B]y legalizing objects which intrinsically lie outside the limits of international law," he writes, "scholars strive to provide themselves with extra raw material to work with, and therefore reduce the number of scholars focusing on the same object of study. They thus extend the topics which qualify for legal study, thereby easing the strain on all legal scholars."[21] The problem he points to is undoubtedly real: consider that Oxford University Press publishes as many books on international law (in a broad sense, not restricted to traditional, general, interstate international law, and thus also comprising the current book) as they do in all other fields of the law taken together. The competition for publishing in good places for international law is higher than in many other legal fields. Incentives clearly exist to craft new fields of international law. More generally, the disciplinary limits between law on the one hand and, on the other hand, political science, economics, sociology, philosophy, literature, and even theology, are waning in many places and on many subjects, in the name of interdisciplinarity, except in some of the more reactionary continental European universities. To be sure, the label of law, or the scope of legality, matters very much for legal scholars as a means to justify that they are legitimate in working on certain subjects and with certain types of norms. Now, is it necessarily a bad thing that academic lawyers deal with more or vaster fields?

D'Aspremont's denunciation seems driven by an almost overwhelming eagerness to keep law, or at least international law, within relatively narrow confines. The eagerness manifests itself in his waggish and pivotal use of the word "intrinsically." Surely nothing—no norm or normative system—is intrinsically law or non-law? A norm or norm system merely matches a paradigm of what counts as law at a given time in a given community. The fate of paradigms is to be replaced at a certain stage in a certain way. This is precisely one of the points this book seeks to show, and it leaves no place for intrinsic elements.

Let me repeat, and I offer no apology for the repetition because the argument is important: nothing is intrinsically of a legal nature or not of that nature. As Paul Bohannan puts it, law is a noetic unity: it is a concept not represented by anything

---

[20] Lon L Fuller, *The Law in Quest of Itself* (Foundation Press 1940) 3.
[21] Jean d'Aspremont, "Softness in International Law: A Self-Serving Quest for New Legal Materials" (2008) 19 *European Journal of International Law* 1075, 1091.

except our ideas about it.[22] Nothing prevents us, scholars, to settle on an odd, even harebrained definition—for instance that every norm that emerges within a group is law, or that every norm that directs the behavior of businesspeople is law, or that law is whatever a distinct community of scholars says it is. Definitions of law may validly be grounded exclusively in conventions among scholars.

Beyond emphasizing that freedom we have to call law what we wish (and thus to define as we wish species of that genus such as transnational law and stateless law), and beyond signaling that this freedom may be misused and abused, we should see that we do not necessarily have to be cynical about attempts to embrace broad understandings of legality. After all, expanding the meaning of law to discuss a greater share of reality seems to have more advantages than drawbacks. As long as we lawyers can contribute to advancing the reasoning about a given subject, it seems valuable from the sociological viewpoint we have adopted just here.

6. A Promise of Predictability

Although we may theoretically define law as we wish, the use of the word law in discourses about a regime, a regulation or a regulatory policy will usually be understood to carry certain promises. Chapter 2 will make that argument in detail. For now, at this introductory stage, I want to focus on just one simple promise that is routinely associated with the idea of law. It is a particularly salient problem in the field of international arbitration and stateless law. It is the idea of law's predictability.

When you enter the realm of law, you would usually expect that realm to be predictable to a certain degree. When you agree that a dispute is resolved according to law, as applied by an arbitral tribunal for instance, you would usually expect the outcome to be predictable to certain degree. I might have to mention that the argument can on occasion be heard that dispute resolution is never predictable anyway, since you do not know in advance what a tribunal's decision will be. Predictability, then, should not be part of the picture representing international arbitration's relation with legality. That argument is asinine. Predictability is a property that obtains by degrees; it is a scalar property; norms and norm systems are more or less predictable. The expectation of predictability that accompanies us as we enter the realm of law is no outlandish hope for perfect, mechanical predictability, be it only because of the indeterminacy of language and the argumentative character of the exact meaning of many legal directives. But it is not rolling the dice either. If something is called law, one would in principle take it to exhibit a certain degree of predictability.

One of the important reasons why law itself is often considered an achievement, as having value for society in and of itself, is that it is reasonably predictable. As Neil McCormick puts it, "among the many values that [the rule of law] can secure, none

---

[22] Paul Bohannan, "The Differing Realms of the Law" (1965) 67 *American Anthropologist* 33.

is more important than legal certainty."²³ With "pre-announced rules that are clear and intelligible," "consistency among [these] rules" and "coherence of principle in the system as a whole," one can achieve "reasonable predictability in one's life." Law is thus "of considerable value because of the quality of life [it] facilitate[s] for citizens." Indeed, he maintains, "[w]here the law prevails, you know where you are, and what you are able to do without getting yourself embroiled in...litigation." Hence law, he considers, is "a signal virtue of civilized societies."²⁴ In sum, law is one of the best instruments a social field can have to predict and plan; law is one of the most predictable types of normative systems. In a benign regime, law as predictability has moral value.²⁵ That moral value is usually expected when something called law is defended; it is usually expected when the legality of that something is defended. "Being law" matters because law is taken to come with the promise of that moral value.

This idea is the basis of an argument Michael Reisman makes in an article on stateless law and international arbitration. The object of his study is to ask whether it is appropriate in international arbitration to refer to and apply soft law—a general concept which encompasses various forms of law beyond state law. His answer is a resounding no: "for those who perform the specialized jobs of international judge or arbitrator," he contends, "and for those who entrust their lives and treasure to them, soft law should be off-bounds."²⁶ The arguments he musters to make his point nicely illustrate the nexus between the importance of legality and the idea of law's predictability.

Michael Reisman starts off by taking position in a significant debate in legal philosophy. Taking jurisprudence to a welcome level of humor, he writes that "[t]he adjective 'soft', when used to modify the word 'law', brings to mind the adverb 'slightly', when used to modify the word 'pregnant'."²⁷ What is meant here is that legality is not a scalar property, but an on/off property: something is law or it is not law; it is not more or less law, a little bit law or very much law, law to 20, 50, or 70 percent.²⁸ Why is this debate, which Chapter 3 will take further, important in fact? One reason is that if we admit that the property of being law is scalar, a great deal of the analysis of what law is, of what the rule of law is and how to achieve it becomes muddled. You no longer know what law really is, almost everything can be

---

²³ Neil McCormick, *Rhetoric and the Rule of Law* (Oxford University Press 2005) 16.
²⁴ McCormick, *Rhetoric and the Rule of Law*, 12.
²⁵ On the restriction of that moral value to benign regimes, not evil regimes, see Matthew H Kramer, "For the Record: A Final Reply to N.E. Simmonds" (2011) 56 *American Journal of Jurisprudence* 115.
²⁶ W Michael Reisman, "Soft Law and Law Jobs" (2011) 2 *Journal of International Dispute Settlement* 25, 26.
²⁷ McCormick, *Rhetoric and the Rule of Law*, 26.
²⁸ On the debate, see for instance Ronald Dworkin, "Philosophy, Morality, and Law—Observations Prompted by Professor Fuller's Novel Claim" (1965) 113 *University of Pennsylvania Law Review* 668, 677–8; Lon L Fuller, *The Morality of Law* (rev edn Yale University Press 1969) 122–3; Joseph Raz, *Practical Reason and Norms* (Oxford University Press 1999) 150; Matthew H Kramer, *Objectivity and the Rule of Law* (Cambridge University Press 2007) 105–9.

a little bit law, traces of legality could be discerned in a wide range of mostly meaningless norm systems.

The distinctiveness of law, the feature that should not be tainted and diluted by the scalability of legality, Michael Reisman finds in what he considers to be one of law's prime functions: the facilitation of social activities by allowing us to make meaningful plans.[29] Drawing examples from the settlement of economic disputes and from investments in politically problematic countries, he notes that "[u]ncertainty about the law is a very effective disincentive for investing wealth. It can also chill human rights. The cultivation of uncertainty is a favoured technique of intimidation by authoritarian governments."[30]

Uncertainty really is, he considers, the antithesis of legality. And on this basis he inveighs against what he sees as a possible basic fraud in international arbitration: the resolution of disputes, in the name of law, according to insufficiently predictable norms or norm systems. He writes this about international arbitrators: "Part of their compact is that those who are designated to resolve their disputes will not evade that mandate by deciding *ex aequo et bono*, *lege mercatoria*, by 'international public policy', *ordre public international* or by any other impressive-sounding but inherently vague principle."[31] The problem he sketches does not relate to the use per se of vague principles, but to the use of vague principles, unworthy of legality, as if they were law. Such a use of vague principles, he maintains, amounts to "taking formulations which happen to be in the subjunctive mode but are not law, christening them soft law and then applying them as if they were law."[32]

Christening, no less. This is no simple dubbing, or semantic clarification, but the admission into an order, the elevation of norms to a higher class where it is granted the attributes that are reserved to and are specific to law. Law is clearly seen here as something superior. Becoming law, being affixed the label of law, is a significant promotion for a norm or a norm system.

As to why overly vague principles do not deserve this elevation into legality, he considers that this would amount to "unfair law"[33] and so "[t]here is a reason deriving from morality that militates against an arbitral tribunal taking soft law and applying it to a dispute for which the parties had designated a specific legal system. This is retroactive law-making."[34] In sum, the argument is that if we do away with the distinctiveness of law and forgo law's property of being reasonably predictable, we engage in retroactive law-making.

Two basic considerations emerge from Michael Reisman's argument: the first is that law is intimately associated to fairness, to a form of justice; the second is that retroactivity is antithetical to the notion of law. If we combine the two considerations and take the argument one step further, we see that retroactive law runs against law's basic aspiration to fairness and justice and should therefore not be considered law at all. Put differently, the label of law, when affixed to a dispute

---

[29] On law as an institution to allow us to make plans, see Shapiro, *Legality*.
[30] Reisman, "Soft Law," 26.   [31] Reisman, "Soft Law," 26.
[32] Reisman, "Soft Law," 27.   [33] Reisman, "Soft Law," 29.
[34] Reisman, "Soft Law," 29.

settlement mechanism, signals operations conducted prospectively, not retrospectively, and this signal is grounded in basic expectations of fairness that are intimately associated with the concept of law.

One of law's fundamental functions, which could not be severed from what we view as law without adulterating it beyond recognition, is that it serves, as Fuller puts it, to provide "dependable guideposts for self-directed action," which form a "sound and stable framework for [people's] interaction with one another."[35] Law increases possibilities for self-determination because when the subjects of a given normative order are treated, in the words of Matthew Kramer, "with law-derived regularity and predictability, it allows them to know where they stand," it makes them "free to plan and lead their lives as they please ... [w]ithin the confines of their established duties to others."[36] And, seen from the other side, it allows to make individuals responsible for their own actions.[37] By allowing you to predict and plan, by telling you what the consequences of your actions are, law treats you with dignity.[38] To achieve these results, law has to be followable, and to be followable it has to be predictable.[39] One reason why we cherish law is that we expect it to be predictable. The lack of predictability is one of the things that is patently missing in the agonizing world of Franz Kafka's *The Process*, assuredly one of the most eloquent expositions of the antithesis of law.

If we call something law, that characterization carries an expectation of predictability, of opportunities for self-determination. The label of law matters because it carries a promise of predictability. The same reasoning—if you call something law, one would take it to exhibit certain properties, which may or may not accord with what is agreed in analytic jurisprudence—applies to law's legitimate authority. This forms the substance of the next section.

7. The Legitimate Authority Associated with Legality

Let us once more start with an idea expressed by Joost Pauwelyn, an idea that prima facie seems straightforwardly sensible and almost self-evidently correct, almost commonplace. On closer inspection, the idea allows us to draw some basic distinctions and to see a deeper point about the nature of law.

"In any domestic legal system worth that name," Pauwelyn argues, "the fact that a norm passed through parliament or other constitutional processes before being minted as formal law gives it an aura of legitimacy that demands respect." But, he continues, in international law the situation is different because "given the neutrality and value-free architecture of international law ... merely elevating an instrument to the status of international law does not necessarily make it more

---

[35] Fuller, *Morality*, 229, 210.
[36] Matthew H Kramer, *In Defense of Legal Positivism: Law Without Trimmings* (Oxford University Press 2003) 41.
[37] Kramer, *In Defense*, 41.
[38] See also David Luban, "The Rule of Law and Human Dignity: Re-examining Fuller's Canons" (2010) 2 *Hague Journal on the Rule of Law* 29.
[39] Kramer, *In Defense*, 42.

legitimate. A treaty signed by the military juntas of North Korea and Burma is as much international law as a treaty ratified by the democratically elected parliaments of The Netherlands and India."[40] Let us slightly caricature the argument in order to bring out more clearly the underlying quandary (note that I am not placing a straw man in Pauwelyn's argument, since the point is not to animadvert on it but merely to take it as an illuminating starting point for our theoretical investigations): it makes no difference, the caricatured argument would become, from a moral-political point of view whether something is international law or not.

The point taken from the military juntas seems barely objectionable, yet you may still be skeptical—persuaded but not convinced. The puzzle comes from the fact that we usually think of law as a cultural achievement, as human progress, as something valuable, as a sign of civilization, that is conducive to individual dignity and fairness: they are all signs of law's lack of neutrality from a moral-political viewpoint.

To make sense of that conundrum, it helps to distinguish between the legitimacy of a norm and of a legal system, where "legitimacy" is taken to mean that it should be obeyed for reasons other than the threat of a sanction. Joost Pauwelyn's argument will, again, help us illustrate that distinction.

7.1 The legitimacy of a norm

One typical reason why we may consider a norm to be legitimate is that it belongs to a system that on the whole is viewed as legitimate. For instance, you may disagree with certain provisions of your domestic legal system's tax law because you think it is a bad rule, or because it is not in accord with your political preferences. Yet you would usually recognize that the norm has a certain form of legitimacy, which it derives from the fact that it is part of a legal system that on the whole is perceived as legitimate. You may rebuke French or Swiss employment law, depending on your political orientation, but you would consider these laws to have a certain legitimacy because they belong to the French and Swiss legal orders, which on the whole are legitimate. Call it the package deal effect of the law, if you will: you may lambaste specific elements of a legal system, but you would consider these elements to have a certain legitimacy because the legal system comes as a package deal, and that package deal seems legitimate to you. Consider Ronald Dworkin: "no general policy of upholding the law with steel could be justified if the law were not, in general, a source of genuine obligations."[41] Individual elements of a legitimate normative system demand respect because of their belonging to the system. Recall Pauwelyn's point: "In any domestic legal system *worth that name*,"[42] norms admitted into the system have "an aura of legitimacy that demands respect."

Let us apply that reasoning to international law, as an illustration.

---

[40] Pauwelyn, "Is it International Law," 148.
[41] Ronald M Dworkin, *Law's Empire* (Harvard University Press 1986) 191.
[42] Emphasis added.

Either we accept the idea that a norm of international law has a certain legitimacy because it belongs to the legal system that international law is, and that legal system on the whole we consider to be legitimate.[43] If we accept that idea, then we should be careful about what we consider to be part of international law, because international law's legitimacy extends to its norms. This may precisely be the problem one may wish to avoid when looking beyond formalism in defining international law: we may feel uncomfortable granting a norm created by military juntas a form of legitimacy that demands respect regardless of possibilities of constraint.

Or we take the opposite starting point and consider that a norm does not become more legitimate by being called a norm of international law. It does not derive any legitimacy from its belonging to the legal system that international law is. That position, however, causes disquietude for two reasons, the first of which leads to the second.

The first reason for unease is that if a norm cannot derive legitimacy from its belonging to international law, this means that there is no legitimacy to be derived, that international law itself has no legitimacy that demands its respect, that demands the respect of its different parts, its norms.

The second reason for unease, which follows from the first, relates to international law's identity as law. To see the point, we may recall Pauwelyn's felicitous formulation: "[i]n any domestic legal system *worth that name*," the fact that a norm forms part of the system grants it legitimacy. "Worth that name": that is to say, worth the name, the label of "legal system," in other words a system or regime properly characterized as law. There seems to be no reason not to apply that reasoning to international law. Now if that premise is true, and I believe it is, then the logical consequence would be that international law is not a legal system worth that name; international law is not a legal system; international law is not law.

Let me repeat: If a norm acquires no legitimacy from its being part of international law, the logical consequence is that international law has no such legitimacy, does not have the legitimacy that we usually associate with law. Logically, we then have only three choices.

First, we may think differently about law's inherent legitimacy that demands respect. We write off the arguments that say that law is a cultural achievement of universal significance. We dismiss the idea that it is desirable to promote the rule of law. Fair enough. There is not doubt that analytically we can come to this position. But such a position would divorce analytical or technical discourses about law from the understanding of law in the mind of the layman and the laywoman. We would dissever what we mean when we speak about law from what an ordinary audience would understand when we characterize something as law, for instance when we argue that a given instance of stateless law is law. We would simply no longer be

---

[43] The argument that international law is not a system but a set of different systems, possibly self-contained (Bruno Simma and Dirk Pulkowski, "Of Planets and the Universe: Self-contained Regimes in International Law" (2006) 17 *European Journal of International Law* 483), does not change the argument. It would merely require more qualifications. They are ignored for the sake of the argument's lucidity and because international law is here merely an example, not an object of study.

talking about the same thing. Such a situation would not necessarily be the result of a definitional mishap. A gap between, on the one hand, what is technically meant by an academic assertion of legality ("this is law") and, on the other hand, what is understood from that assertion by a general audience may also be caused by a purpose to mislead. The implications I have in mind when I call something law may be very different from the implications you have in mind when you hear such a characterization. As Chapter 2 will argue, legality can indeed be used as a rhetorical argument: then the implications associated with a pronouncement of legality, in the minds of the addressees of such pronouncements, have to be taken into consideration when we define law in the first place.

Second, we may consider that, indeed, international law is not law. Such a position, however, seems unlikely to advance our understanding of anything.

Third, we consider that, after all, international law norms have a certain legitimacy, derived from the legitimacy of international law as law, a legitimacy that norms that are not international law have not. Then we have to be careful about what we call law, because calling something law accords it a certain legitimacy which demands respect.

Of course, these sundry considerations also apply to non-state legal systems. I merely use international law as an example to show a general point about the nature of law. That point remains, admittedly, rather theoretical in international law, but it becomes acute when we deal with law without the state.

7.2 The legitimacy of a system

We have seen that one form of a norm's legitimacy—the type of legitimacy that demands respect regardless of possibilities to force compliance—depends on its belonging to a legal system. The equivalent for a *system*'s legitimacy depends on it being law, on it being "worth that name" in the language used above. Something called law is perceived, understood to have a form of inherent legitimacy. It matters to call something law, the label of law is of significance, legality carries weight, among other reasons because a normative system characterized as law, as a legal system, is generally understood to have a certain legitimacy. I mean the legitimacy that we normally associate with law, with the value of promoting the rule of law, with the idea that we live in a better world today where we have law, than we would, or did, in a world without law. We *need* law and therefore it is legitimate that it tells us what to do: as Scott Shapiro puts it, "[t]he law is morally valuable ... because we face numerous and serious moral problems whose solutions are complex, contentious, and arbitrary. The only conceivable way for us to address these moral concerns is through social planning. Morally and prudentially speaking, we desperately need norms to guide, coordinate, and monitor our actions."[44] It is that desperate need for the type of normative system that can best orient our behavior—followable, predictable rules—that makes law legitimate and that

[44] Shapiro, *Legality*, 396.

demands that we respect it, lest we undermine its authority and reduce its power to guide behavior.

That legitimacy extends to all the elements of the legal system in question, that is to all its norms. Conversely, we cannot say that a given norm has the sort of legitimacy and demand for respect that characterizes law without that norm being part of any legal system. So the label of law has a legitimizing purpose, because we more or less consciously accord value to that which is law, we more or less consciously associate a sense of desirability to legality. This idea of the perceptions of law's value deserves, now, further attention and clarification.

7.3 Perceptions of the value of legality

It matters to call something law, to affix the label of law to a given regime, because we have a different relationship to legal rules than we have to other rules. Indeed, the ultimate justification for the authority that the smallest legal rules have over you is to be found in the understanding of what law is. What is law has authority because we believe, deep down, that law is something good, something intrinsically valuable.

This may prove to be wrong: to be sure, exploitative officials can, purely instrumentally, use the "direction-providing and incentive-promoting and coordination-facilitating advantages of the rule of law"[45] to reinforce the grip of their evil regime over their society. Put differently, that particular society would credibly be better off without law to help the repressive, malevolent officials, since they would thus lack one essential tool of social structuring and power assertion. Put very simply, law may merely be "an instrument for the effective realization"[46] of political goals, which may be benign or evil. Brutally simplified, law may reinforce the benignity or evilness of a regime, since law is necessary, in Matthew Kramer's words, both for many morally worthy projects and for the "long-term perpetration of certain large-scale projects of evil" (typically "far-reaching enterprises of iniquity that are carried on for many years").[47] Consider the former regime in East Germany, for instance, which likely was strengthened by the regime's instrumental recourse to law. Consequently legality is, strictly analytically speaking and in the abstract, morally neutral.

But that is not the way law is usually perceived. The psychosocial perception of legality undoubtedly is a positive, welcoming one in most countries today, arguably even in many oppressive regimes and radical theocracies. The vast majority of ordinary citizens—in the sense of not being legal theorists, legal philosophers, or political philosophers—would consider it a positive when told that something (a norm, a norm system) qualifies as law. There is a general perception that law has value, the sort of value that demands respect of its rules, regardless of a threat of a sanction. I repeat: we are musing on these questions here at the level of sentiments of right and wrong, from a psychosocial viewpoint, and are not engaging

---

[45] Kramer, "On the Moral Status," 76. [46] Kramer, "On the Moral Status," 76.
[47] Kramer, "For the Record," 124, 125. See further Kramer, *In Defense*.

in an analytical jurisprudential discourse on whether law indeed has moral value in itself. The perspective is a descriptive one, considering how ordinary citizens think when told that something is law. The argument does not proceed at a metaphysical level, starting from a system of ethics, and determine whether, and if so under what conditions, people have a moral duty to obey the law. The argument is to say that most people most of the time in most situations will feel morally pressed to obey legal rules because they are legal rules. This may sound like a trivial assertion. Such paltriness is caused by the fact that we usually have state law in mind when we speak about law. But if the argument holds, and I believe it does, it becomes significant when applied to stateless norms: if the label of law is affixed to them, their power to orient behavior increases.

The generally perceived value of legality, prompting respect for that which is legal, is plain in the widespread non-analytical contentions and proclamations, on every front, extolling the virtues and stressing the importance of law and the rule of law. They are indications that indeed we believe that law is something good that should be respected.

Consider theorists first: for John Locke, "[w]herever law ends, tyranny begins";[48] for HLA Hart, there is a "normally fulfilled assumption that a legal system aims at some form of justice";[49] for Jerold Auerbach, the prominent historian, the occurrence of law is a "glorious triumph...over inferior forms of communitarian extra-legal tyranny";[50] and for EP Thompson, the celebrated historian, British peace activist and socialist intellectual, law is a "cultural achievement of universal significance."[51] As Judith Shklar, the political theorist who became the first tenured woman at Harvard's Government Department, put it, the Western political tradition essentially boils down to "freedom under the rule of law."[52]

Then consider political figures and institutions, seeking to garner support by mobilizing the symbols of desirability and legitimacy that ordinary citizens associate with the rule of law. As Brian Tamanaha shows, such recourse to the appeal of law traverses all political and ideological fault lines:[53] he points to the *Declaration of Democratic Values*, issued by seven heads of states of the West, stating "[w]e believe in a rule which respects and protects without fear";[54] to George W Bush, when he declares that "America will always stand for the non-negotiable demands of human dignity: the rule of law";[55] to the World Bank and the International Monetary Fund requiring the implementation of the rule of law for the provision of financial assistance; to Vladimir Putin when he places "the full implementation of the

---

[48] John Locke, *Second Treatise of Civil Government* (first published 1690, Prometheus 1986), ch XVII, section 202.
[49] HLA Hart, "Positivism and the Separation of Law and Morals" (1958) 71 *Harvard Law Review* 593, 622.
[50] Jerold S Auerbach, *Justice Without Law?* (Oxford University Press 1983) 14.
[51] Edward Palmer Thompson, *Whigs and Hunters: The Origin of the Black Act* (Allen Lane 1975) 265–6.
[52] Judith N Shklar, *Legalism* (Harvard University Press 1964) 22.
[53] Brian Z Tamanaha, *On the Rule of Law: History, Politics, Theory* (Cambridge University Press 2004) 3.
[54] *Washington Post*, June 9, 1984, A14.
[55] George W Bush, State of the Union Address of January 28, 2002.

principles of the rule of law among the country's highest priorities";[56] to the repeated assurances of Chinese leaders that "we must build a system based on the rule of law, instead of pinning hopes on particular leaders";[57] to an Indonesian president, boasting of his nascent achievements, claiming that "we are beginning the rule of law";[58] and even to Robert Mugabe of Zimbabwe when he recognizes the idea that "[o]nly a government that subjects itself to the rule of law has any moral right to demand obedience from its citizen."[59] Clearly, law is invoked here as much more than John Austin's idea of a command backed up by the threat of a sanction. Surely, those of the political leaders just mentioned who are not normally considered liberal democrats were not telling their citizens that they were pragmatically, instrumentally going to resort to the rule of law to carry out their plans of evil over a long period. More realistically, they were dwelling on the legitimate authority of their regime, obtaining as a consequence of it qualifying as rule of law, thus as law. Referring to the legality of a regime is politically thought to be only good.

The rule of law is an "accepted measure worldwide of government legitimacy."[60] Legality is thus arguably one measure of legitimacy of a regime, of a system of governance, of a normative system, and of a norm that is part of such a system. This finds expression, for example, in the fact that international dispute settlement mechanisms are in principle established to further or sustain the international rule of law:[61] one dimension of their legitimacy is thus the extent to which they do indeed create, strengthen, or further a regime that qualifies as law, that amounts to an instantiation of the rule of law. That is one of the basic questions underlying this book, with a focus on international arbitration.

Now, to better grasp the notion of legitimacy that was adumbrated heretofore, let us bring in the distinction between prudential and moral reasons-for-action.

7.4 Prudential vs moral reasons-for-action

Because of the perceived or assumed value of legality, we in principle entertain different relations to legal rules than we do to social norms. One way to see how is to briefly go back to the basic question of why in fact we should engage in analytic jurisprudence.

As Shapiro explains, ordinary citizens and ordinary lawyers often think that legal theorists, and more precisely scholars engaging in analytic jurisprudence, are largely useless because after all it is obvious what law is.[62] Indeed, why be such a nerd, when we can point to courthouses, parliaments, policemen, law books, contracts,

---

[56] Robert Cordy, "Gulags Give Way to the Rule of Law," *Boston Herald*, November 18, 2002, A25.
[57] Wang Xiangwei and Gary Cheung, "Keeping Economic Drive on Track Will Require Huge Effort, Warns Hu," *South China Morning Post*, March 8, 2003.
[58] "We are Beginning the Rule of Law," *Business Week*, May 29, 2000, 70.
[59] Marie Woolf, "Mugabe Told He Has Lost Moral Right to Govern," *The Independent*, August 1, 2002, A8.
[60] Tamanaha, *On the Rule of Law*, 3.
[61] See for instance Cesare PR Romano, "A Taxonomy of International Rule of Law Institutions" (2011) 2 *Journal of International Dispute Settlement* 241.
[62] Shapiro, *Legality*, 4.

prisons and confidently say, with a trace of exasperation, that all of this obviously is law. Don't bother defining law, I know it when I see it.

Fair enough, Shapiro responds in substance, but precisely drawing the contours of legality nevertheless does matter because we may have to know why it is binding.[63] In such case, we may have to engage in a chain of regress through hierarchically superior norms. In Shapiro's story, a fictional character relentlessly asks why a legal norm is binding. The answers are initially easy: A norm is binding because it is in conformity with the norm that is immediately superior to it. A contract is binding because a norm of contract law says so, and that norm is binding because it is in conformity with the constitution. N1 (the lower norm) is binding, and has to be interpreted according to, N2 (the higher norm); N2 according to N3, and so on. But what happens when you get to the top of the hierarchy? Why is the constitution binding? There is no higher norm to justify its binding character. So why is it binding? Because it is the law. At that juncture, you have to resort to the arsenal of jurisprudential theories: why is *all of this* binding. And indeed that is where you do find a number of analytic jurisprudential theories.

It is like a child who asks his father, or mother, why he has to do something, and the father (mothers have more intelligent answers) responds that he so decided. "But why do I have to do what you decide?" asks the child. "Because I'm your father," says the father. "But why must children do what their fathers decide?" asks the child. And here the theorizing starts. "Because it is the natural order of things" would be the answer of a proponent of natural law. "Because fathers have the coercive power to constrain their children to do as they have decided" would sound like a positivistic, John Austin style, answer.

Hans Kelsen, from whom this example is borrowed,[64] refers at that stage to the *Grundnorm*, whose validity is "a presupposition of those who treat posited law as valid *qua* law," as John Gardner puts it.[65] To crack that presupposition open—that is, to investigate why the *Grundnorm* is valid qua law, or simply put why it is law at all—is one way to think about what we should call law. It is one way to ponder what sort of normative systems we want to affix the label of law to. Affixing that label triggers the chain of logical entailments that eventually tells you why you are bound by a given contract or any other norm.

So thinking about what law is seems warranted to make sense of what happens at the end of the logical regress of the bindingness of norms. Yet you may still be skeptical about the usefulness of such theorizing. Frankly, you may ask, who engages in this sort of logical regress, except the obtrusively bad-faithed character in Scott Shapiro's story, the one who systematically asks why a norm is binding? Is this not a purely theoretical problem, which shows ordinary citizens and ordinary lawyers to have a point in considering legal theorists to be wasting their intellectual

---

[63] Shapiro, *Legality*, 25–30.
[64] Hans Kelsen, "The Function of a Constitution" in Richard Tur and William L Twining, *Essays on Kelsen* (Clarendon Press 1986) 112.
[65] John Gardner, *Law as a Leap of Faith* (Oxford University Press 2012) 9.

capabilities? Wondering whether the constitution of a country is in fact really binding is not a prevalent preoccupation of ordinary citizens and ordinary lawyers.

The importance of thinking about what law is may indeed be clearer elsewhere. The understanding (which for ordinary citizens and ordinary lawyers is almost systematically implicit) of the "binding" character of the constitution in fact colors the whole way in which we understand and relate to legal rules on a daily basis. To see the point, we need to swap the term "binding" for the term "authority." "Binding" is often (though not necessarily) taken to mean that you have to obey a norm in the sense that if you do not there will be a sanction, that a norm is binding because it can constrain you to do something. Bindingness is often equated with power, more precisely with coercive power.

Authority, on the other hand, is something more subtle. In Robert Paul Wolff's words, "To *claim* authority is to claim the right to be obeyed. To *have* authority... may mean to have that right, or it may mean to have one's claim acknowledged and accepted by those at whom it is directed." In the descriptive sense of the word, he continues, authority is about "what men *believe* they *ought to* do."[66] Authority, in this sense, relates to what we *believe* we *morally ought to* obey. For example, the coercive power of the rule that says you have to pay for a bus ticket when you go to work is in the hands of the relevant public transport company, and ultimately in those of the police to seize your assets. But even if all checks by bus conductors are cancelled for a year, the authority of the rule is not altered during that period: if you break that rule you are, to a small extent, a bad citizen, because you break a legal rule. If we transpose that to a criminal organization, the question of authority disappears and is replaced by a simple rule of power: you have to obey the rule because otherwise you are harmed. You have to pay 10 percent of the revenues of your restaurant to the local mafia because otherwise they harm you. If the mafia becomes unable to monitor the respect of that rule and to force you to obey it, the rule, which has no authority, loses all binding character. Wolff offers a similar example: "When I turn over my wallet to a thief who is holding me at gunpoint, I do so because the fate with which he threatens me is worse than the loss of money which I am made to suffer. I grant that he has power over me, but I would hardly suppose that he has authority, that is, that he has a right to demand my money and that I have an obligation to give it to him. When the government presents me with a bill for taxes, on the other hand, I pay it (normally) even though I do not wish to, and even if I think I can get away with not paying. It is, after all, the duly constituted government, and hence it has a *right* to tax me. It has *authority* over me."[67]

Authority, in this sense, is unconcerned by the morality of the rule to which authority attaches: you may find the rule that you have to pay for a bus ticket immoral,

---

[66] Robert Paul Wolff, "The Conflict Between Authority and Autonomy" in William Atkins Edmundson (ed), *The Duty to Obey the Law: Selected Philosophical Readings* (Rowman & Littlefield 1999) 63, 64 (the emphasis on the words "believe" and "ought to" is mine).
[67] Wolff, "The Conflict Between Authority and Autonomy," 64.

because you think bus rides should be free for users and financed instead by the general taxpayer, but nevertheless the rule has authority because it is a legal rule.

Authority is nevertheless a question of morality. To make the argument apparent, it helps to distinguish between moral and prudential reasons-for-action. Prudential reasons-for-action relate to the pursuit of the actor's own interests. People act in a certain way for prudential reasons if they believe it is in their interest to do so, that they would be better off for reasons that do not include having a good or bad conscience (which is precisely a moral question). People act in a certain way out of moral reasons-for-action if they believe it is morally correct to act in such a way, which ultimately amounts to an intent to further other people's interests.[68]

You do not only have prudential reasons to obey the law (the bus conductors asking you for your ticket). There is also a moral reason to obey that which is legal, regardless of the morality of the legal rule in question, because it is generally believed that it is good thing, a moral pursuit, to preserve the rule of law by abiding by it. There is a general perception in society—to be precise: in benign societies—that obeying the law is good for society even when it is unpleasant for oneself. Obeying that which is legal is thought to be promotive, among other things, of other people's interests, which signals a moral reason-for-action.

Obviously I am not maintaining that the moral reasons for obeying the law are always stronger than the prudential reasons not to obey it. But I am arguing that if you map, consciously or unconsciously, all the reasons you have to engage or not to engage in a certain course of action that comes within the realm of law, there likely will be one vector representing law's authority as law. In the terms of Wolff's language used above to describe authority, that vector is based on "what men *believe* they *ought to* do." That vector is a moral reason-for-action.

If we now revisit Shapiro's argument, we see this: I should obey a given legal rule because a statute says it is a valid rule (where valid means it is part of the legal system); and the statute itself is constitutional (where constitutional means is part of the legal system); and the legal system itself bears the label of law and therefore has the sort of authority that law has; and law has that authority because we assume, at least in benign societies, that law is something good and valuable and should therefore be respected as a whole.

To be clear, the argument is this: in most settings, calling something law grants it the authority that law usually has and thus creates a moral reason to comply with it. Legality creates moral reasons-for-action.[69] Accordingly, it matters a great deal what

---

[68] Kramer, "On the Moral Status," 66: "Somebody's prudential reasons-for-action are focused exclusively or primarily on his own interests and only derivatively if at all on the interests of other people. Somebody's moral reasons-for-action are focused exclusively or primarily on other people's interests and only derivatively if at all on his own interests (apart from interests, such as a concern for acting in a morally proper fashion, which are themselves defined by reference to the well-being of other people)." See also Kramer, *In Defense*, 81–3, Raz, *Practical Reason and Norms*, 155–6.

[69] It is irrelevant in the context of this argument whether the moral reasons-for-action are justified or not, that is whether obeying the law is indeed more promotive of society's interests than disobeying it.

we decide to call law and we should take this effect of legality into consideration when we cogitate about what we want to call law.

We started this section by arguing that in principle we entertain different relations to legal rules than we do to social norms. Now we can see the difference: law is often credibly obeyed for reasons other than prudential reasons-for-action. This understanding in turn allows us to better grasp the meaning of legitimacy used heretofore, or more precisely to see another dimension of it. Law's "legitimacy which demands respect" is an expression of this idea: legality (the label of law) creates moral reasons to obey that which it characterizes (that to which the label is affixed) because law is generally perceived to be something useful and valuable for society.

7.5 A generally perceived legitimate authority

One way to tie the strings from above together is to consider that law has a generally perceived legitimate authority. Let me briefly elaborate on each of those words.

By "general" I mean that the approach adopted here is largely an empirical, not a metaphysical one. Most of the tenets of my theorizing up to now in this book would be testable in empirical social science studies. In addition, my purpose at most junctures was not to apprehend elements of legality that are necessarily true, in all possible worlds. I was rather trying to elucidate elements of legality for which there are more hypotheses in which they are credibly correct than hypotheses in which they are not credibly correct.

By "perceived" I mean that my ruminations, though directly inspired by analytic jurisprudence, are aiming less at being correct studies in analytic jurisprudence than correct representations of the laypeople's (ordinary citizens and ordinary lawyers, not legal philosophers) understanding of what law is.

By "authority" I mean that people will credibly infer from the label of law moral reasons to obey the norms and norm systems to which that label is affixed.

By "legitimacy" I mean that the label of law creates the moral reasons just mentioned because law, as a mechanism that effectively directs behavior, is understood as valuable, as a social achievement. Hence it must be allowed to direct behavior. Hence it ought to be respected and obeyed. Clearly, this is not a substantive form of legitimacy referring to the contents of law. It is unrelated to a Kantian approach for instance, or to the idea that law's legitimacy is measured by the correspondence between the law's mandates and the addressees' basic moral, social, cultural, or theological values.[70] Just as clearly, it is not a procedural form of legitimacy, interested in law as process. It is unrelated, for instance, to Habermas's ideal speech situation[71] or his discourse ethics[72] or the democratic legitimacy of

---

[70] For such an approach to legitimacy, see for instance François Ost, "Essai de définition et de caractérisation de la validité juridique" in François Rigaux, Guy Haarscher, and Patrick Vassard (eds), *Droit et pouvoir:* vol 1: *La validité* (Story-Scientia 1987) 97.

[71] Jürgen Habermas, "Wahrheitstheorien" in Helmut Fahrenbach (ed), *Wirklichkeit und Reflexion* (Neske 1973) 211; Jürgen Habermas, *Between Naturalism and Religion* (Polity 2008).

[72] Jürgen Habermas, *Justification and Application* (MIT Press 1993).

law.[73] What I mean here is, on the contrary, a socio-institutional form of legitimacy, relating to law as a social institution, based on the belief, in most of our modern societies, that law per se is something good and valuable and that it has a specific role in society which requires that it be obeyed.

To the main points: Such generally perceived legitimate authority obtains as a consequence of the fact that a normative system qualifies as law. It extends to all the individual parts of the system labeled as law, to all its norms, regardless of their contents, thus regardless of whether we even know their contents. When a normative system qualifies as law, it creates a moral reason to obey its norms. That moral reason may be trumped by other moral reasons, taken from the contents of the rules. Indeed, other moral reasons may for instance push, antagonistically, for disobedience if the values expressed by the contents of the rules are at odds with our own moral values. Clearly then, I do not maintain that a legal norm, by dint of its legality, "can reasonably be judged morally binding even by those who regard it as unwise," as John Finnis would say.[74] Its legality does not make it morally binding, it merely creates at least one and in principle several reasons-for-action, one of which is of a moral nature.

8. Why it Matters that Legality Matters

Why is it important to understand why the label of law matters? Why have we done this? The point of this discussion was not only to understand that defining stateless law is a meaningful question. It is also important to see why legality matters because we cannot really understand what we may want to call law—that is, how we want to exercise the freedom we have in defining law—unless we understand the implications of calling something law. The meaningful character of the label of law influences how we understand law and where we should see law. Chapter 3 will take this argument further.

I must repeat one point, because it is important. Note that we have focused on certain aspects of what law typically is: it is predictable, it is associated with a sense of legitimacy, it has authority because it is law, and so on. Now, these are not necessarily features of law that make law *law*. Indeed, we may come, analytically, to the conclusion that legality has no necessary connection with legitimacy or morality. We may realize that certain legal regimes may stop to claim authority and in fact no longer have authority (consider a domestic legal system in case of an extreme war or natural catastrophe). It is nevertheless important to focus on what is typically associated with legality. For if we define a chair without yielding to its consequences, for instance that people may try to sit on it, we may well lead people to fall on their bottom—this in fact, without irony, may precisely be certain people's purpose when they use the label of legality. The label of law can indeed be used as a rhetorical argument. That will be the story for Chapter 2.

---

[73] Jürgen Habermas, *Between Facts and Norms: Contributions to a Discourse Theory of Law and Democracy* (MIT Press 1996).
[74] John Finnis, *Philosophy of Law Collected Essays Volume IV* (Oxford University Press 2011) 46.

2
Legality as Rhetorical Argument

Some time ago, in the context of a debate on whether international arbitration forms a legal system of its own, Ralf Michaels took the view that my arguments "seem[ed] unobjectionable" and were "almost obviously right."[1] I felt elated. I had argued that international arbitration does not comport with a given set of principles of legality (namely Lon Fuller's classical, even ordinary "inner morality of law"[2]) and should therefore not be considered an instance of transnational law.[3] I expected disagreement and disputation. So I was surprised, though of course content, that anyone of Michaels's caliber could think I was so positively correct. But it was not a praise. It rather was a criticism, albeit gentle. Michaels was in fact pointing to a problem and to an important question. He put it thus: "Is the law created by the regime of transnational dispute resolution *of the nature* that is addressed [by the set of conditions that Schultz chose]?"[4] His argument, in essence, was that the concept of law I had used to conduct my analysis was less than ideal because it led, unobjectionably it seemed, to the conclusion that arbitration does not form its own legal order without territory.

Michaels is an earnest and upstanding scholar. He was not playing Humpty Dumpty. (Recall Lewis Carroll: "'When *I* use a word,' Humpty Dumpty said, in rather a scornful tone, 'it means just what *I* choose it to mean—neither more nor less.'") He was not lamenting my choice of a concept of legality because it failed to serve his interests, because it failed to lead to the conclusion that the arbitral normative order qualifies as a legal order. His point was not that we should play with the meaning of "law" until it tells us what we need—for instance until it leads to the determination that there is indeed a transnational arbitral legal order. As we will see, arbitration partisans may have reasons and might be tempted to do just

---

[1] Ralf Michaels, "A Fuller Concept of Law Beyond the State? Thoughts on Lon Fuller's Contributions to the Jurisprudence of Transnational Dispute Resolution—A Reply to Thomas Schultz" (2011) 2 *Journal of International Dispute Settlement* 417, 418.
[2] Lon L Fuller, *The Morality of Law* (rev edn Yale University Press 1969) 33–41.
[3] Thomas Schultz, "The Concept of Law in Transnational Arbitral Legal Orders and some of its Consequences" (2011) 2 *Journal of International Dispute Settlement* 59.
[4] Michaels, "Fuller Concept," 426 (the emphasis is mine). The full passage goes as follows: "Once we take a broader perspective, however, a prior, and potentially more interesting question arises. That question is this: Is the law created by the regime of transnational dispute resolution of the nature that is addressed in the second chapter of the Morality of Law (i.e. comparable to enacted law), or is it of a different nature (e.g. adjudicatory law, or customary law, or contractual law), for which different criteria of legitimacy are appropriate?"

that, but not Michaels.[5] No, his concern is a fair one. Certainly, he does mean that the concept of law we use to determine the legality of arbitration as a regime should be adapted to that regime. He does mean that the definition should be adapted to the object of study. But his concern is that we do not learn quite enough about arbitration by saying it fails to meet the standards I had chosen for what amounts to law. My choice of a concept of legality was, to put it simply, too ordinary.

My claim is that ordinariness is critical in discussing law at its frontiers. If we want to grapple with international arbitration as a legal order, as transnational law without the state, then we should subject arbitration to the conditions we ordinarily use to determine whether a regime is a legal regime. (So long, of course, as we do not endorse the postulate that law is necessarily state law, making stateless law an oxymoron.) It does matter to see how arbitration fails ("obviously" or not) to meet the threshold of what we would ordinarily be content to call law, that it fails to accord with what everyday discourse would assume is law. Fuller's inner morality of law is appropriate for discussing law without territory precisely because it was developed with no consideration for law disconnected from territory and government. It was developed for what we would ordinarily call law.

My aim is not to embark, for the time being, on a discussion of what exactly Fuller's principles of legality say and what they mean for international arbitration—Chapter 8 will handle that discussion. I offered this brief account of my exchange with Michaels in the hope that it sketches enough to see a far more general point, a point about law that is particularly relevant in the context of transnational law, a point quite plainly illustrated in debates about arbitration being non-state law.

This general point is that a pronouncement of legality (the act of characterizing a given regime as a legal regime) creates rhetorical effects. We may call something law for intents of persuasion. The persuasion operates by mobilizing the signals that an accession to legality exhibits. This rhetoric of legality draws on the characteristics and regulatory qualities that we ordinarily and by default associate with that which is called law. This is most germane to regimes that are not evidently called law, such as transnational regimes disconnected from territory and government.

To see where this point comes from, the first main section of this chapter broaches some preliminaries relating to the way the label of law connects to the object it labels. It briefly concretizes an idea I floated in the background of Chapter 1 about better and worse definitions of law and whose interests are served by definitions of law. In a second main section, we shall examine the general idea that something called law is perceived in a certain way because it is called law, and how this labeling effect of legality, operating on a rhetorical plane, may be divorced from analytic jurisprudence—a point that was also adumbrated in Chapter 1. I then want to offer, in a third main section, eight signals that the label of law

---

[5] Michaels's other writings are sufficiently critical of arbitration to dispel that sort of concern. See for example Ralf Michaels, "Rollen und Rollenverständnisse im transnationalen Privatrecht" in *Paradigmen im internationalen Recht: Implikationen der Weltfinanzkrise für das internationale Recht* (Müller 2012).

creates. This will lead us to underscore, in a fourth main section, the importance of defining law in accordance with its political and ethical signals. The chapter ends with an illustration of the theoretical ruminations we will have expounded until then in the context of transnational law and in particular with regard to international arbitration.

1. Better and Worse Definitions of Law

Let me recall from Chapter 1: when scholars define the word law and ponder what to affix it to, they do not merely give in to "labeling anxieties," as Scott Shapiro puts it.[6] They do not simply engage in lexicography and attempt to contribute to a language dictionary.[7] The point of asking what is law is not just to settle semantics. Contrariwise, one reason why it matters to define law and to map its whereabouts is that it leads us to ask what we should call law, which in turn forces us to excogitate the implications of a pronouncement of legality. If we start thinking about the implications of calling something law, we inevitably come across the point that there are better and worse definitions of law. The implications of calling something law, whether agreeable or disturbing, inform our assessment of the commendable or deplorable character of a definition of law. Let me elucidate: if we call something law, this has certain consequences, as we have seen in the preceding chapter, and we may find these consequences either desirable or inconvenient. If these consequences are all in all inconvenient (provided of course the characterization as law was correctly derived from the definition), then the definition of law that was used is all in all deplorable—and vice versa.

This focus on the varying desirability of definitions of law leads in turn to another question: desirability for whom and for what? Definitions of law may be convenient for some because they advance their interests, and inconvenient for others. When we pass judgment on definitions of law being better or worse, we usually have in mind the interests of scholars, and even more specifically legal philosophers. Their purpose in defining law, as Shapiro puts it in the passage already quoted, is usually "to understand the nature of a social institution and its products."[8] A desirable definition of law is then one that clarifies more than it muddles the understanding of the nature of the social institution that law is. A good definition of law, here, is one that has strong explanatory power. But we should not too easily surmise that only legal philosophers, or even more broadly scholars, are interested in definitions of law. For there are other often, though not always, less estimable uses of the label of law than understanding social institutions. Certain actors may find a political or economic interest in having a given regime called law. They accordingly may, and in fact do, attempt to push a non-scholarly agenda by dint of the implications of a pronouncement of legality, more precisely by means of the rhetorical effects that follow from calling something law.

---

[6] Scott J Shapiro, *Legality* (Belknap Press 2011) 30.
[7] Shapiro, *Legality*, 7.   [8] Shapiro, *Legality*, 7.

Brutally simplified, a definition of law may serve given interests because it exhibits certain distinct signals about what we decide to call law. These signals are by default determined by our ordinary understanding of law. What these signals are, and how the implications of calling something law can and have been used in the context of transnational law, and in regard to international arbitration in particular, will be propounded in the coming sections.

2. Signals of the Label of Law

Something called law is perceived in a certain way because it is called law. Indeed, affixing the label "law" to a given regulatory regime makes us assume, in the absence of analytic investigation, that this regime possesses the characteristics that ordinarily attach to that which is of a legal nature. Our collective conscience associates certain features with law; we then naturally expect to find these features in the various incarnations of law. In other words, labeling a regime as law sends signals about this regime. These signals are informed by the characteristics we assume instantiations of law to have, and these assumptions, in turn, are informed by the meaning of law in our collective conscience.

Given as much, pronouncements of legality can be used to take advantage of the signals they send. When the purpose, or one of the purposes, of mobilizing these signals is to bolster the persuasiveness of an argument, then the label of law is used, primarily or among other purposes, for its rhetorical effects. So legality may be used as a rhetorical device, as rhetorical argument. This is a credible use of the label of law because, as we will see, the assumed characteristics of that which is law are primarily virtues.

Put less precisely but perhaps more plainly, we may call something law so that one believes it is virtuous, in the sense of possessing the virtues that are normally associated with law. We may call a regime a *legal* regime in the hope that the addressees of our utterance will assume that this regime displays the characteristics that a non-analytical understanding of law ascribes to that which it characterizes as law. Illustrated with the utmost terseness, if told that something is law, you may be (mis)led to intuitively assume that this something has certain characteristics, for instance that it is good and valuable and must be respected.

This labeling effect of legality, operating on a rhetorical plane, is divorced from analytic jurisprudence on two fronts. First, the validity of theories about law's characteristics differs between analytic jurisprudence and reflections on law as a label. A theory about the properties of a regime signaled by the label of law is not falsified if we identify a counter-example—for instance a regime that cannot reasonably be denied the qualification of law yet fails to display one or several of the properties that the theory ascribes to law. Indeed, like other labels, a non-fallacious pronouncement of legality indicates that, in principle, the properties we associate with law will be found in the regime characterized as law. But, as with other labels, we might find instances that actually do not display one or several of these properties. The signals sent by the label pointed to a wrong state of affairs, but they nevertheless were sent as the theory predicted and the theory holding that the signals were sent is not in trouble.

Contrariwise, a jurisprudential theory on the concept of law typically puts forward the conditions that are jointly both necessary and sufficient for a regime to qualify as law, and the identification of a counter-example falsifies such a theory.

The point matters because it clarifies the fact that the theory expounded below describes the features that are usually associated with law, not any necessary or sufficient conditions of legality. That theory would not be falsified by the possible identification of a regime that fails to display one or several of the features it associates with law.

The second way in which analytic jurisprudence and theories about law as a label differ, which is intimately connected to the first, relates to the object of the theories, which may differ but do not necessarily do so. They describe something else. Analytic jurisprudence, as far as it is concerned with the concept of law, typically seeks to apprehend the "state of affairs that obtains when a legal system exists and functions."[9] A theory about the properties signaled by legality, on the other hand, seeks to describe the psychosocial expectations of properties in the regimes labeled as law; such a theory has no direct ambition to discern the actual properties displayed by legal regimes. It is based on an ordinary understanding of law, on what non-legal philosophers—ordinary citizens, but also law-makers and lawyers of other specialties—understand by law.

To be sure, non-specialists may have an understanding of law that is reasonably distinct from the findings of legal philosophers. For instance, ordinary citizens will often not include in their reasoning about law the idea that it may, in fact, be serviceable for the pursuit of evil ends because the rule of law allows heinous governments to consolidate their power and better control their citizenry (that part of George Orwell's *1984* has not made it into our collective imagination).[10]

However, it is also evident that an ordinary understanding of law is not by necessity different from a jurisprudential one. Fuller's "inner morality of law," for instance, comports quite straightforwardly with what nearly every non-specialist would agree is law; here the meaning of "law" is equivalent, or at least overlaps in many respects, in everyday discourse and in philosophical argumentation. It should now be plain that my arguments developed below do not seek to contradict, and cannot be contradicted by, jurisprudential theories (including, I hope, my own).

There is a last preliminary to settle. The preceding paragraphs have repeatedly referred to broad notions of "our" understanding of law, "our" collective conscience, the meaning of law for ordinary citizens, and the characteristics that are "normally" associated with law. It is readily acknowledged that the meaning of law and the characteristics associated with it may vary markedly across cultures and within a single culture from one individual to another. For instance, most things legal will likely be perceived as hurdles by the libertarian ("law is what prevents me

---

[9] Matthew H Kramer, "On the Moral Status of the Rule of Law" (2004) 63 *Cambridge Law Journal* 65, 65.

[10] Kramer, "On the Moral Status," 66ff.

from doing what I want") but as means of empowerment for the communitarian ("law protects the weak against the strong"). Now, if it were important for this chapter's argument to map all the precise variegated understandings of law by non-legal philosophers, then a lot of social-scientific, empirical research would plainly be needed, so as to determine what their representations exactly are when told that something is law. However, my chief purpose is to delineate a commonsensical understanding of the rhetorical effects of being law, based largely on the writings of legal theorists that have given rise to no or few controversies. It appeals to commonsense and reason, rather than evidence, and may thus validly remain at a relatively high level of abstraction and generality. To be fair, the theory propounded here does not rely on elements so broad as to be unfalsifiable. But if controversies there are, it seems improbable that the identity of the signals of the label of law will be a cardinal point in them.

3. Eight Signals

A pronouncement of legality, at least when made to an audience of non-legal theorists, usually will trigger a rich symbolism associated with law—symbols of justice and of power, mental images of decrees, of vengeance, and eventually of peace. For instance, Lady Justice in her fullest apparel, blindfolded with sword and scales, figures prominently in our collective imagination about law. Discussions about the legality of a regime summon her to our conscience. In truth, the *poiesis* of the societal essence of law (the "bringing-forth," as Heidegger would call it,[11] of what the basic nature of law is to society) can be found in our collective imagination perhaps more than in doctrines and theories, nurtured as that imagination for instance is by pregnant symbolic literature. Consider Shakespeare's work, as François Ost encourages us to do, when it aspires to bring together the core values that law stands for and to bind them in a symbolic narrative that ordinary citizens can adhere to: such accounts shape, through symbols, our non-technical understanding of law.[12] Now, naturally, this symbolism can be mobilized in argumentative discourse for rhetorical effect.

When we move from this general understanding of law's symbolic dimension to its more specific articulations, we can discern at least eight such rhetorical effects. That is, our collective conscience associates at least eight features with law, which flesh out the aforementioned symbolism; everyday discourse associates at least as many characteristics with that which is law. Accordingly, when a pronouncement of legality is made, when the label of law is affixed to a regime, eight signals are sent about this regime. They are the following:[13]

---

[11] Martin Heidegger, *The Question Concerning Technology and Other Essays* (trans W Lovitt, Harper & Row 1977) 10–11.
[12] François Ost, *Shakespeare, la comédie de la loi* (Michalon 2012).
[13] Undoubtedly there are more such assumed characteristics and signals, but, although I am arguing a general point about law, my focus is on an argument about transnational law, and the path to that argument requires no more than the characteristics and labels I identify.

(1) law is a superior mode of social regulation,
(2) law is something desirable,
(3) law carries expectations of justice,
(4) law is normatively meaningful from an external point of view,
(5) law is normatively meaningful from an internal point of view,
(6) law relies on an underlying organization or system,
(7) law carries an opposition to legal intervention from outside, and
(8) law carries a claim for normative and political autonomy.

Before we probe them, two brief observations must be entered. The first is that a pronouncement of legality signals that the regime in question is a qualified normative social system.[14] Not every normative system is a legal system, but every legal system is a normative system. Not every social system is a legal system, but every legal system is a social system. A legal system has something more to it than an unqualified normative social system. It is in that sense that law is a label, a certification. It signals that the normative social system in question has certain distinct properties that make it law.

The second preliminary observation is that the level or strength of these signals varies from one understanding of what law is to another. For many, following Austin and Bentham, a legal regime necessarily has a regulatory sway that is such that the regime has actual coercive force.[15] For others, like Joseph Raz, the idea that law is to be taken normatively seriously and that it tries to orient behavior goes so far as to imply that the legal regime claims authority to intervene in all facets of its addressees' lives—this is regarded as law's virtual comprehensiveness.[16] Then Hans Kelsen would argue that the opposition to legal intervention is not quite a gentle push in a battle for regulatory dominance, but a fight for legal exclusiveness. In his words, "a system of norms can only be valid if the validity of all other systems of norms with the same sphere of validity has been excluded."[17] Accordingly, as Jean Carbonnier would present this view (though he does not share it), "Either the phenomena depicted as forming another body of law are taken into consideration by the overall system, which takes over the whole; or the phenomena of an alleged other body of law remain outside, not integrated into the system ... and cannot be truly classified as law."[18] The basic idea that law is a superior mode of regulation is sometimes taken to the extreme that law purports to be the highest normative order within a given sphere of application and a given subject-community: law, as Joseph Raz puts it, "claims authority to regulate the setting up and application of other institutionalized systems by its subject-community."[19]

---

[14] Evgeny Pashukanis, *Law and Marxism: A General Theory* (first published 1929, Ink Links 1978).
[15] John Austin, *The Province of Jurisprudence Determined and the Uses of the Study of Jurisprudence* (first published 1832, Weidenfeld & Nicolson 1954) 13–14; Jeremy Bentham, *Of Laws in General* (first published 1782, Athlone Press 1970) 2.
[16] Joseph Raz, *The Authority of Law* (2nd edn, Oxford University Press 2009) 116–18.
[17] Hans Kelsen, *General Theory of Law and State* (first published 1945, Harvard University Press 1949) 410.
[18] Jean Carbonnier, *Sociologie juridique* (A Colin 1972) 213.
[19] Raz, *Authority of Law*, 118.

Let us, then, ponder these eight assumed characteristics of law.

(1) *Law is a superior mode of social regulation.* The label of law signals the presence of a superior mode of regulation. It is, intuitively, something more sophisticated, more attractive than an unqualified social system. If we had to choose between living in a regime where there is law and a regime devoid of law, we would be more likely to choose the former.

(2) *Law is something desirable.* If we take that line of reasoning just one step further, a qualification of legality elevates the regime in question to something desirable, an achievement to be respected. Recall the discussion from Chapter 1,[20] and these quotes: "Wherever law ends, tyranny begins";[21] "the glorious triumph of law over inferior forms of communitarian extra-legal tyranny";[22] law is a "cultural achievement of universal significance."[23] Brian Tamanaha puts it simply: "everyone is for [the rule of law]."[24] Everyone is for law. Law is perceived to be something good.

(3) *Law carries expectations of justice.* We may take that reasoning again a step further, and see that the label of law is associated with the presence or at least the expectation of justice. Matthew Kramer, for instance, speaks of the Rule of Law, as a political ideal, "with its expressed values of human equality, individual dignity, and fairness."[25] HLA Hart, despite his strict insistence on the separability of law and morality, evokes the "assumption that a legal system aims at some form of justice[, which] colours the whole way in which we interpret specific rules in particular cases."[26] Ordinary citizens are uncomfortable when told that Nazi law was law. The cyclical revival of the natural law tradition is another sign that, regardless of what analytic philosophy tells us, we intuitively seem to want to associate law with justice, and we normally do if we have not studied or are not convinced by modern legal positivism.[27]

(4) *Law is normatively meaningful from an external point of view.* The fourth thing that a pronouncement of legality signals is that the regime so labeled is to be taken seriously, on a normative level and from an external point of view: law is perceived

---

[20] See Chapter 1, Section 7.3 "Perceptions of the value of legality."
[21] John Locke, *Second Treatise of Civil Government* (first published 1690, Prometheus 1986), ch XVII, section 202.
[22] Jerold S Auerbach, *Justice Without Law?* (Oxford University Press 1983) 14.
[23] Edward Palmer Thompson, *Whigs and Hunters: The Origin of the Black Act* (Allen Lane 1975) 265–6.
[24] Brian Z Tamanaha, *On the Rule of Law. History, Politics, Theory* (Cambridge University Press 2004) 3.
[25] Matthew H Kramer, *Objectivity and the Rule of Law* (Cambridge University Press 2007) 160.
[26] HLA Hart, "Positivism and the Separation of Law and Morals" (1958) 71 *Harvard Law Review* 593, 622.
[27] Joseph Charmont, *La renaissance du droit naturel* (2nd edn, Librairie de jurisprudence ancienne et moderne 1927); Charles G Haines, *The Revival of Natural Law in America* (Harvard University Press 1930); Heinrich A Rommen, *Die ewige Wiederkehr des Naturrechts* (J Hegner 1936); Scott M Buchanan, *Rediscovering Natural Law* (Center for the Study of Democratic Institutions 1962); Hayden Ramsay, "The Revival of Natural Law Theories" (1994) 35 *Analytic Philosophy* 153. Also Hart, "Positivism," 595, who speaks of "all the principles for the defence of which the terminology of natural law has in our day been revived."

as normatively meaningful from the standpoint of external observers.[28] The presence of something called law in a given social field is likely to figure prominently in the regulatory reasoning of an external observer about that social field.

The prime example of law that ordinary citizens, and mostly everyone, will have in mind when thinking about law is state law. Up to a certain point, when we characterize a regime as law, we make it comparable to the prime example. Nowhere is that metaphorical effect of legality as plain as it is here. Non-state law acquires a certain equivalence to state law by the fact that the word "law" is used in both cases. That equivalence is not called to mind when we compare social norms with state law: there is no plausible reason for ordinary citizens to think that social and legal norms are on the same footing or of a proximate nature. And except under extreme circumstances of anarchy and statelessness, the law of any state is taken, by external observers, to matter normatively. Credible reasonings by external observers on the overall conduct of the citizens of a state will include a reference to the law of that state. So if the label of law calls to mind the symbol of state law, and if state law is considered central in regulatory reasonings, then a pronouncement of legality about a regime makes that regime figure prominently in the considerations of outside observers examining how a social field is regulated and how it should be regulated. For a regime, to qualify as law gives it a special place in regulatory reasonings.

The mental invocation of state law, however, is not the only source of this effect of the label of law. Admittedly, law is a regulator just like market forces, social norms, and the spatial and temporal constraints of the built architecture (walls, doors, etc)—with this difference, however, that law often will have a claim and usually will have the capacity to influence and trump all other types of norms.[29] In a confrontation between law and social norms or market forces or the built architecture, law usually can (in the strict sense of having the power but not necessarily in the broader sense of being justified in doing) orient, displace, or otherwise alter these other types of norms. Social norms, market forces, and the built architecture are each subject to law.[30] Law in fact often regulates by instrumentalizing these other regulators. In terms of power then, law is perceived as a higher calling: it has the potential of being the most powerful regulator—a position that unqualified social norms usually do not claim to have.[31] Again, this actual or potential power gives things called law a special place in regulatory reasonings by external observers.

(5) *Law is normatively meaningful from an internal point of view.* The fifth consequence of the label of law, which mirrors the fourth, is the expectation that if you come under the sway of something called law, it will orient, or at least it will seek to orient your behavior. Scott Shapiro for instance writes that "the law normally claims the right to use force to ensure compliance with its rules."[32] Law

---

[28] HLA Hart, *The Concept of Law* (2nd edn, Clarendon Press 1994) 86ff.
[29] Lawrence Lessig, "The New Chicago School" (1998) 27 *Journal of Legal Studies* 661.
[30] Lessig, "New Chicago School," 666ff.
[31] Raz, *Authority of Law*, 118.   [32] Shapiro, *Legality*, 5.

is not something that we can normally ignore when we predict and plan. Law is understood as something authoritative and constraining or empowering. Law is normatively meaningful from an internal point of view (from the point of view of the addressees of the norms). It makes little sense to call a regime a legal regime if that regime does not, on the whole, seek to direct people's conduct. So Matthew Kramer for instance infers essential characteristics of the rule of law (elements of the state of affairs that needs to obtain for a regime to qualify as a legal regime) from the observation that their absence would lead to situations in which the regime is "thoroughly inefficacious in channeling people's behavior" and "[t]he existence of the system would make no difference to anyone's reasoning about appropriate courses of conduct."[33]

As we have seen in Chapter 1, the normative meaningfulness and authority of law also imply that there is an inherent violence in elevating something to the status of law.[34] It increases the power of social control in the hands of those who hold the scepter of legality, those who control the ultimate determinants of what counts as law and what does not. There may be a dark instrumental side to calling law a given norm or norm system.

(6) *Law relies on an underlying organization or system.* A legal rule is not usually perceived to exist in isolation.[35] It is curious to think of just one isolated rule as a legal rule. From a theoretical perspective, this is a consequence, for instance, of the Hartian need to have primary and secondary rules in order to have law. From a pragmatic perspective, it is also a consequence of law's inherent purpose to orient behavior (which I listed as the fifth consequence of the label of law), for which it needs some form of organization that at least applies and enforces the norms. Hence the usual opinion that the words "law" and "legal system" refer to the same object, simply with a different semantic focus, used in different linguistic situations.[36] It is difficult to conceive of law outside of a legal system, of law without a system, of law without some sort of organization.[37]

---

[33] Kramer, *Objectivity*, 113.
[34] Chapter 1, Section 3 "Does Legality Affect Power Relations" and Section 7 "The Legitimate Authority Associated With Legality."
[35] Norberto Bobbio, *Teoria dell'ordinamento giuridico* (Giappichelli 1960) 7, 186; Michel van de Kerchove & François Ost, *The Legal System between Order and Disorder* (Clarendon Press 1993); François Ost & Michel van de Kerchove, *De la pyramide au réseau? Pour une théorie dialectique du droit* (FUSL Publ 2002) 284–5; Brian Z Tamanaha, "The Folly of the 'Social Scientific' Concept of Legal Pluralism" (1993) 20 *Journal of Law and Society* 192, 206; Kelsen, *General Theory of Law and State*, 3; François Ewald, "The Law of Law" in Gunter Teubner (ed), *Autopoietic Law: A New Approach to Law and Society* (de Gruyter 1988) 36; Jacques Chevallier, "L'ordre juridique" in Jacques Chevallier and Danièle Loschak (eds), *Le droit en procès* (Presses universitaires de France 1983) 8; Michel Troper, "Système juridique et Etat" (1986) 30 *Archives de philosophie du droit* 2, 30; Santi Romano, *L'ordinamento giuridico* (first published 1917, Sansoni 1918).
[36] Shapiro, *Legality*, 4–5.
[37] For a noteworthy rejoinder, but focusing on a nearly straw-man-ish understanding of a legal order as necessarily requiring the capacity to exercise physical constraint, see Alec Stone Sweet and Florian Grisel, "L'arbitrage international: du contrat dyadique au système normatif" 2009 (52) *Archives de philosophie du droit* 75.

(7) *Law carries an opposition to legal intervention from outside.* A pronouncement of legality is a form of opposition to legal intervention. Legality repels legal intervention. Two legal systems are like water and oil, they oppose one another's intervention. As Joseph Raz puts it, "[s]ince all legal systems claim to be supreme with respect to their subject-community, none can acknowledge any claim to supremacy over the same community which may be made by another legal system."[38] Since the Westphalian order, we have come to think of law as something exclusive, usually as something territorially exclusive (there can be only one law that applies within a given territory).[39] To put it colloquially, law does not like to overlap. Lawyers intuitively are against overlaps of legal regimes. The lawyers' terminology is telling: such overlaps are called *conflicts* of law. This consequence of legality creates an intuitive reaction that a legal system should refrain from interfering in the affairs of another legal system.[40]

Admittedly, many strands of legal pluralism precisely posit that there routinely are more than one legal system in existence and in effective operation within a given social field. As a consequence, conflicts between legal systems are commonplace. Real conflicts are practically ingrained in the workings of the law in a real-life societal context. Potential conflicts of legal systems are inherent in the workings of legal systems. But as Raz points out, to ask whether two legal systems can coexist in fact is not to ask whether they can coexist as a matter of law.[41] Let us go one step further: to ask whether they can legally coexist from an external point of view is not to ask whether each of them, from their relative point of view, accepts legal intervention from outside. Raz again: "Can one legal system acknowledge that another legal system applies by right to the same community or must one legal system deny the right of others to apply to the same population?"[42] Law's claim to supremacy, he concludes in substance, prevents it from acknowledging the claim to supremacy from a competing legal system. We will see in Chapter 4 that this idea of law's supremacy seems analytically debatable, but it remains the way in which law is usually understood, which is what matters in the context of the current argument.

(8) *Law carries a claim for normative and political autonomy.* If we take the last argument just one step further, we see that law signals a claim for autonomy, for political and normative autonomy. Legal sociologists like Boaventura de Sousa

---

[38] Raz, *Authority of Law*, 119.

[39] Matthew H Kramer, *In Defense of Legal Positivism* (Oxford University Press 1999) 97; Hans Kelsen, *Pure Theory of Law* (University of California Press 1967) 329; Kelsen, *General Theory of Law and State*, 410. Chapter 4 examines this question in greater detail.

[40] Thomas Schultz & David Holloway, "Retour sur la comity I—Les origines de la comity au carrefour du droit international privé et du droit international public" (2011) 138 *Journal du droit international* 863.

[41] Raz, *Authority of Law*, 118.   [42] Raz, *Authority of Law*, 118.

Santos call this "emancipation through law."[43] The doctrine of legal pluralism, which in essence may be equated with the characterization as "law" of non-state normative systems, is perceived as "a critical instrument...of emancipation" for groups other than nations.[44] If law is expected to be something just, something organized that opposes legal intervention from outside, then the doctrine of legal pluralism can be used as an attempt for the norms of a group to accede to some degree of autonomous legal dignity, to some degree of normative autonomy.

The argument works as follows. In a world dominated by states and state law, where the dominant model of law is state law, to call a regulatory system "law" is to consider it comparable to, indeed equivalent in certain respects to state law. The connection between law and states in turn evokes the symbolism associated with states and inherited from the intellectual developments that occurred at the time of the Peace of Westphalia.[45] The Westphalian Treaties, by ending the Thirty Years' War and the Dutch Revolt in the seventeenth century, helped lay the foundations of what Wolfgang Friedmann later called the "law of coexistence."[46] He meant the rationale of early international law, whose purpose was primarily to implement the principle of sovereignty through rules of abstinence from interference with the affairs of other sovereign states. The law of coexistence promoted and reinforced the symbolism of the international legal order being one of "billiard balls," as Arnold Wolfers was one of the first to put it: in other words firmly juxtaposed states.[47] This symbolism has remained deeply anchored in our understanding of the proper relations that legal orders should entertain, even when we speak of non-state law. Alain Pellet, for instance, wondered whether "transnational legal orders...just like national legal systems...remain juxtaposed to each other?"[48]

In short, the symbolism of "billiard balls," which remains very much present when we think of law beyond the state, triggers the intuitive reaction that a legal system should refrain from interfering in the affairs of another legal system. I will elaborate on this point in a few pages, but for now notice its salient implication. In terms of policy, it means this: claiming that a non-state normative system is a legal system favours a policy of laissez-faire with regard to that normative system.

---

[43] Boaventura de Sousa Santos, *Toward a New Legal Common Sense: Law, Globalization, and Emancipation* (2nd edn, Butterworths 2002) 90: "the reduction of law to state law was, more than anything else, the result of a political fiat."

[44] Anna di Robilant, "Genealogies of Soft Law" (2006) 54 *American Journal of Comparative Law* 499, 545.

[45] On these connections, see Schultz & Holloway, "Retour sur la comity I: les origines de la comity" and, to a lesser extent, Thomas Schultz & David Holloway, "Retour sur la comity II: La comity dans l'histoire du droit international privé" (2012) 138 *Journal du droit international* 571.

[46] Wolfgang Friedmann, *The Changing Structure of International Law* (Columbia University Press 1964).

[47] Arnold Wolfers, *Discord and Collaboration: Essays on International Politics* (Johns Hopkins University Press 1962) 19–24.

[48] Alain Pellet, Foreword to Frank Latty, *La lex sportiva* (Martinus Nijhoff 2007) xi.

4. Defining Law in Accordance with its Political and Ethical Signals

My argument so far in this chapter has been the following: if we characterize a given regime as law, it signals that this regime is a superior mode or regulation, which is desirable, from which we should expect justice, which is normatively meaningful for external observers and for the regime's addressees, which relies on some form of organization, which opposes the intervention of other legal regimes, and which harbors a claim for autonomy.

These eight signals form the contours—blurred contours to be sure—of our common, intuitive non-analytic understanding of law, our understanding of what we are presented with when we are presented with something that bears the label of law.

Many of these signaling effects of a label of law are of a political and ethical nature. Characterizing something as law, granting something the label of law creates political and ethical signals. It is an ethical and political act to characterize something as law, because that characterization sends political and ethical signals.

At this juncture, we should recall that these signals are rhetorical effects of a pronouncement of legality. As rhetorical effects, they draw on our collective conscience, our common, non-analytical understanding of law. As rhetorical effects, they are as invariable as our collective imagination is: they do not vary because of a sudden scholarly change in the underlying definition of law. If scholars alter the definition of law that they use to make a pronouncement of legality, the rhetorical effects very likely will remain the same. This divorce between the contents of an analytic definition of law and its rhetorical effects naturally becomes only greater when the definition of law remains implicit, or is merely addressed briefly in passing, in the discussion of the legality of a regime.

Let me repeat: In ordinary, non-jurisprudential discourse, affixing the label of law to something has certain rhetorical effects which do not depend on the underlying jurisprudential stance that we take about law. If we change the concept of law with which we work, to increase its explanatory power, or for advocacy reasons, the political and ethical signals of an attribution of legality will remain just the same.

Hence, in ordinary discourse (that is, outside of jurisprudential discussions among legal theorists), the definition of law we use in order to characterize a certain normative regime as law, or to deny it that label, should be adapted to the political and ethical signals that such a characterization would send. In other words, in ordinary, non-jurisprudential discourse about the nature of a given normative regime as either law or social order, our analytic stance on the concept of law should be adapted to the rhetorical effects of a pronouncement of legality. Chapter 3 takes this argument further. But before we continue that theoretical discussion, I want to focus on some illustrations of what we have seen so far.

5. Illustrations

When Berthold Goldman first came up with his account of the lex mercatoria,[49] he undoubtedly attracted, intentionally or not, attention to the existence of a societal phenomenon we had not thought about, that we had not seen. By calling law a normative system used in certain commercial circles, he triggered the effect of the label of law that consists of saying: "observers of the regulation of the economic world, take this seriously." Intentionally or not, simply by characterizing it as law, he signaled that the lex mercatoria should be considered normatively meaningful from an external point of view. The effect of his observation (or characterization) is that people seeking to understand or to influence the regulation of certain commercial circles should take these non-state norms into account. That is the fourth effect of the label of law in my list discussed above. His observation likely also contributed to our understanding that private economic actors form societal organizations and behave in a normatively self-reflexive way to a greater degree than we expected (sixth effect in my list above).

This echoes forty years later: certain studies in private international law today suggest that one of the reasons why private economic actors have become so disproportionately powerful is that, on the one hand, public international law largely ignored them, because they are non-state actors, and, on the other hand, private international law largely ignored their normative production.[50] Private international law is still very much marked by legal statism, or classical legal positivism. As a consequence, it fails to exert any regulatory function over phenomena that do no appear on its radar. It cannot regulate non-state law if it ignores it. So to come up with a theory that says that we should recognize the transnational regime of arbitration as a legal regime is an attempt to allow private international law to regulate it.

When the current French school of arbitration claims that there is an arbitral legal order, I suspect that they have a quite different agenda. As a prominent French arbitration scholar and practitioner puts it, "arbitrators must always strive to maintain, or to reinforce, the reputation they enjoy from states."[51] Only thus, he continues, can arbitration secure the "systematic and lasting delegation of power in the field of justice" that arbitration enjoys from the state.[52] Put more straightforwardly, the arbitration community has to show that they do a good job, that they have created a desirable regime from which parties can expect true justice, and that arbitration forms a system that is sufficiently normatively meaningful to orient the behavior of its addressees (and thus allows them to predict and plan their actions, in other words to engage in reliable business activities). On this basis, the arbitration

---

[49] Berthold Goldman, "Frontières du droit et lex mercatoria" (1964) 9 *Archives de philosophie du droit* 17.

[50] Horatia Muir Watt, "Private International Law Beyond the Schism" (2011) 2 *Transnational Legal Theory* 347.

[51] Christophe Seraglini, *Lois de police et justice arbitrale internationale* (Dalloz 2001) 69.

[52] Seraglini, *Lois de police*, 67.

community can claim a certain degree of laissez-faire on the part of the state—it can claim autonomy through liberal arbitration laws.

Labeling the arbitral regime as a legal regime in and of itself mobilizes many symbols that are useful to push such an agenda. By characterizing the arbitration system as law, the French school of arbitration triggered multiple effects of the label of law: arbitration, as law, is desirable (second effect), parties can expect justice from it (third effect) and can rely on it as a guidepost for self-directed action (fifth effect). The organization or system that underlies it (sixth effect) should be taken seriously by regulators (fourth effect), who should preferably interfere as little as possible (eight effect), as this would be tantamount to a legal system (the public state system) interfering in the affairs of another legal system (the private arbitration system) (seventh effect).

One important insider of the French school of arbitration—a particularly distinguished and sophisticated one, member of the *Académie française*—recognized almost as much in a bout of candid self-deprecation. It is all a matter of the "time-honored prestige of one word," Jean-Denis Bredin writes, for "what we call law gets a promotion. And so the arbitrator himself is glorified... and rises to full dignity. He becomes a proper judge. It may well be that the best function of [this talk of stateless law and arbitration] is to flatter the arbitrator."[53] Bredin sees in it a "gain in authority, in seriousness."[54]

But we can go further. It is generally agreed that the French school of arbitration has been instrumental in the progressive withdrawal of the state from intervention in the regulation of arbitration, in the liberalization of international arbitration as it were.[55] States were encouraged to refrain from intervening in the world of arbitration because the world of arbitration already had its own law. The rationale is this: if there already is law, with the aforementioned presupposed implied virtues, then there is less need, and even justification, for the state to interfere in this legal system. Chapter 8 explores this question in greater depth, so I want to simplify it brutally here. By the characterization of the arbitral regime as law, governments are led to believe—rightly or wrongly—that arbitrators produce a normative ordering that is more or less equivalent, in terms of regulative quality, to the workings of other legal systems. Hence a laissez-faire policy is in order: don't fix arbitration if it "ain't broke," and it "ain't broke" because it is law.

Conventions among scholars for the definition of law may have at least two very different goals: one sort of convention seeks to determine the concept of law that will have the greatest explanatory power, that will bring to light as many features as possible of the object characterized as law and help understand the nature of the social institution that is law and its specific incarnations. This is a properly scientific

---

[53] Jean-Denis Bredin, "La loi du juge" in Philippe Fouchard, Philippe Kahn, & Antoine Lyon-Caen (eds), *Le droit des relations économiques internationales—Études offertes à Berthold Goldman* (Litec 1982) 15, 27.
[54] Denis Bredin, "La loi du juge".
[55] William W Park, *Arbitration of International Business Disputes* (2nd edn, Oxford University Press 2012) 129: "To a large extent, laissez-faire judicial review remains the legacy of two great French thinkers, Professors Berthold Goldman and Philippe Fouchard, who during the 1960s began to explore notions of 'delocalized' arbitration autonomous from national law."

sort of convention about the definition of law. The other is rather one of advocacy: we may define and use legality as a qualifier in order to take advantage of its rhetorical power, of the symbols it mobilizes, of the moral-political effects it has.[56]

So we should ask ourselves this: when we fight, scientifically, for the recognition of international arbitration as an autonomous arbitral legal order, what are we really fighting for? Are we trying to explain arbitration? But then what have we really learned about arbitration by speaking about arbitration being an autonomous legal order? Or are we trying to make arbitration more autonomous by calling it a legal regime of its own? But then is this really what we, the scholars, the observers, the critics, want? Arbitration practitioners may well seek to obtain greater regulatory laissez-faire that way. Fair enough. Such manipulative uses of law are not devoid of risks, as they may trigger a regulatory backlash if autonomy goes too far, but that is another matter. To be sure, when we are not pushing a business agenda, we may want to think again about whether we really think that it is desirable to call the arbitration regime a legal order, with all the political and ethical consequences that attach almost inevitably.

What, then, is an appropriate choice of legality? How demanding should the concept of law be that we use to characterize a given norm system, for instance the international arbitration regime, as either law or social norms? The answer depends on the purpose of the question about the regime's legality. It depends on what the person affixing, or not, the label of law wants to show. If the purpose is to underscore the risk of granting arbitration greater autonomy, to leave the parties in arbitration to greater self-regulation through arbitration, then my sense is that a rather strict understanding of legality, based on what we would usually be content to call law, seems to be the right choice. If the purpose were to exhort states to treat the arbitration regime as a regime deserving respect, deference and non-intervention, then a lighter, less demanding definition of law would naturally be more appropriate.

My contention is that arbitration should not be considered a legal system because it does not meet the standards of regulative quality that one usually expects from a legal system. Calling it a legal system would be, in many circles, selling the arbitration regime for what it is not. An important part of the balance of this book tries to show just why. But for now we need to see how the rhetorical effects of a pronouncement of legality, and some other implications of legality, can be worked back into the way in which we define the concept of law. The next chapter takes up that task.

---

[56] There is also a more general point to think about, one that on the surface seems more quirky than important. In fact it has significant consequences for the way lawyers think. When scholars with no vested interests in arbitration speak of international arbitration as transnational law, their point often will be that academic lawyers should take it seriously, that law schools should take it seriously (fourth effect). The law curriculum at most law schools is quite regrettable in this regard. The study of transnational law is rarely a mandatory part of a law school curriculum, although it would usefully help studying the transformation of the forms of legal normativity. It would help see regimes that are normatively meaningful and often will actually determine and thus explain the conduct of, for instance, private economic actors (fifth effect). By brandishing the label of law, it becomes easier to convince a dean that certain forms of private regulation should indeed be studied by law students.

3
Shaping Legality

In the previous two chapters, the heart of my argument was that law ought not to be trivialized. Calling a regime "law," I said, has certain implications: it creates expectations of predictability and of justice; it engenders moral reasons to obey the regime; it gives the regime increased authority; it accords power to those who produce or control the regime or some of its norms; it facilitates policies of laissez-faire with regard to that regime; and overall it fashions the lawyers' appropriate field of expertise. Affixing the label of law to given rule systems is not a neutral matter of merely settling the semantics.

Outrageous as it may be, many people did not wait for my elucidation of this point to understand the idea that labeling something as law has real-life implications. Some of these people sought then, occasionally in a very successful way, to shape legality in a certain manner, so as to activate some of the implications of characterizing regimes as law. Sometimes this was done because of justice beliefs associated with certain law-producing actors. Sometimes it was done to pursue a more straightforward political agenda.

In this chapter, I map some of the ways in which legality has been shaped in order to achieve these ends. I do that in a laconically selective way given the size of the matter, but I hope just extensively enough to make my point. I start with a key reason why law has been confined to state law: a justice belief, which was prominently expressed by Hans Kelsen and Léon Duguit in 1926. I then move to the flip side of that story, to review some of the ways in which legality has been used for stateless regimes in order to promote certain values and powers. On the basis of that review, the chapter goes to a higher degree of abstraction and delineates some of the principal parameters of the battle to replace state law as the paradigm of legality. As a coda to this discussion, the chapter ends with an important clarification: law ought not to be considered scalable (that is, the character of law does not obtain by degrees). Such a position would indeed largely amount to a return to the trivialization of the question of what we call and do not call law.

1. Justice Beliefs in State Law

The confinement of law to norm systems made by states was initially, to a large extent, the consequence of the political doctrines that surrounded the Westphalian

Treaties, which ended the Thirty Years War.[1] We briefly encountered the Treaties in the previous chapter. Brutally simplified, these political doctrines were the independence of nations and their legal orders and a duty of non-interference in the affairs of other nations. These ideas are captured by the concept of sovereignty and the modern state system, which fully emerged or rather got traction at that time.[2]

The purpose of these doctrines, at the time, was essentially to minimize regulatory overlaps among the various political entities that preceded states.[3] Such overlaps had been one of the causes of the Thirty Years War.[4] The idea, simply put, was to recognize only one regulatory authority (the state) and one type of regulation (state law). States and state legal system nearly completely displaced the earlier overlapping "transnational" layers of legal regulation.[5]

So equating law with state law sought to cure the political context that had led to an extremely brutal and destructive war—the Thirty Years War was one of Europe's most devastating conflicts until the World Wars. Such a political objective undoubtedly constituted a very legitimate raison d'être for an idea of what counts as law.

But later the equation between law and state law became, at least in part, the consequence of a simpler belief of ethical order—more precisely a belief of justice. Léon Duguit and Hans Kelsen for instance expressed it in 1926 when they wrote this: "we believe to have serious reasons to be convinced that the only means to

---

[1] The Westphalian Treaties of October 1648 are considered by most commentators to have brought about the birth of modern international law, marked among other elements by a clear separation between the internal affairs of a State and its external relations with other states, and by the concept of territorial sovereignty. It was in fact not the Treaties themselves that brought about any change in regard to sovereignty or territoriality, as they happened to be completely silent on these matters, but the general context of their negotiations did indeed foster the shifts that are ascribed to them. See for instance Nico Schrijver, "The Changing Nature of State Sovereignty" (1999) 70 *British Year Book of International Law* 65, 68–9; Antonio Cassese, *International Law* (Oxford University Press 2001) 19ff; David Boucher, *Political Theories of International Relations* (Oxford University Press 1998) 224–5; Stephen Neff, "A Short History of International Law" in Malcolm D Evans (ed), *International Law* (Oxford University Press 2003) 33, 42; John M Gillroy, "Justice-as-Sovereignty: David Hume and the Origins of International Law" (2007) 78 *British Year Book of International Law* 429; John M Kelly, *A Short History of Western Legal Theory* (Clarendon Press 1992) 158ff, 175; Malcolm N Shaw, *International Law* (5th edn, Cambridge University Press 2003) 21, 25.

[2] See for instance James Crawford, *The Creation of States in International Law* (2nd edn, Oxford University Press 2007) 10: "the early law of nations had its origin in the European State-system, which existed long before its conventional date or origin in the Peace of Westphalia (1648), ending the Thirty Years' War. The effect of the Peace of Westphalia was to consolidate the existing States and principalities (including those whose existence and autonomy it recognized or established) at the expense of the notion of the *civitas gentium maxima*—the universal community of mankind transcending the authority of States."

[3] See for instance Andreas Osiander, *Before the State: Systemic Political Change from the Greeks to the French Revolution* (Oxford University Press 2007).

[4] Stéphane Beaulac, "The Westphalian Legal Orthodoxy—Myth or Reality?" (2000) 2 *Journal of the History of International Law* 148, 160: "Th[e] large number of increasingly powerful actors in Europe, in addition to the multilayered system of political authorities, as well as the religious dimension of the different polities, made the violent solution of the situation virtually inevitable."

[5] Philip Allott, "Self-Determination—Absolute Right or Social Poetry?" in Christian Tomuschat (ed), *Modern Law of Self-Determination* (Martinus Nijhoff 1993) 177, 184–5; Markus Fischer, "Feudal Europe, 800–1300: Communal Discourse and Conflictual Practice" (1992) 46 *International Organization* 427, 449; George Clark, *Early Modern Europe from about 1450 to about 1720* (Oxford University Press 1957) 28.

satisfy our aspiration to justice and equity is the resigned confidence that there is no other justice than the justice to be found in the positive law of states."[6]

Put differently, Duguit and Kelsen thought, and their opinion is arguably still widely shared among law-makers and policy-makers, that to admit of law outside of state law would jeopardize our "aspiration to justice and equity." Transnational stateless legality would as a consequence almost necessarily seem to raise ethical concerns. The rise of transnational law would per se amount to a rising ethical threat. Similarly, Hobbes and Bentham, these two great believers in the state, "regarded valid laws," according to John Gardner, "as necessarily endowed with some moral value just in virtue of being valid laws."[7] Nothing should be law if it is not made by states, because there is a connection between legality and morality: not an analytical connection, but a belief that there is something moral in law, and that only states can be expected to provide that something.

Duguit and Kelsen acknowledged indeed that they had expressed a belief. This belief amounted to a political argument quite different from the duty not to interfere in the affairs of others states, drawn from the concept of sovereignty for the purposes of advancing peace. Duguit and Kelsen's belief really amounted to a political ideology. Let me repeat: seen in this light, classical legal positivism (a school of thought that they, in particular Kelsen, so strongly contributed to promoting) implicitly contends that the only law there is, is state law, because only systems of rules produced by a state or a collectivity of states deserve the label of law. It is based on the belief that only states can produce the kind of justice or fairness that we have come to associate with law.

Arguably, then, Duguit and Kelsen *did not want to be* legal pluralists, *did not want to see* law outside of state law. It is not so much, as it is on occasion claimed, that they, or Kelsen at least, seemed to have understood that something was wrong with legal statism but could not figure out how legal pluralism would work in theory.[8] It rather seems, based on what we just discussed, that the objective was precisely not to allow the label of law to attach to stateless regimes. This is a relatively straightforward example of how legality may be shaped starting from real-life, social implications of calling something law: what the label of law *ought to* be affixed to, because of the consequences of this affixation, determines the meaning to be given to legality, and thus what the label of law *can be* affixed to.

2. Some Uses of Legality for Stateless Regimes

So we have seen how certain people believed that legality ought to be shaped in such a way as to admit only of state law, because, to put it bluntly, it seemed

---

[6] Léon Duguit and Hans Kelsen, "Avant-propos" (1926–1927) 1 *Revue internationale de la théorie du droit* 1, 3 (translated by the author).
[7] John Gardner, "Legal Positivism: 5½ Myths" (2001) 46 *American Journal of Jurisprudence* 199.
[8] As asserted for instance by John Gardner, "What is Legal Pluralism?" paper delivered at Osgoode Hall Law School, May 8, 2013, available at <http://www.youtube.com/watch?v=q-aTJgTTOA8>.

necessary to safeguard the aspiration to justice and equity we place in law. Let us now consider how other people pushed the opposite idea—the idea that we should embrace certain stateless regimes as law—often in a similar pursuit of a certain kind of justice and equity.

Before we properly start, I should mention that "legal pluralism" is probably the terminology most often used in attempts to extend the shape of law beyond the state. I do not particularly like that term. I use it rarely in this book, because of the diversity of meanings it has been given: legal pluralism has been used alternatively to cover almost every aspect of law's plural nature—for instance the plurality of its sources, the diversity in the types of legal norms, the multiple kinds of legal systems, and many more aspects of law's non-monolithic character.[9] "Pluralism," after all, is a fashionable word. It smacks of open-mindedness, or humanism, of embracing human diversity. Worthy ideals to be sure.

The point here is clearly not to review this diversity. The point merely is to anchor our discussion in a certain strand of literature dealing with legal pluralism. I mean the strand of literature that revolves around the idea that "two or more legal systems coexist in the same social field":[10] there is more than one legal system on a given territory at a given time, one at least of which is not produced by the state.

Now, to be analytically precise, and this is a further reason why I generally refrain from using the phrase "legal pluralism," stateless law may of course exist even if there is no other legal system that exists within the same social field or territory, in which case there would perforce be no "pluralism." Stateless law does not require the presence of "overlapping normative communities."[11] No overlap is needed. Legal *pluralism*, however, does need it, at least in the branch of legal pluralism we have now followed.

So within that branch of legal pluralism, we should simply retain the idea, as Michaels puts it, that "the state is not the only producer of law; non-state communities can produce law as well."[12] More precisely, legal pluralism is taken here in its meaning that non-state communities can produce their own legal systems, not merely contribute to the state's legal system. (Recall the distinction from the first main section of Chapter 1 between participating in a given legal system and creating a normative system which is legal in itself, not because of its belonging to another legal system.)

This understanding of legal pluralism has been used to pursue at least four main bold objectives: local cultural diversity, socialism, economic liberalism, and, counterintuitively, the strengthening of the state.[13] Let us consider them in turn.

---

[9] Francis G Snyder, "Governing Economic Globalization: Global Legal Pluralism and European Law" (1999) 5 *European Law Journal* 334; Francis G Snyder, "Economic Globalisation and the Law in the Twenty-First Century" in Austin Sarat (ed), *Blackwell Companion to Law and Society* (Blackwell 2004).

[10] Sally E Merry, "Legal Pluralism" (1988) 22 *Law and Society Review* 869, 870.

[11] Paul S Berman, *Global Legal Pluralism. A Jurisprudence of Law Beyond Borders* (Cambridge University Press 2012) 3.

[12] Ralf Michaels, "The Re-State-ment of Non-State Law: The State, Choice of Law, and the Challenge from Global Legal Pluralism" (2005) 51 *Wayne Law Review* 1209, 1221.

[13] For a much more extensive review of the meaning of legal pluralism, see for instance Emmanuel Melissaris, *Ubiquitous Law: Legal Theory and The Space for Legal Pluralism* (Ashgate 2009) 27ff.

2.1 Law without the state for local cultural diversity

Law is an important instrument of colonization. Sally Engle Merry provided a good example of this in her studies of the colonization of Hawaii.[14] Indigenous Hawaiian law was elbowed aside to make place for Anglo-American law, with its carriage of state courts, prisons, and new ideas of discipline. It steered the culture of the islands towards global capitalism and Christianity. Questions as culturally intimate as the role of women, representations of appropriate sexuality, and the contours of marriage were altered, sometimes quite profoundly. Conducted in the name of civilization, this cultural imperialism descended on the islands in many forms. Chief among them, and that is what is of interest to us, were legal reforms. A new blanket of law covered Hawaii and smothered its culture. But not completely.

True, Western states imposed their legal systems in many colonies. But as Ralf Michaels puts it "below those, with or without the acknowledgment of the official law, other legal orders lived on."[15] (Michaels is a comparative lawyer. Comparative lawyers sometimes have to think about what law is in order to figure out what to compare when comparing legal systems.) In other words, there are often niches of "stateless law" surviving under the umbrella of the state that covers the same territory.

Stateless *law* it is meant to be indeed. And not merely because of lexicographic clarification. Situations such as the Hawaiian colonization prompted certain people to take a harder look at legality, at what amounts to law. They were in the main legal anthropologists, at least as far as our argument is concerned. In many colonies, legal anthropologists said in substance, we find local communities, typically indigenous communities, which live to a significant extent according to their own rules. They deem these rules to be "law" or something that in their worldview is roughly equivalent to "law."[16] We should recognize these rules as law, and not just as unqualified social norms, because that recognition may well play a key role in protecting cultural diversity.

Their reasoning goes more or less like this: first, we should see these normative systems as law because these local communities often interact with these norms, behave vis-à-vis these norm systems, in a way that is comparable with the way in which we Westerners interact with what we call law.[17] On that basis, we colonial powers lose an important rhetorical justification for interfering with these communities.[18] Consider this famous quote from Carl von Linné: "American[s are]

---

[14] Sally E Merry, *Colonizing Hawai'i: The Cultural Power of Law* (Princeton University Press 2000).
[15] Michaels, "The Re-State-ment," 1221.
[16] See for instance the classic Bronislaw Malinowski, *Crime and Custom in Savage Society* (first published 1926, Littlefield Adams 1985).
[17] See for instance the introductory chapter of John L Comaroff, *Rules and Processes* (University of Chicago Press 1981).
[18] Consider Norbert Elias, *Der Prozess der Zivilisation* (Suhrkamp 1976), who considered that state-building and thus state law was the main vehicle of "civilization," and the many reactions to Elias, such as Hans-Peter Duerr, *Nacktheit und Scham. Der Mythos vom Zivilisationsprozess* (Suhrkamp 1988).

regulated by custom. European[s are] governed by laws. Asiatic[s are] governed by opinions. African[s are] governed by caprice."[19] Rhetoric like this justified colonization: recall the idea from Chapter 1 that law is generally perceived to be a superior mode of regulation, a cultural achievement. So legal anthropologists took on to temper such worldviews by reconsidering the notion of law, in order to help protect legality (in the sense of that which is of a legal nature) in all its variegated manifestations, which are to a certain extent equivalent.[20] The argument "they do not have law so we will bring it to them, because it will civilize them" no longer flies, since they already have law. We should respect what they have for what it is, namely law. We should respect legal pluralism. If we trump their local norms, we simply replace their law with ours; legal monism replaces legal pluralism: that is more difficult to justify in terms of "civilizing" a people, a community. Stateless law must be left to survive, as law, under the broader umbrella of state law, because law without the state contributes to local cultural pluralism.

This sort of legal pluralism, sometimes called "state legal pluralism,"[21] essentially expressed a policy of self-restraint: brutally simplified, we should not destroy valuable institutions in colonies, and law intuitively is valuable. One reason to call this "*state* legal pluralism" was that it barely represented a threat to the power or central authority of states. This sort of legal pluralism did not really seek to assert the power of local communities, at least not straightforwardly.

Let me caricature the reasoning once more, to bring out the salient aspect we should notice on our way to this chapter's argument: consider these local communities, they are precious and fragile, we shall protect them, leave them alone, respect them as we respect biodiversity, like the remnants of a forgotten, harmless world.[22] That sort of legal pluralism does not change the way a state governs, does not alter relations of power, does not challenge those in power. It is a simple carve out in the regulatory scope of the state, a carve out limited in space, typically to specific regions, and often limited to specific ethnic groups.

Notice however, in this line of reasoning, an appeal to the argument that law is valuable, is a sign of sophistication: we should not trample on these norms because they are legal norms.

But delineating the contours of law can also have a more assertive, more challenging intent. Let us consider how.

2.2 Law without the state for socialism

Marc Chagall was a rather free-thinking painter, even by artistic standards. His style, though influenced by cubists, surrealists, and fauvists, remained very much

---

[19] Carl von Linné, *A General System of Nature* (Lackington, Allen & Co 1806) I, 6.
[20] Margaret T Hodgen, *Early Anthropology in the Sixteenth and the Seventeenth Centuries* (University of Pennsylvania Press 1964).
[21] John Griffiths, "What is Legal Pluralism?" (1986) 24 *Journal of Legal Pluralism* 1, 5; Gordon R Woodman, "Legal Pluralism and the Search for Justice" (1996) 40 *Journal of African Law* 152, 157–8.
[22] Merry, "Legal Pluralism," 869–70.

independent of any school of art. He was one of the greatest too, having been one of the very few artists to exhibit their work at the Louvres during their lifetime. More importantly for our discussion, he was a Jew. He lived in France at several points of his life, including before both World Wars, at a time when France, too, was devoured by antisemitism. His first stay in Paris took place shortly after the Dreyfuss Affair and Zola's "J'accuse!".

Jewish culture influenced Chagall quite significantly. Jewish images and personages figure prominently in his paintings, as do depictions of Jewish martyrs and refugees. His work was, in part, a defense of Jewish culture against the dominant antisemitism of his time, a resistance, in an artist's way, against the then dominant creed.

Chagall was close friends with another person who engaged in a form of resistance against central powers: Georges Gurvitch, a lawyer and sociologist. Gurvitch and Chagall had a common history of active political revolt. Both were born in Russia, and engaged in the Russian revolution of 1917, ousting the Tsarist autocracy. Bolshevik rule, however, was barely more satisfactory, and Gurvitch and Chagall escaped to France. There Gurvitch later continued his forthright opposition to ruling powers, as an outspoken advocate of Algerian decolonization. He strongly supported the Algerian revolt against France, and thus against French law. To the point that his apartment was bombed by a French paramilitary organization, the OAS,[23] leading him to go into hiding, with his wife, at Chagall's apartment.

Just like Chagall, Gurvitch also engaged in a subtler, more scholarly form of revolt, partly influenced by his disappointment with the Bolshevik authoritarianism he had helped put in place. Where Chagall painted to help preserve the identity of a persecuted community, Gurvitch sought to advance the political interests of a subdued group by reshaping the contours of legality. He embraced, once again, the cause of the working class, and hence contributed to creating, almost incidentally, the field of legal sociology.

Gurvitch produced a somewhat byzantine work.[24] But at its heart is a simple and important claim: law is the expression of a sociality's order. Determining what counts as law (that is, shaping legality) is one way in which a sociality asserts its power and defends its values and interests. A sociality, in that sense, is in essence a community loosely defined, possibly as broad as a social class, with overarching shared values and interests. Each sociality also forms a power structure, an entity that has certain means to advance the shared values and interests. In each sociality, certain individuals, groups of individuals or institutions hold the "scepter": the symbol of power, the means to identify power. Those who hold the scepter determine the official, accepted discourse or position about the values and interests to be pursued, and thus about what is law.

---

[23] "Organisation de l'armée secrète," whose motto was "Algeria is French and will remain so."
[24] Georges Gurvitch, Sociology of Law (first published 1942, Transaction Publishers 2001); Georges Gurvitch, L'idée du droit social: notion et système du Droit Social; histoire doctrinale depuis le XVIIe siècle jusqu'à la fin du XIXe siècle (Sirey 1932).

To see how law is the expression of a sociality's order, and thus how communities can use the shaping of legality to push their interests, we need to consider two main types of sociality: Gurvitch calls them organized and spontaneous.

Organized sociality, to put it simply, is the state. Or more precisely it is the ruling class, which controls the state and imposes it on others. Organized sociality produces organized law in a centralized and hierarchical way. Here's how Gurvitch puts it: "Organized sociality... is linked with collective behaviors in so far as they are guided by patterns crystallized in deliberate schemes, which are fixed in advance and impose hierarchized and centralized conduct."[25] The ruling classes impose a view of what law is, of where legality starts and where it ends, of what is part of the "official," and thus only, legal system.

Organized sociality produces law and imposes it by relegating all other norm systems to the rank of unqualified social norms, with a corresponding loss in authority. The official discourse maintains that only organized sociality can produce what counts as law. And the official discourse is controlled by an organized sociality, in other words by the ruling class. Undoubtedly Gurvitch had seen enough real-life examples of this to craft such a theory, during, before, and after the Russian revolution of 1917.

This delimitation, or shaping, of legality, has effects on two types of addressees. First on the primary or final addressees, those who receive the hard end of the rules. They obey the ruling class by obeying the norms they call law. They obey these norms because they are deemed to be law, and that qualification mobilizes symbols of justice and legitimacy and authority (recall the discussion from Chapter 1). Ruling classes use the generally perceived legitimate authority of law to impose their will. The contours of what counts as law also affect the law's secondary addressees, those who apply the rules, such as judges and the administration. They obey the ruling classes by applying the norms they call law. They apply these norms because it is their job to apply what is called law in the official discourse about what law is.

But the reality beyond the official discourse, Gurvitch argued, is that spontaneous sociality also produces law—spontaneous law. Gurvitch's idea is basically this: we need to embrace legal pluralism (recall: more than one legal system on a given territory at a given time) in order to look beyond the prevailing power structure, to apprehend it from an external point of view. This would help us see the determination of law's contours for what it really is: the imposed will of the ruling class, disguised as the only law there is. Legal pluralism would allow us to become cognizant of law beyond state-made law, to perceive stateless legality, and thus to fully recognize the force of spontaneous sociality without the state.

Gurvitch's purpose, in accord with his political inclination, was that we notice in particular the spontaneous sociality revolving around unions and worker's councils. We should see different power structures than those of the ruling classes and of the state. They also produce rules. If we embrace legal pluralism, we can conceptually

---

[25] Gurvitch, *Sociology*, 203.

have access to the view that there are other rules than the rules of state law; we can see that these other rules have a great degree of autonomy; we can see that these other rules may be equivalent, in many respects, to state law; we can see that these forms of sociality may be equivalent, in a number of ways, to the organized sociality that produces state law.

In fact, and here the argument moves more openly to a rhetorical, political discourse, there is no reason not to recognize the equivalence of these different social groups, these socialities. It is a way to tell the proletariat that their spontaneous sociality, their social group, is worth just as much, is as legitimate, as the social group forming the ruling class. The pitch would go more or less like this: "Members of the working class, your spontaneous sociality is just as normatively relevant as the one of the ruling class. There is 'their law', the official law of the state, but there is also 'your law'. And there is no a priori, principled, prevalence of one over the other, there is only imposition through power. Which legal system prevails is just a question of power, and power can be overthrown." Anna di Robilant, in her discussion of Gurvitch, frames this as "social life taking revenge against state law."[26]

In sum, Gurvitch's hope was that legal pluralism, by challenging the unity of law, would help us see power structures. It should help us discern the power monopoly in the hands of those who hold the scepter of legality, those who say what law is, those who shape the contours of legality. His aim was that the recognition of the power implications of defining legality would engender a change in power structures, would bring about socialism in France.

Understanding Gurvitch, of course, was not the point of this discussion. The point was to see one way in which legality was shaped, in theoretical discourse, in order to achieve practical political results. Legal pluralism, or more precisely the possibility of stateless law, was proffered to advance the cause of socialism. It was meant to help workers revolt by changing our understanding of law, by extending it to law without the state.

This idea that legal pluralism is a tool to reveal and push back imposed law, to liberate socialities other than the state, has also been used for other political aims. Let me describe one that pertains to the other end of the political spectrum.

2.3 Law without the state for economic liberalism

The idea is neither new nor complicated to grasp: some people believe that states are, at least in their current incarnation, slow, heavy creatures that constitute obstacles to the economic development of a country, a region, or a trade. Small government would help the economy to flourish. State law, it follows, is a cure that should be used homeopathically. International commerce, precisely because it is international, is particularly unsuited to government regulation. It should be subject as little as possible to state law. It needs its own rules. It is best off with rule systems it primarily makes itself.

---

[26] Anna di Robilant, "Genealogies of Soft Law" (2006) 54 *American Journal of Comparative Law* 499.

So we have here again a claim of inappropriate subjugation by the state and an ensuing call for freedom. In a sense it is quite similar to the one made by Gurvitch for the working class, though of course it pursues vastly different axiological objectives. Oftentimes, and these are the instances that are relevant to my argument, the appeal to freedom is not a plea to take a few steps towards the state of nature, towards fewer rules per se. Economic actors are not necessarily averse to rules. The aversion, oftentimes, is directed at rules made by the state. They should make place for rules made by the economic actors themselves. The buzzword for this is "self-regulation." Elevated to theoretical reasoning, it is also, in many cases, a push for legal pluralism, for law without the state.

Here is one example of how it is a push for legal pluralism, for *law* without the state. The starting point is the argument that state law and stateless law are just instances of law. They are law to the same extent. There is an equivalence of everything juridical. Gilles Cuniberti has shown how this manifests itself in the work of organizations producing model contracts: the label of law is invoked as a justification for side-stepping mandatory rules of national law.[27] The rhetorical operations of the argument are these: since private agreements and regimes amount to law to the same extent that national law amounts to law (they are on the same footing of legality, if you will), mandatory rules of national law should not interfere with the work of their private counterparts, the private legal regimes.

Now, stateless law is supposed to be better than state law for the economy because, as Anna di Robilant nicely sums it up, non-state law allows "the greatest degree of flexibility and revision accommodating rapid change."[28] Stateless law is the only type of law that can satisfactorily "respond to rapidly changing market needs."[29]

Think of it as economic actors arguing that they already have their own regulation, their own law, and that they should be left alone with it because that law can boast of the quickest reactions, is closest to its main actors, etc. That sort of reasoning is in fact fairly frequent among members of the international arbitration community.[30]

As I said, this whole line of thought is remarkably conventional. It thus barely needs further explication, given that its mention is merely an illustration to mark a place on the way to the argument I make in this chapter. (The general idea of markets as regulators is of course a great deal more complex than it is represented in the foregoing, as Gralf-Peter Calliess and Peer Zumbansen for instance show,[31] but

---

[27] Gilles Cuniberti, "Three Theories of Lex Mercatoria" (2013) 52 *Columbia Journal of Transnational Law*, forthcoming.

[28] di Robilant, "Genealogies," 550.

[29] di Robilant, "Genealogies," 550.

[30] Catherine Rogers, "The Vocation of the International Arbitrator" (2005) 20 *American University International Law Review* 957, 963: "failures to voluntarily take up efforts at self-regulation have provoked other potential regulators to step in to fill the perceived gap... I propose certain innovations that would increase the rigor and transparency in the market for services and in international arbitrators' self-regulation." In other words: self-regulate and they will go away.

[31] Gralf-Peter Calliess and Peer Zumbansen, *Rough Consensus and Running Code. A Theory of Transnational Private Law* (Hart 2010) 59–64.

we shall keep from that distraction here.) Let me now describe, in the wake of this idea, a use of a certain theory of stateless legality, made among others by the arbitration community, that is, ironically, in complete opposition with the intents of the theory's author.

2.4 Law without the state for a stronger state

What should hopefully be clear at this stage is that legal pluralism and the shaping of legality, is not only an epistemological project. It does not only seek to achieve different understandings of the social phenomenon that law is. It is not only a neutral descriptive project (assuming, for a moment, that descriptive projects can be neutral at all). Shaping legality is also a political project, in the fullest sense of the word.

Noberto Bobbio, a devotee of structuring ideas, sought to mark out two archetypal, ideal-type political projects in legal pluralism.[32]

Either, he contended, stateless legality is embraced as a rebellion against the establishment, against the established power, following a subversive agenda. Non-state law is meant here as an instrument to help "liberat[e] social groups from the oppression of the state."[33] Gurvitch is a case in point. The defense of stateless law's legality in the name of the market is another—admittedly less clearly so, but that does not matter.

Or, Bobbio argued, stateless legality can be alleged for the exactly opposite purpose: to strengthen the state. Stateless law can indeed be pointed at as an unpalatable state of affairs, legal pluralism a disorder crying out for reordering, a fragmented legal landscape in want of unity, the tell-tale sign of the winds of anarchy. Counterintuitive as it may sound, a finding of legal pluralism, of law without the state, can be a way to conjure fears of the collapse of the state and an ensuing "lawlessness": the state must react and reassert its power and authority. Signaling the occurrence of non-state law can proceed from a reactionary ideology and nurture it.

Michel Foucault had a nice word to catch a similar idea, which helps us see the point: "logophobia,"[34] literally the fear of discourse, of orders and knowledge. It means the angst often provoked by the non-unicity of discourse in a given area, perceived as an "incessant, disorderly buzzing."[35] Foucault calls it a "dumb fear... of everything that could possibly be violent, discontinuous, querulous, disordered even and perilous in it."[36] In substance, a plurality of conflicting ideas (or discourses, or norms expressing ideas) about a subject-matter can cause angst, which can entice attempts to impose unity. Unequivocalness is psychologically reassuring, and thus rhetorically appealing.

---

[32] Norberto Bobbio, "Teoria e ideologia nella dottrina di Santi Romano" in Paolo Biscaretti di Ruffia (ed.), *Le dottrine giuridiche di oggi e l' insegnamento di Santi Romano* (Giuffrè 1977) 35–9.
[33] di Robilant, "Genealogies," 551.
[34] Michel Foucault, *L'ordre du discours* (Gallimard 1971) 32–4.
[35] Foucault, *L'ordre du discours*, 32–4.   [36] Foucault, *L'ordre du discours*, 32–4.

Bobbio was aiming at a specific author, who did engage in a culture of unicity of thought, when he expounded this pro-state use of stateless legality: Santi Romano, the great hero of the French doctrine on arbitration as a separate legal order.

Two longer quotes are warranted here. Here's how Emmanuel Gaillard puts it, giving a brief abstract of the places where international arbitration and legal theory have met:[37]

Unlike the views of Maurice Hauriou, whose institution theory seemed somewhat dated in the second half of the twentieth century, Santi Romano's work, which was also based on an institution theory and dated back to 1918 but had only been translated into French in 1975, was still considered new and appealing... [M]ost of the studies on this subject by international arbitration specialists referred to Santi Romano's definition of a legal order, be it to justify the existence of transnational rules or to deny the legal nature of transnational rules without their recognition as such by a national legal order. This shows how Santi Romano, at least in this context, acquired a belated reputation in the circles of positive law scholars in France.

Filippo Fontanelli, a young scholar who recently completed a brilliant study on the legacy of Santi Romano, echoes the story from the Italian camp:

From the beginning, the debate [on the existence of a transnational arbitral system and the lex mercatoria as a legal order] often turned to Romano's theory, which provided a theoretical foundation for the emergence of a system removed from the State model... Romano's theory has enjoyed increasing currency, most often to support the conclusion [that] *lex mercatoria* is indeed an autonomous legal order.[38]

A great, influential scholar, then. But there is another side to Romano, a darker side that is usually ridden roughshod over. In October 1928, Romano became a member of the *Partito Nazionale Fascista* (the Italian National Fascist Party). Two months later, Benito Mussolini appointed him to the high political office of President of the *Consiglio di Stato* (the Italian State Council, a combination of a Supreme Administrative Court and a Ministry of Justice, and thus an important political organ). Six years later, in 1934, he made it to the Senate of the Kingdom. He remained in both posts, during a very troubled time in Italy, until 1944. At that time the Italian High Court of Justice for Sanctions Against Fascism removed him from his office in the Senate, on charges of having furthered the cause of fascism.[39] For his distinguished services, he was decorated at least nine times by King Vittorio Emanuele III. Against this background, he hardly comes across as the archetype of a liberal democrat, let alone of a revolutionary seeking to push back the state to allow other communities than the nation to flourish.

Bobbio thus describes Romano as "*teoricamente un pluralista, ma ideologicamente un monista*": "theoretically a pluralist, but ideologically a monist."[40] A credible

---

[37] Emmanuel Gaillard, *Legal Theory of International Arbitration* (Martinus Nijhoff 2010) 4.
[38] Filippo Fontanelli, "Santi Romano and *L'ordinamento giuridico*: The Relevance of a Forgotten Masterpiece for Contemporary International, Transnational and Global Legal Relations" (2011) 2 *Transnational Legal Theory* 67, 108–9.
[39] See the page on Santi Romano at <www.senato.it>.   [40] Bobbio, "Teoria," 41.

reading of his life and ideology, then, also supported by Italian legal philosopher Giovanni Tarello, is that he pursued a conservative agenda and defended, in fact, a strong centralized state.[41]

So the French school of international arbitration as a transnational, stateless, arbitral legal order, built an important part of their theoretical edifice on a thinker his own compeers, scholars of the highest caliber, depict as a reactionary author (he was, it is said, "desperately holding on to old certitudes"[42]). An author who wanted a stronger state. An author who wanted stateless law to be muffled, smothered.[43] Ironic, no?

Ironic but understandable. If Romano indeed meant to trigger state-consolidation reactions by his portrayal of uncontrolled stateless legal orders, he may well have misevaluated the way in which most people would read the label of law: it more often than not evokes representations of justice and desirability, as I discussed in the first two chapters of this book.

In any event, we should not make too much of the irony. It does not, of course, undermine the strength of the theory on arbitration as a transnational stateless legal order. Nor does the irony explain, let alone cure, its flaws. These are matters for the discussions in Chapters 5, 7, and 8. The point in the current chapter has merely been to point the way to a few manners in which the shapes of legality have been influenced by political aspirations, by objectives of power shifts.

We shall, in the next main section of this chapter, move on to a general mapping of the types of forces at play in the shaping of legality—or more precisely its reshaping as we move beyond state-shaped legality.

But before we do that, I want to briefly point the way to a place in international law scholarship. It is a place where a similar depiction of legal pluralism seeks to conjure fears of non-unicity, to evoke logophobia, with the aim of increasing the power of those who hold the scepter of a dominant discourse. That place is the fragmentation of international law.

Roughly simplified, the fragmentation of international law is international law being increasingly subdivided into specialized and conflicting or contradicting systems—legal pluralism within international law, if you will. Now, Mario Prost convincingly argues that, on the lips of certain people, "'fragmentation' is a rhetorical device used by general/public international lawyers as an instrument of symbolic legitimation in their ongoing struggle for professional recognition and dominance."[44]

---

[41] Giovanni Tarello, "La dottrina dell'ordinamento e la figura pubblica di Santi Romano" in Paolo Biscaretti di Ruffìa (ed), *Le dottrine giuridiche di oggi e l'insegnamento di Santi Romano* (Giuffrè 1977) 256.
[42] Maurizio Fioravanti, "Per l'interpretazione dell'opera giuridica di Santi Romano: Nuove prospettive della ricerca" (1981) 10 *Quaderni fiorentini per la storia del pensiero giuridico moderno* 169, 181.
[43] di Robilant, "Genealogies," 551–2.
[44] Mario Prost, "All Shouting the Same Slogans: International Law's Unities and the Politics of Fragmentation" (2006) 17 *Finnish Yearbook of International Law* 1, 28.

The point is simple: the rise of specialized branches of international law (WTO law, EU law, international criminal law, etc) causes a "progressive marginalization of general/public international law and its 19th century categories (territory, statehood, treaties, state responsibility)."[45] This marginalization, in turn, may easily cause a lowered social standing and decreased income, and thus reduced power, for scholars and practitioners of general public international law—taken as a whole of course, not necessarily individually.

An obvious response to the problem, then, is to demonize the competing, specialized fields as "threats to the legitimacy and the efficacy of the legal order."[46] The fragmentation of international law, or legal pluralism within international law, is portrayed as "endanger[ing] the very legitimacy and efficacy of international law itself."[47]

The reasoning is akin to Romano's: flag legal pluralism, and hopefully it will be seen as the herald of chaos, which just might pre-emptively increase the power of the (old) establishment.

3. A Battle of Candidates for Paradigm

So shaping legality can be a battle with political implications. We may well create political effects when we alter the label of law while determining what to affix it to, when we change the concept of law while contemplating what counts as law, in other words when we change the major and not the minor premise in the syllogism that applies the concept of law to a given regime.

A consensus seems to be spreading ever more widely on the idea that we should indeed alter the label of law. We need to break with the idea that law has a necessary connection to territory, that law is nothing more and nothing less than the law made by states. In a recent book entitled *The Concept of Law from a Transnational Perspective*, Detlef von Daniels, a young legal philosopher, goes as far as to contend that reconstructing "a concept of law from a transnational perspective" is "a way to save jurisprudence as a philosophical discipline."[48] While the main effect of this overstatement is to cast doubt on the efforts in acknowledging and responding to alternatives that went into that author's work, like a feminist claiming that all men oppress women, he points in the right direction. The debate about what paradigm of legality should replace the paradigm of legal statism still is a real and important one.

To see the point, let us again look slightly sideways and zoom in on international law. Andrea Bianchi recently examined, from a meta-theoretical point of view, the field of international law as a whole.[49] The point was, since it was a *meta*-theory, to

---

[45] Prost, "All Shouting the Same Slogans," 25.
[46] Prost, "All Shouting the Same Slogans," 27.
[47] Prost, "All Shouting the Same Slogans," 29.
[48] Detlef von Daniels, *The Concept of Law from a Transnational Perspective* (Ashgate 2010) 4.
[49] Andrea Bianchi, "Reflexive Butterfly Catching: Insights from a Situated Catcher" in Joost Pauwelyn, Ramses Wessel, and Jan Wouters (eds), *Informal International Lawmaking* (Oxford University Press 2012).

provide a theory about the theories of what international law is. In Bianchi's compelling account, international law, as a scientific discipline, is in what Thomas Kuhn called "a state of growing crisis."[50]

Let me first recall Kuhn's theory, which deals with the state and evolution of scientific disciplines. In a nutshell, it goes as follows: in scientific disciplines, periods of "normal science" alternate with periods of "scientific revolution."

Periods of normal science are times of stability and consensus within the discipline, which is then marked by a dominant paradigm.

A paradigm is a central idea, accepted for a time by the discipline's community, which determines the appropriate choice of method and terminology within a discipline.[51] It also includes a number of key examples, or "exemplars"[52] in Kuhn's terminology, of what the paradigm is meant to explain.[53] If a bit of lexicological laxness on my part is permitted, paradigms also extend to at least two further types of items. (Kuhn more precisely speaks of "disciplinary matrices," but it is not apposite here to go into the equivocal relations between disciplinary matrices and paradigms.[54]) First, during a period of normal science, a community has certain shared beliefs (recall Duguit and Kelsen) which "supply the group with preferred or permissible analogies and metaphors":[55] think of the "billiard balls" of national legal systems in international law, or of Kelsen's "pyramid." Second, the community of a discipline has shared values: consider, for instance, the political values we have discussed throughout this chapter, but also values such as order and obedience, and how they translate into hierarchies of norms. (Notice also, in passing, the value of respecting the established social order, which means to respect the establishment, and how it affects the number of legal provisions and authors that should be cited in an appropriate academic text, or in other words how black letter law it should be. Just a rant. Sorry.) Paradigms have a profound impact on a field: they amount to "competing modes of scientific activity."[56] Adhering to a paradigm is typically essential to become part of the discipline's dominant community.[57]

But over time, anomalies appear. These are phenomena that are not satisfactorily explained by the dominant paradigm, revealing weaknesses in the paradigm, falsifying it. The first reaction of the discipline is then to stretch the explanatory

---

[50] Thomas S Kuhn, *The Structure of Scientific Revolutions* (2nd edn, University of Chicago Press 1970) 67.

[51] Kuhn, *The Structure of Scientific Revolutions*, viii: paradigms are "universally recognized scientific achievements that for a time provide model problems and solutions to a community of practitioners."

[52] Kuhn, *The Structure of Scientific Revolutions*, 186–8.

[53] Kuhn, *The Structure of Scientific Revolutions*, 10: "some accepted examples of actual scientific practice—examples which include law, theory, application, and instrumentation together—provide models from which spring particular coherent traditions of scientific research. These are the traditions which the historian describes under such rubrics as 'Ptolemaic astronomy' (or 'Copernican'), 'Aristotelian dynamics' (or 'Newtonian'), 'corpuscular optics' (or 'wave optics'), and so on."

[54] Kuhn, *The Structure of Scientific Revolutions*, 181ff.

[55] Kuhn, *The Structure of Scientific Revolutions*, 184.

[56] Kuhn, *The Structure of Scientific Revolutions*, 10.

[57] Kuhn, *The Structure of Scientific Revolutions*, 10: "The study of paradigms, including many that are far more specialized than those named illustratively above, is what mainly prepares the student for membership in the particular scientific community with which he will later practice."

power of the paradigm by all sorts of analytical, argumentative, or rhetorical tricks. When that goes too far, a revolution ensues: times of instability and outspoken dissensus within the discipline. The paradigm is put in question and alternative explanatory theories, or "candidates for paradigm"[58] are propounded. One of them eventually prevails, typically encompassing the older paradigm, which has become marginalized. At this juncture the scientific discipline returns to a period of normal science: there is a general consensus, within the community of the relevant scientific discipline, on the validity of the new paradigm.

Notice, first of all, that when Bianchi says that "international law is experiencing a crisis,"[59] this is not necessarily a bad thing. Crises, in the Kuhnian sense, are good for a discipline. They are a sign of the "vitality of a discipline," as it is put by François Ost and Michel van de Kerchove, two other champions of Kuhn's theory for the understanding of legal disciplines.[60] Paradigm crises are in fact even necessary for a discipline to really evolve; the fact that they happen is testament to a discipline's continuing attempt to be in sync with reality.

Bianchi, then, shows how formalism in international law, in the sense of the mainstream positivist doctrine, is increasingly considered an unsatisfactory account of reality, is under-representative of reality. It fails, he says, "to supply a satisfactory framework of analysis."[61] But, and this is important, it "is still in many ways the prevailing lingua franca of international law."[62] Put differently, it still serves as the dominant paradigm, despite the growing "state of disarray and confusion in which the scientific field of international law seems to be."[63] A new paradigm has not yet gained consensus: "no new set of paradigms has yet achieved sufficient power to impose itself as the scientific paradigm."[64] Hence the "state of growing crisis" mentioned above.

What happens now is in accord with Kuhn's model of what a discipline would do in reaction to such a crisis: we see a host of competing theories on what international law is, or to be more precise what "law" is in the discipline of international law. In other words, there is a battle of discourses taking place, of paradigm-candidates of legality for international law. Clearly this is not merely intellectual jousts at college high tables, or in faculty clubs: there are stakes in the battle. Bianchi explains it thus: the "scientific field is currently engaged in a power battle, in which conflicting claims to academic authority and discourse control are being put forward."[65] Recall the discussion with Mario Prost, in the previous section of this chapter, on the practical impact of academic authority and discourse control.

---

[58] Kuhn, *The Structure of Scientific Revolutions*, 15.
[59] Bianchi, "Reflexive Butterfly Catching," 210.
[60] François Ost and Michel van de Kerchove, *Jalons pour une théorie critique du droit* (Publication des Facultés universitaires Saint-Louis 1987) 541–2.
[61] Bianchi, "Reflexive Butterfly Catching," 207.
[62] Bianchi, "Reflexive Butterfly Catching," 207.
[63] Bianchi, "Reflexive Butterfly Catching," 210.
[64] Bianchi, "Reflexive Butterfly Catching," 210.
[65] Bianchi, "Reflexive Butterfly Catching," 210.

To be sure, it is not only international law that is in a growing state of crisis. The same phenomenon takes place in law in general: there is a need for a new paradigm of what law is, which will be selected among existing or future paradigm-candidates of legality. Law without the state has to be accounted for, but the question is of course what, then, "law" without the state should be.[66]

So we come to the question: what are the parameters of the battle of these candidates for paradigm? Can we itemize the main types of forces at play that may determine which of the understandings of law is likely to prevail, and which one we should support?

First, and most obviously, one force in the tussle for the next paradigmatic understanding of law is the explicative power, or analytical purchase, of candidates for paradigm. Notice at least two dimensions of law's analytic purchase.

On the one hand, our idea of law should help us understand what directs behavior in a given field. This invites a broader concept of law: a more encompassing notion of law (a larger shaped legality, if you will) provides a more encompassing understanding of what directs behavior.

On the other hand, legality serves to distinguish legal from social norms. Hence, the narrower the understanding of law, the stronger or more concentrated the features are likely to be of that which counts as law. Put differently, a less expansive notion of law makes it likelier that the characteristic of legality (something being law) is more distinctive. Thus a finding of legality will be more meaningful. Lawyers, in the sense of both practicing and academic lawyers, have a distinct social responsibility. That responsibility should not be muddled by washing out law's colors.

The second force in the tussle is the advancement of interests. As I have sketched in this chapter, different understandings of law advance the interests of different groups and individuals. Consider two types of interests, and thus two types of views on legality.

On the one hand, certain understandings of law are advocated as a result of moral reasons-for-action. Recall from Chapter 1: "Somebody's moral reasons-for-action are focused exclusively or primarily on other people's interests and only derivatively if at all on his own interests."[67] Understandings of law of that type are focused on advancing the interests of others, where "others" means those who do not lobby for them. Duguit and Kelsen's approach, outlined near the outset of this chapter, would be one example. Gurvitch's support of the working class, to which he did not belong, is another. Supporting stateless legality in order to further economic liberalism can also be done for moral reasons: it is meant to be good for the economy and thus for society.

---

[66] Since paradigms also include, as I said above, determinations on appropriate methods, at least some of the current paradigm-candidates also include candidates for new methodologies. On methodologies associated with transnational stateless law, see Peer Zumbansen, "Defining the Space of Transnational Law: Legal Theory, Global Governance, and Legal Pluralism" (2012) 21 *Transnational Law & Contemporary Problems* 305.

[67] Matthew H Kramer, "On the Moral Status of the Rule of Law" (2003) 63 *Cambridge Law Journal* 65, 66.

On the other hand, certain understandings of law are advocated as a result of prudential reasons-for-action. Recall again: "Somebody's prudential reasons-for-action are focused exclusively or primarily on his own interests and only derivatively if at all on the interests of other people."[68] Understandings of law of that type are focused on advancing the interests of those who lobby for them. This is what Bianchi and Prost pointed at in the discussion above. Romano's approach is a likely example: Romano, a high-ranking state official, adherent of fascism and thus of univocity in discourse and a strong state, supported a theory of legality which eventually sought state empowerment. The proponents of arbitration as transnational law, as I argued in Chapter 2, promote a notion of law that serves their interests, or at least is meant to.

The third force is what we may call the social construct of legality. To see the point about law, consider money first. What we understand under the rubric of "money" today is very different from what was considered money in, say, the Middle Ages. Think of the "virtual" aspects of money today, for instance. We have a different "paradigm" of money than they had. But we barely could, today, reach an academic consensus on the idea that, tomorrow, money will start meaning something radically different. The meaning of money, as John Searle explains, is strongly influenced by what the system's actors, the people who use money, collectively believe is money, and treat as such. He put it thus: "in order that the concept 'money' apply to the stuff in my pocket, it has to be the sort of thing that people think is money. If everybody stops believing it is money, it ceases to function as money, and eventually ceases to be money."[69] That quote from Searle leads Bianchi to argue that "collective beliefs play a central role in international law as they direct the use and the understanding of fundamental legal categories. What the actors believe the law is may not coincide with how law is defined in the abstract by theorists."[70] In other words, what counts as law depends on the beliefs of a regime's subjects. This is in fact a very Jellinekian idea: Georg Jellinek, at the dawn of the twentieth century, had already sketched its basic tenets.[71] In sum, the point is this: law is just a collective belief; it is what the members of a community consider and treat as law; its meaning is constructed by society.

Now, this does not mean that theoretical discourses about legality are useless: theoretical discourses mold collective belief, though of course only over time. (Yes, students actually believe what we tell them! At least sometimes...) What this means for our discussion of the battle of paradigm-candidates of legality is twofold.

First, theoretical discourses about what law is should not be too remote from collective belief, too disconnected from society's general understanding of law. Such aloofness would be self-defeating if the discourses are meant to have an influence in practice, to mold collective belief. If we craft a financial discourse

---

[68] Kramer, "On the Moral Status," 66.
[69] John Searle, *The Construction of Social Reality* (Penguin Press 1995) 32.
[70] Bianchi, "Reflexive Butterfly Catching," 211.
[71] Georg Jellinek, *Allgemeine Rechtslehre* (2nd edn, O Häring 1905) 324ff.

using a concept of money that bears little resemblance to what people at large believe to be money, the discourse likely will remain divorced from the real world, irrelevant to it.

Second, theoretical discourses about what law is should take into consideration the *implications* of legality as collectively believed. I mean this as a social construct variant of what Scott Shapiro calls the Implication Question.[72] Shapiro contrasts the Implication Question with the Identity Question. The Identity Question is an inquiry into "what makes the object the thing that it is,"[73] "what it is about X that makes it X."[74] It focuses on the set of properties that make instances of X instances of X and not of Y, on the conditions that need to obtain for something to qualify as X. The Implication Question, however, is an inquiry into "what necessarily follows from the fact that [a thing] is what it is and not something else."[75] For instance, coming after 2 is the necessary and sufficient condition for something to be 3. That is an Identity Question. Now if a certain number is the number 3, it follows that it cannot be evenly divided by anything other than 1 and 3—it is a prime number. That is an Implication Question. Applied to law, the Identity Question is about what makes law *law*; and the Implication Question is about what necessarily follows from the fact that something is law.

The type of implications I mean are not those that necessarily follow in the abstract, the logical analytical consequences of something being law. What I mean are those *empirical* implications that *usually* follow, in *collective belief*, from something being called law. This is for example the fact that something called law is usually associated, in the social construct of legality, with some form of justice and that it has some legitimate authority, that it commands respect more than non-legal norms, all other things being equal. The focus here is not on analytic jurisprudence, but on the perception of those who "read" the label of law, the perception of the addressees of statements of legality.

Not taking into account the implications of legality as collectively believed would amount to selling something ("yes, this is law") for something it is not perceived to be ("I thought I had a moral reason to obey it, because it is law"). Addressees of pronouncements of legality ("this here is law") will assume that the thus characterized rules or system display the properties usually associated with law. Our analytic stance about the concept of law should thus be adapted to such implications of a pronouncement of legality. This is the idea I adumbrated in Chapter 2 when I argued that the definition of law we use in ordinary discourse should be adapted to the political and ethical signals that the label of law sends.

The first two types of forces—understandings of law based on moral or prudential reasons-for-action—are also attempts to delineate legality starting from its consequences or implications. Each paradigm-candidate of legality creates certain implications and some of these implications are the advancement of interests: these interests may be those of the proponents of the theories of legality (prudential versions) or those of other people (moral versions). The candidate for paradigm that

---

[72] Scott J Shapiro, *Legality* (Belknap Press 2011) 8–10.
[73] Shapiro, *Legality*, 9.   [74] Shapiro, *Legality*, 8.   [75] Shapiro, *Legality*, 9.

will prevail will bring along, when it comes to rule the discipline, a retinue of interests.

The point here was merely to sketch some of the main forces that may influence the shaping of legality, influence which candidate for paradigm of law might prevail in the next "normal science" phase of the discipline. A complete social sciences endeavor should of course have listed all of the existing paradigm-candidates of legality, then examined the interests advanced by these paradigm-candidates, and finally evaluated which of these interests are appropriate and which are not. This would help make explicit some of the political strategies, and rhetorical manipulations behind alternative concepts of law. But for the purposes of my argument, pointing the way is enough.

4. The Non-scalability of Law

Roger Cotterrell has this to say about the concept of "soft law," a concept often associated with the idea of transnational legality: is the use of the word "soft," he asks, "something whose half-hearted designation as law...suggests that *some* account has to be taken of it, if only as doctrine (rules, principles, guidelines, etc.) perhaps *on the way to becoming law* and acquiring some legal authority?"[76] He thus points at the issue that legality, in "soft law," comes across as scalable, as obtaining by degrees. This is an idea we should resist. Let me respond here to a few arguments that could support law's scalability.

There are certain concepts to which scalability attaches, and certain concepts to which it does not, as Dworkin for instance remarked.[77] Baldness comes by degrees: one can be more or less bald, or bald to a greater or lesser extent. Speed is another example: objects move more or less quickly. Other concepts are not matters of degrees. A house for instance cannot be more a house than another. It cannot be a house to a greater or lesser degree. A chair, also, is a chair or it is not, but a given chair cannot be twice as much a chair as another one. It can however, as Wittgenstein for instance observed, be more or less *clearly* a chair.[78]

It is true that some elements of law are scalar, in the sense that they can be satisfied to varying degrees. As Raz writes: "The general traits which mark a system as a legal one are several and each of them admits, in principle, of various degrees."[79] This seems true in a great variety of approaches to the constituent elements of law, be the approach focused on, for instance, the presence of sanctions, unity, autonomy, or the concept of secondarity. All of these cardinal elements are

---

[76] Roger Cotterrell, "What is Transnational Law?" (2012) 37 *Law & Social Inquiry* 500, 503 (emphasis in the original).

[77] Ronald Dworkin, "Philosophy, Morality, and Law—Observations Prompted by Professor Fuller's Novel Claim" (1965) 113 *University of Pennsylvania Law Review* 668, 677.

[78] Ludwig Wittgenstein, *Philosophical Investigations* (first published 1953, Blackwell 1974) aphorisms 80ff.

[79] Joseph Raz, *Practical Reason and Norms* (Oxford University Press 1999) 150.

scalar: sanctions can be more or less effective and thus present; a normative system is marked by more or less unity or autonomy;[80] and the concept of secondarity, as we will see in Chapter 7, clearly functions by degrees.

Yet it is not because some of the constituent elements of a concept are scalable that the concept itself obtains by degrees. To hold the contrary view would mean, to use Dworkin's words, that "whether something is a novel, or a room, or an army is always a question of degree, because size is one of the criteria of each."[81] Ten pages of fictional narrative is clearly not a novel, but rather a novella or a short story. At fifty pages, it seems unclear whether we should call it a novel. At 200 pages, all doubt is quieted. But it would seem very wrong to say that *Great Expectations* (592 pages in the Penguin Classics edition) is a novel to a greater extent than *Hard Times* (369 pages in the same edition), or that one of these novels becomes a novel to a greater extent when it is translated into French, which requires more pages. It would also be quite amusing to think of Alexander the Great's army on the plains of Gaugamela to be an army to a lesser extent than Darius's. (The size of Alexander's army is estimated at 47,000 troops. Darius's force is put at 1,000,000 troops in Plutarch's starry-eyed account, and at 52,000 to 120,000 in modern estimates. In all cases it is simply an army. And Alexander won the battle.)

One may fail to make law. But that too does not mean that law itself is scalar. Lon Fuller got that one wrong. The purposeful enterprise of doing X is not necessarily equitable with X itself. Fuller claims that "to speak of a legal system as an 'enterprise' implies that it may be carried on with varying degrees of success... This would mean that the existence of a legal system is a matter of degree."[82] He considers that law is like education: if you ask whether education exists in a given country, the answer would hardly be yes or no. It would rather be a description of the achievements in this respect.[83] So it would be for law, Fuller contends, which necessarily would be appreciated as a "performance falling between zero and a theoretical perfection."[84] But this is wrong.

The addressee of the question about education necessarily would speak of achievements because the obvious answer to the question is yes. The question would then be reinterpreted as asking how good the education system is, which is a different question entirely. The dichotomous question about the presence of education can only fairly be asked, in its true meaning, to a chimpanzee specialist, for instance, to inquire about the presence of an educational system in ape communities. There the answer may well be yes or no, or some other reply expressing degrees of clarity. In this latter situation, the question would be about X itself, whereas in the situation envisaged by Fuller, the question is about the purposeful enterprise of doing X.

---

[80] See for instance Michel van de Kerchove and François Ost, *Legal System Between Order and Disorder* (Oxford University Press 1994) 135–42; Mireille Delmas-Marty, *Global Law: A Triple Challenge* (Martinus Nijhoff 2003) 74.
[81] Dworkin, "Philosophy," 678.
[82] Lon L Fuller, *The Morality of Law* (rev edn, Yale University Press 1969) 122.
[83] Fuller, *The Morality of Law*, 123.   [84] Fuller, *The Morality of Law*, 123.

Similarly, if we contrast the education system of the United Kingdom and a Saharan tribe, we may well conclude that *there is more* education in the United Kingdom, but it does not mean that *it is more* education. The British system of education can be more thorough than the other one, but its educational nature may be expected to be the same.

Let me illustrate this with more immediate examples: the differences in musical achievement between Madonna and Ludwig van Beethoven are clear (to most people), but we cannot say that the 9th Symphony is "more" music than *Ray of Light*. Similarly, Shakespeare's opuses are not "more" plays than Feydeau's. And Marius Petipa's ballets are not "more" ballets than Maurice Béjart's.

So if we can quite clearly be more or less successful in the purposeful enterprise of doing anything, this does not mean that the object of the enterprise is scalar itself. The purposeful enterprise of creating law may be more or less successful, but this does not mean that the result is more or less legal.

A scalar nature of law may not, either, be inferred from the gradualness of the evolution of normative systems. Let us assume that a normative system evolves gradually over time to become a legal system. Let us further assume that, once it is a legal system, it continues to evolve to form "developed and . . . less highly developed legal systems," as Paul Bohannan would say.[85] (Discussing the details of this, by the way, will be the job for Chapter 7.) Now, one might think that the only approach consistent with such a developmental view is to acknowledge the scalability of legal systems qua *legal* systems. The following examples should show why this is wrong, why gradualness of evolution does not necessarily entail scalability of the underlying property.

The physical phenomenon of water becoming water vapor is gradual: the thermal motion of water molecules increases, gradually, up to the point where the kinetic energy overcomes the surface tension and molecules evaporate. But of course this does not imply that the concepts of water or water vapor are obtained by degrees. Even though the transition from one state to the other has a scalable component (speed), each of the two states are non-scalar. The evolution reaches a threshold and then the difference in degree becomes a difference in kind.

Over the threshold, the continued evolution to a more or less highly developed state does not, either, imply the scalar character of the underlying concept. For example, a muscle can be more or less developed, it can achieve its functions to a higher or a lesser degree, but this does not mean that we may speak in such cases of something that is more or less of a muscle. As Matthew Kramer argues, over the threshold of legality, a legal system may admit of various degrees not of legality, but of "straightforwardness," "robustness," or "vibrancy," which determine how "full blown" it is.[86] In sum, something can be more or less *clearly* a legal system, but it cannot be more or less a legal system.

---

[85] Paul Bohannan, "The Differing Realms of the Law" (1965) 67 *American Anthropologist* 33, 37.
[86] All these terms are used in the second chapter of Matthew H Kramer, *Objectivity and the Rule of Law* (Cambridge University Press 2007).

There is such a thing as an epitome of a legal system: no one would deny its legal character to a standard, off-the-shelf public legal system of a modern state,[87] one that does not have any particular flaws. By epitome I mean a legal system that is most clearly a legal system, what is typically understood as a legal system, a legal system par excellence, a paradigmatic example. It is not, though, an ideal of perfection that is never attained in reality, such as a geometrical figure existing only in abstraction.[88]

Even from a pluralist's point of view, the public legal system likely is that epitome. But to recognize the existence of a given object's epitome is not to recognize that the object itself is of a scalar nature. We might be able to assign degrees to the difference between the epitome and an examined instance of the object. We might be able to intellectually measure the distance between any given instance of a concept and its most typical instance. But that does not imply that the concept itself is scalar.

An apple can be more or less like the archetype of an apple (the paradigmatic example that we would describe to someone who would not know what an apple is) but this does not mean that an apple can be an apple to a greater or a lesser extent.

A woman and a man are not more or less of that nature depending on their differences with respect to those represented on the so-called "Pioneer Plaques" (the pictorial greetings from Earth's inhabitants sent out into space on board unmanned spacecrafts Pioneer 10 and Pioneer 11, representing what a woman and a man typically look like). Even if a given person looks half man and half woman, his or her appearance being halfway between a typical man and a typical woman, the person would still be either one or the other, however unclear it is to which one he or she belongs.

If a legal system is quite different in its aspect to an ordinary public legal system, it does not follow that it is less legal, that it is a legal system to a lesser degree. But it may be less clearly a legal system or simply not of that nature at all.

The preceding paragraphs are not meant to imply that a clear threshold distinguishes social normative system from legal systems. On the contrary, it seems that it is not possible to position such a threshold precisely. It seems that it is merely a "rough and shifting minimum" as Ronald Dworkin said,[89] an "unspecifiable threshold" as Matthew Kramer puts it.[90] The boundaries of legality, these authors contend in essence, are unspecifiable, and I would tend to agree. Where I do not agree with Dworkin is when he considered that, within this zone of unspecifiability, legality is scalar, while outside it, it is not.[91] Indeed, it seems odd to consider that law is, at certain stages of its development, a scalar property and, at other stages, a non-scalar property. The degree of development of a concept's instantiation does not change the nature of the concept.

---

[87] Andrei Marmor, *Positive Law & Objective Values* (Oxford University Press 2001) 39–42.
[88] Nigel Simmonds, "Straightforwardly False: The Collapse of Kramer's Legal Positivism" (2004) 63 *Cambridge Law Journal* 98, 118–19.
[89] Dworkin, "Philosophy," 678.   [90] Kramer, *Objectivity*, 107.
[91] Dworkin, "Philosophy," 678.

4

Analytic Obstacles in Legal Positivism to Stateless Law

Is non-state law conceptually conceivable at all in a world where public legal systems cover all meaningful portions of territory? Do we have to forfeit legal positivism—a profound, sophisticated, rich and widely shared tradition in the way we understand law—in order to make room for law without the state? What is it that would make stateless law conceptually impossible in a world full of states and adhering to legal positivism?

There is, of course, the postulate in the most classical branch of legal positivism (legal statism) that law necessarily is state law.[1] It is a postulate often based on the moral-political belief that only the state can satisfactorily provide the level of justice without which it would be an abuse of language to speak of "law." As it is a postulate, which is by definition not demonstrated but considered to be self-evident, we do not need to attend to it very closely. However, I want to point out that this postulate and the belief it is based on inform the entire current book, in the sense that the public legal system is recurrently used as the main reference point of legality. The public legal system certainly appears to be the most advanced regulatory system, an ideal of perfection of legality if you will, against which non-state normative systems can meaningfully be assessed.

A more serious set of objections to the conceptual possibility of transnational legality without the state follows from arguments, made by many legal philosophers, that the essence of law includes certain properties that indirectly make it impossible, in the geopolitical situation of the world today, to conceive of law outside of the state. A normative system, these legal philosophers contend, must bear certain essential attributes in order to partake of legality. These attributes cannot attach to the kind of non-state normative systems we may conceive of today.

These properties, which would threaten the conceptual possibility to recognize the existence of stateless legal systems, are the following: comprehensiveness, exclusiveness, and supremacy. Legal systems, it is argued, in order to be legal systems, must display the features of comprehensiveness of their regulatory scope, of territorial exclusiveness, and of supremacy. If one of these features is indeed essential, then most if not all stateless normative systems would fail as legal systems,

---

[1] On legal positivism as state law and its origins, Arnold Brecht, *Political Theory: The Foundations of Twentieth-Century Political Thought* (Princeton University Press 1959).

could not qualify as law. This is of particular clarity with regard to arbitral regimes. Their regulatory scope always is relatively narrow, they overlap with a large number of national legal systems, and they do not claim supremacy over public legal systems. Accordingly, the following needs to explain why these three features are not essential features of legality.

1. Comprehensiveness, Exclusiveness, Supremacy

The feature of comprehensiveness means that law, in order to be law, must claim authority to intervene in all facets of its addressees' lives. It does not mean that law must actually regulate all aspects of life, it is only about claiming the authority to do so. Joseph Raz, for instance, maintains that legal systems "claim authority to regulate any type of behavior" and that they "do not acknowledge any limitation of the spheres of behavior which they claim authority to regulate." One element that sets legal systems apart from other normative systems is that legal systems "claim such an authority [to regulate all forms of behavior], whereas other systems do not claim it."[2] Matthew Kramer argues that if a normative system does not claim to rule over "virtually all aspects of social and individual life in a given region," if its norms do not "encompass most aspects of human life," then "they do not together constitute a full-blown legal system."[3] "[T]he regulatory sway of a full-fledged legal system," he continues, "must encompass most aspects of life (even if that regulatory sway is not actively exercised in regard to some aspects)."[4]

Territorial exclusiveness means that there cannot be two legal systems that regulate the same territory. There cannot be, the assertion goes, legal systems within or across legal systems: a population cannot be governed by several legal systems at a time. Kramer, for instance, rejects the possibility that "two conflicting legal systems reign over a single portion of territory."[5] We may also recall Hans Kelsen's famous tenet that "no one can serve two masters."[6] This is meant in the sense that "a system of norms can only be valid if the validity of all other systems of norms with the same sphere of validity has been excluded."[7] This is also known as the monistic conception of law, as opposed to legal pluralism: law only would exist as law in the form of a single and all-encompassing system.[8] With regard to private normative systems, this position leads to the view that, if you recall the quote from Jean Carbonnier in Chapter 2, "[e]ither the phenomena depicted as forming another body of law are taken into consideration by the overall system, which takes over the whole; or the phenomena of an alleged other body of law remains

---

[2] Joseph Raz, *Practical Reason and Norms* (Oxford University Press 1999) 150–1.
[3] Matthew H Kramer, *In Defense of Legal Positivism: Law Without Trimmings* (Oxford University Press 2003) 97.
[4] Kramer, *In Defense*, 98.
[5] Kramer, *In Defense*, 96.
[6] Hans Kelsen, *Pure Theory of Law* (University of California Press 1967) 329.
[7] Hans Kelsen, *General Theory of Law and State* (first published 1945, Harvard University Press 1949) 410.
[8] See for instance Norberto Bobbio, *Teoria dell'ordinamento giuridico* (Giappichelli 1960) 186.

outside, not integrated into the system... and cannot be truly classified as law."[9] One, and only one, legal system could thus reign over any portion of territory. Non-state law would only be able to exist in stateless territories.

Law's purported claim to supremacy means that each legal system recognizes no higher authority in the field it regulates, that it is the highest normative order with respect to its subject-community.[10] Accordingly, law, to be law, would have to claim to reign alone like Hobbes's Leviathan, with no limits within its territory but self-imposed ones. As Andrei Marmor puts it, law would be the "final arbitrator of its own domain."[11]

Marmor further points out that these three features are often claimed to be interdependent. Law's claim to supremacy is, then, viewed as one side of the coin of which comprehensiveness is the other. The argument is that a normative system would not be able to claim authority to regulate all aspects of life, with no external limit, without at the same time claiming to be the highest normative order in its field.[12] Supremacy and comprehensiveness would, in turn, necessarily imply a claim to exclusiveness, a claim to exclude all other legal systems on the same territory. Put differently, in Hans Kelsen's term, "a monistic construction is inevitable."[13]

2. Misconceptions

There are reasons to believe that these features—supremacy, exclusiveness, comprehensiveness—are incorrectly attributed to law, or are conceived in a way that leaves much room for doubt.

The feature of comprehensiveness may only be understood realistically as virtual comprehensiveness. I mean this in the sense not only of the feature being a claim to authority rather than an actual exercise thereof, but also in the sense of it being understood as widely ranging as opposed to all-encompassing. The range of life's facets that law typically claims authority to rule over is very broad, but it sometimes does not cover every facet of life; it is about very variegated types of behavior, but not necessarily all behavior. This is evidenced in federal systems, where there are two wide-ranging but not all-encompassing co-occurrent legal systems. Certain types of behavior are regulated by the federal system, others by the legal systems of the federated entities. The latter do acknowledge limitations, set by the federal legal system, of the spheres of behavior they claim authority to regulate. The systems of

---

[9] Jean Carbonnier, *Sociologie juridique* (A Colin 1972) 213.
[10] Recall Raz from Chapter 2: law "claims authority to regulate the setting up and application of other institutionalized systems by its subject-community": Joseph Raz, *The Authority of Law* (2nd edn, Oxford University Press 2009) 118.
[11] Andrei Marmor, *Positive Law & Objective Values* (Oxford University Press 2001) 39–42 (Marmor does not share this view, does not maintain that a claim to supremacy is an inherent feature of legality).
[12] Marmor, *Positive Law*, 39.
[13] Hans Kelsen, *Pure Theory of Law* (University of California Press 1967) 333.

the federated entities are not the highest normative orders but they still claim a wide-ranging authority to regulate.

Furthermore, federal legal systems are evidence that supremacy and territorial exclusiveness are not essential properties of a legal system. Federated entities typically each operate their own legal system, while being constitutionally subordinate to federal law. Hence, federated legal systems are not supreme and make no claim that they are. As to territorial exclusiveness, the fact that a federal legal system and federated legal systems are co-occurrent on one and the same territory shows that there are instances where this feature fails to obtain. It therefore cannot be an essential feature of legality—if essential is taken in its formal logical sense of being "present whenever and wherever law exists" and being "invariant in that every legal system is characterized by them."[14]

A brief look at history confirms as much. Lon Fuller reminds us that "[h]istorically dual and triple systems have functioned without serious friction, and when conflict has arisen it has often been solved by some kind of voluntary accommodation. This happened in England when the common law courts began to absorb into their own system many of the rules developed by the courts of the law merchant."[15] So historically there were non-exclusive legal systems. Andrei Marmor further explains that in the Middle Ages "positive law was seen as an exception to customs, traditions, religion, and in general, social practices long in force[, t]hus the law, as a relatively exceptional normative source, only could intervene within the narrow space left open by these other normative sources."[16] Such legal systems, Marmor concludes, "had no ... claims to supremacy."[17]

As to the feature of virtual comprehensiveness, my sense is that it is not an essential feature of law but a routine property of the law of modern states. To see why, we need to think back to the modern conceptions of political sovereignty as they emerged in the wake of Jean Bodin's *Les six livres de la République* (1576) and later the intellectual developments before and after the Peace of Westphalia (1648), including Thomas Hobbes's *Leviathan* (1651).[18]

These conceptions of sovereignty included a political claim to the supremacy of the state in order to impose unified and centralized structures over separatism.[19] Such central structures of power were needed insofar as nation-states were originally wrestling with groups headed by feudal lords, the church, and local customs. To prevail in the wrestle, it helped to create and later sustain the "imagined community" that we call a nation.[20] The nation-state, as distinguished from the state tout

---

[14] Matthew H Kramer, *Objectivity and the Rule of Law* (Cambridge University Press 2007) 101–2.
[15] Lon L Fuller, *The Morality of Law* (rev edn, Yale University Press 1969) 124.
[16] Marmor, *Positive Law*, 40.
[17] Marmor, *Positive Law*, 40.
[18] For a summary, see for instance Malcolm N Shaw, *International Law* (5th edn, Cambridge University Press 2003) 21, 25.
[19] Marmor, *Positive Law*, 40.
[20] The term "imagined community" is from Benedict Anderson, *Imagined Communities: Reflections on the Origin and Spread of Nationalism* (first published 1983, Verso 2006). On the concept of nation, see also Friedrich Meinecke, *Weltbürgertum and Nationalstaat: Studien zur Genesis des deutschen Nationalstaates* (first published 1908, Oldenburg 1915) 124–57; Jürgen Habermas, *The Postnational*

court, is in this sense modernity's socially constructed equation between an overarching community and a territory. It is the product of a strong connection created, for political reasons, between an imagined community and "imagined geographies" (the territory of the state).[21]

In order to achieve this goal, in order to create and sustain the nation, the modern state sought to "transcend ethnic, religious and other cleavages in a political construction of ample proportions, guaranteeing at least a certain level of solidarity," as François Ost and Michel van de Kerchove put it.[22] Or again, the modern state engaged in a vast effort to achieve a "universalization of collective life."[23] "Universalization" is meant here not, of course, in the sense of cosmopolitan, or global, or worldwide, but in the sense of comprehensive in subject-matter. This is an echo to Jürgen Habermas, when he writes that the purpose of the modern state was to comprehensively "colonize the lifeworld" of its citizens.[24] The idea of the lifeworld, a concept that Habermas took from Alfred Schütz,[25] is that it represents our common understandings and values, a common sense of who we are in a community. The "lifeworld," for Habermas, is that which "stands behind the back of each participant in communication and which provides resources for the resolution of problems of understanding."[26] So the idea here is that the state (and for Habermas the economy, but that does not need to enter our reasoning here) "colonizes" social relations, by replacing subjectively shared backgrounds with objectively defined structures of social reality. These structures of reality are, precisely, based on a unified, "virtually universal rationality," as Ost and van de Kerchove put it.[27]

One of the instruments used to achieve this goal was the public legal system of the modern state, which thus had to be "virtually universal," to use Ost and van de Kerchove's terminology, or in other words virtually comprehensive. The use of law's function in creating and sustaining a unified community is part of the groundwork of political sovereignty in the modern state. In order to allow sovereignty to be comprehensive, the legal system of the modern state also had to be comprehensive.

Assuming, *arguendo*, that virtual comprehensiveness is nevertheless a feature of law, it must be conceived as being limited in scope by the underlying community's

---

Constellation: Political Essays (MIT Press 2001); Hannah Arendt, *The Origins of Totalitarianism* (Harcourt, Brace and Co 1951); Ernest Gellner, *Nations and Nationalism* (Cornell University Press 1983).

[21] Edward W Said, *Orientalism* (rev edn, Penguin 1978). See also Anthony Giddens, *The Nation-State and Violence* (Polity 1985) 125.

[22] François Ost & Michel van de Kerchove, *De la pyramide au réseau? Pour une théorie dialectique du droit* (FUSL Publ 2002) 128.

[23] Ost & van de Kerchove, *De la pyramide au réseau?* 128.

[24] Jürgen Habermas, *The Theory of Communicative Action* (Beacon 1987) 332–73.

[25] Alfred Schütz & Thomas Luckman, *The Structures of the Life-World* (Northwestern University Press 1973). (The book was finished by Thomas Luckman, one of Schütz's disciples, after his death.)

[26] Jürgen Habermas in Peter Dews (ed), *Autonomy and Solidarity: Interviews with Jürgen Habermas* (Verso 1986) 109.

[27] Ost & van de Kerchove, *De la pyramide au réseau*, 127.

boundaries. Virtual comprehensiveness is indeed best understood as the claim to rule over a very large proportion of those facets of life that occur within a community. Let me explain why.

Admittedly, sociability traditionally was mainly territory based, rooted in proximity.[28] It is true that it used to be that groups primarily would form within geographically determined areas. But no necessary relation of entailment exists between territory and sociability. The link is contingent. With the lowering of travel costs and the development of information technologies, in other words with the increasing globalization of commercial and social relationships,[29] sociability indeed gradually shifted, giving rise with increasing frequency to delocalized communities.[30] They emerged because the means to form communities is communication,[31] and communication has become almost entirely independent of geography. This development prompted the French cultural theorist Paul Virilio to come up with a neologism: "social tele-localness."[32] The idea is simply this: groups increasingly engage in societal relationships (for instance of a commercial or more plainly social nature), progressively creating bonds that eventually form communities, almost irrespectively of their geographical localization. Ever more frequently, what matters is not the territorial proximity between people but the "selective ties" that members of such "communities of choice" purposefully develop, as sociologist Manuel Castells puts it.[33] Such ties are typically based on common affinities, interests and goals. In a nutshell: these communities are no longer proximity based, but subject-matter centered. Their boundaries are no longer dependent on territory, but on specific activities.

Given as much, nothing seems to prevent such communities of choice, at least theoretically, from developing to the point of forming what legal pluralists call "[social] entities capable of producing law."[34] In such a case, virtual comprehensiveness would mean that the legal system claims authority to rule over a large proportion of the behavior that occurs within such a delocalized community of choice. Consequently, it would claim to rule over behavior that occurs in the context of certain activities only. Virtual comprehensiveness would be restricted to relatively specific types of behavior.

We do not need to get seriously into legal anthropology to believe in the following postulate: every community, if sufficiently developed, organized, and autonomous from its societal environment, theoretically is able to produce its own normative system and then its own legal system. Starting from there, the current

---

[28] See for instance Manuel Castells, *The Internet Galaxy: Reflections on the Internet, Business, and Society* (Oxford University Press 2001) 125–6.
[29] For an easy discussion of this point, see for instance Thomas L Friedman, *The Lexus and the Olive Tree* (Anchor Books 2000) xvii et seq.
[30] The iconic description of this phenomenon is by early internet-fan Howard Rheingold, *The Virtual Community: Homesteading on the Electronic Frontier* (Addison-Wesley 1993). For a more lawyerly take, see Pascale Deumier, *Le droit spontané* (Economica 2002) 324–48.
[31] On the role of communication in forming nations, see Anderson, *Imagined Communities*, 5–6.
[32] Paul Virilio, *The Information Bomb* (Verso 2000) 59.
[33] Castells, *Internet Galaxy*, 119–25.
[34] Deumier, *Droit spontané*, 324.

development of deterritorialized communities is a real jeopardy to the idea of virtual comprehensiveness in any other understanding than the one just sketched. Indeed, a deterritorialized legal system that regulates only the behavior that relates to the shared interests or common goals of the community's members is, by definition, non-comprehensive if we give this concept an absolute or universal meaning (a very large number of the facets of life generally speaking as opposed to life within a specific community). This leaves open only one of two solutions: either we consider that the model of a legal system is too limiting and the feature of comprehensiveness must be reduced to its guise of virtual comprehensiveness. Or we consider that these communities cannot produce legal systems, regardless of their level of self-organization, autonomy, and overall development. It seems to me that the latter would be unduly restrictive, that it would be an overtly political move to deny such communities the capacity to create law on the basis of a model of law that owes much to conceptions of political sovereignty, whose goal precisely was to assert and establish exclusive and supreme control over a specific portion of territory.

It must, however, be recognized that a legal system that features the three properties addressed in this section is conceptually closer to the epitomical public legal system of the modern state. Accordingly, such a system is more clearly a legal system than those that do not exhibit these features. The public legal system remains the epitome of a legal system because current legal thinking still is very much marked by modern conceptions of political sovereignty. These conceptions, translated into legal thinking, are one of the factors that encouraged the development of the doctrine of classical legal positivism, or legal statism, as a monistic conception of law.[35] Hence, it has appeared very natural for the last centuries to treat law as an all-encompassing normative order.

It is all too tempting, really, to think of law as necessarily having the same characteristics as this epitomical instance of law. But we should resist the temptation, because it leads us into an inductive fallacy. Admittedly, the public legal system of the modern state simply has been so preponderantly present that it has been obscuring all other possibilities of legality. As a consequence it is an easy reflex to take the example of the public legal regime of the state, or more generally of the law made by a state or a collectivity of states, and believe this is how law must be.

Or we may be lured into that position—seeing law only through the example of state law—by the comfort of old traditions. That is in essence the argument Simon Roberts makes. He considers, first, that we have come to deeply associate law with government. On this basis, he considers that to claim the existence of non-state legal systems would be contrary to the way we now think of law. That would, he says, run afoul of "the durability of old understandings."[36] Perhaps, then, we should be older than that and remember that the modern state is only a historical creation[37] and that law pre-dated it.

---

[35] Deumier, *Droit spontané*, 39.
[36] Simon Roberts, "After Government? On Representing Law Without the State" (2005) 68 *Modern Law Review* 1.
[37] See for instance the classical work of Joseph R Strayer, *On the Medieval Origins of the Modern State* (Princeton University Press 1970).

Temptations and lures aside, the main reasons why current legal positivism may make non-state law impossible do not withstand analytic scrutiny. The notion of comprehensiveness (authority to intervene in all facets of its addressees' lives), territorial exclusiveness (one and only one legal system per portion of territory) and supremacy (each legal system recognizes no higher authority within its sphere of application) are not criteria of legality. Normative systems that regulate only certain slices of life, that do not exclude other legal systems within one and the same portion of territory and that admit of higher normative orders, in other words transnational subject-matter-specific normative orders, are not in and of themselves excluded from the scope of legality. Non-comprehensive, non-exclusive, and non-supreme legal systems are possible in theory. If non-state normative systems fail as legal systems, it is not because of these features.

5
Relative and Absolute Legality

Are non-state legal systems existentially dependent on their recognition by states? The answer is likely to be obvious, and it is often written off with the attitude reserved for plain matters: the answer is obviously... yes, for some, and no for others.

The question should be contrasted with and placed outside of the debate between the monist dimension of legal statism and legal pluralism.

The monist dimension of legal statism relates to the relation between the law made by the state and other bodies of law. Recall the quote from French legal theorist Jean Carbonnier: "*Either* the phenomena depicted as forming another body of law are taken into consideration by the overall legal system... and unity is restored through that overall system, which takes over the whole; *or* the phenomena of an alleged body of law remain outside, not integrated into the system, in a primitive state, and cannot be truly classified as law."[1] In other words, norms not created by officials of the public legal system become legal if, and only if, they are somehow integrated into the public legal system. Non-state normative systems would be able to acquire the status of legality, but only if they are recognized by the legal system of the state and made part of it, swallowed up by it, if you will. Such an approach implies, of course, the conceptual impossibility of the existence of non-state legal systems.

By contrast, the current question—whether the existence of non-state legal systems depends on their recognition by states—presupposes that non-state legal systems can exist in this capacity, without being integrated into the public state legal system. That is to say, the current question implies a pluralistic approach.

I have just sneaked in, implicitly, a key distinction: On the one hand, we have the public legal system, recognizing another body of rules and making it legal by integrating it into itself, into the public legal system. On the other hand, we have the public legal system recognizing another body of rules as a discrete, separate legal system. We may now slightly rephrase the question: The matter to be discussed here is whether the own discrete legality of non-state legal systems may depend on the position adopted on it by one or several public legal systems.

The argument is frequently made by very able contemporary private international lawyers that recognition by courts is an essential element for the identification of non-state legal systems. Such authors argue that a given non-state

---

[1] Jean Carbonnier, *Sociologie juridique* (A Colin 1972) 213.

normative order is, or is not, a legal system because one or several court decisions provided that the order in question is, or is not, a legal system.[2]

Consider an argument made by Andreas Bucher, for instance. I had written an article, a few years ago, arguing that the lex mercatoria fails to amount to a legal system and does not qualify as law.[3] Bucher, one of the world's leading private international lawyers and an unusually sharp legal mind, responded a year later in a lecture he delivered at the Hague Academy of International Law. His point, in substance, was this: fair enough, he said, the lex mercatoria is not a legal system, but to say that it is not law is at odds with what courts say. If the public legal system of the state says it is law, then there is no point in arguing any longer: It is law because the state so decided.[4]

The point is persuasive and to be taken seriously, but it is ultimately wrong. It reflects certain important and widespread misunderstandings which are likely due to the sketchiness of the systems theory prevalent in private international law. Analytic jurisprudence may contribute to clarifying these issues.

Help, I believe, is to be found in the distinction between relative and absolute legality.[5] Relative legality relates to what each legal system considers to be legal—a situation that varies from one legal system to another, and is therefore referred to as "relative." Absolute legality relates to the legal character that a normative system has in and of itself. The following three sub-sections first ponder the meaning of these concepts and then briefly examine certain relations between the two concepts.

1. Relative Legality

Relative legality is something prescriptively conferred on a norm, a set of norms, or a normative system through its recognition by a normative order which conceives of itself as a legal system. It refers to the property of which a norm, a set of norms, or a normative order partakes by dint of being regarded as law by a legal system. It is determined by what Jeremy Waldron calls the "retail account of law," which is "the account of what law ... is in a particular jurisdiction"—as opposed to the "wholesale account of law," which is "the account of what law, the institution, is (as

---

[2] See for instance Andreas Bucher, "La dimension sociale du droit international privé" (2009) 341 *Hague Lectures* 9, 144; Emmanuel Gaillard, *Legal Theory of International Arbitration* (Martinus Nijhoff 2010) 60–6; Thomas Clay, *L'arbitre* (Dalloz 2001) 217; Jean-Michel Jacquet, Philippe Delebecque, and Sabine Corneloup, *Droit du commerce international* (2nd edn, Dalloz 2010) 59–61.

[3] Thomas Schultz, "Some Critical Comments on the Juridicity of Lex Mercatoria" (2008) 10 *Yearbook of Private International Law* 667.

[4] Bucher, "Dimension sociale," 144, maintaining that my argument about the lex mercatoria is "sans reflet dans la positivité normative du droit." He further contends that my argument may in fact be valid in legal theory, but not in law, which implicitly means that legal theory and law are somehow divorced. That sort of balkanization of scholarship is, in my view, unfortunate and profoundly sad, in the fullest sense of that word.

[5] For a more succinct discussion of relative and absolute legality, see Thomas Schultz, "Secondary Rules of Recognition and Relative Legality in Transnational Regimes" (2011) 56 *American Journal of Jurisprudence* 59.

opposed to other methods of governance)."[6] Put differently, legality in this relative meaning refers to what the rules of recognition of a specific legal order provide.

A distinction may be entered here, as relative legality may be seen as a genus with two species.

1.1 Two species of relative legality

On the one hand, relative legality may refer to a legal system's recognition of a norm or decision as one of its own laws or legal determinations. If system A considers that norm X or decision Y forms part of the system, then X or Y is law for that system. System A decides sovereignly what it recognizes as law by integrating it or rejecting it as one of its (legal) components. Put more casually, the system decides sovereignly what its blanket of legality should cover.

On the other hand, relative legality may refer to a legal system's recognition of a norm or decision as one of the laws or legal determinations of another system. If system A considers that norm X or decision Y forms part of system B, then X or Y belong to system B as far as system A is concerned. If a French court considers that a certain norm or decision forms part of English law, then English law, as far as the French legal system is concerned, contains that legal rule or determination. Typically, and this not too exceptional a situation, the highest court of a given state may "incorrectly" apply a foreign law. That interpretation of a foreign law, deviating from the way in which the courts of that foreign country would likely have interpreted it, is nevertheless a valid interpretation in the system whose courts have performed the interpretive act. System A decides sovereignly with which contours it sees system B. (This is so even if there were an international convention or customary international law providing the contrary, as in such a hypothetical case an issue of state responsibility may occur, but not of interpretive validity.) To make a lighter parallel, the matter is comparable with the inquiries that polyglots occasionally make about the way in which Latin is pronounced in English, French, German, or Italian. The "rules of recognition" of the English language, for instance, determine sovereignly how Latin phrases (or French, German, and Italian phrases for that matter) are to be pronounced within a statement made, for the rest, in English.

The argument can be taken one step further, and be extended to another system's legality itself. If system A considers that system B is not law, that it is not a legal system, then B is not a legal system for A; normative system B is not law as far as legal system A is concerned. Again: if the secondary rules of recognition of normative system A, which considers itself a legal system, provide that normative system B is (respectively is not) law, then B is (respectively is not) law for legal system A and for legal system A only. (It may be pointed out that the question whether the pretense of legality of the recognizing normative order—the legality of system A in this example—is successful or not is irrelevant in this context. In other

---

[6] Jeremy Waldron, "Normative (or Ethical) Positivism" in Jules Coleman (ed), *Hart's Postscript: Essays on the Postscript to The Concept of Law* (Oxford University Press 2001) 410, 415.

words it is meaningless for this argument whether system A actually is a legal system or not. But let us leave that point aside until the next sub-section.)

The point becomes clearer if we attribute a meaningful value to variables A and B: if, for instance, Argentine law (variable A) recognizes the lex mercatoria (variable B) as law, then the lex mercatoria is law for the Argentine legal system, but this has no effect whatsoever on the question whether the lex mercatoria is law for the Croatian legal system, for example.

The point may further be illustrated by a state refusing to recognize the existence of another state: if for instance part of a state has seceded and enacted its own laws, a foreign country may refuse to recognize the existence as law of these new sets of rules, and consider that only the laws of the mother state apply within the territory of the seceded territories.

Let me recap. Relative legality is a matter for the internal point of view of a legal system: what a legal system considers to be law is law within the recognizing legal system. Hence, we may also think of relative legality as a form of normative or political legality, insofar as the qualification as law of a normative system is a normative and performative statement.

The characterization as law, in application of the secondary rules of recognition of the characterizing system, is the necessary and sufficient condition for the recognized system to be law for the characterizing or recognizing system. It follows that the power to determine (prescriptive dimension) relative legality belongs to the officials of the recognizing system. The identification (descriptive dimension) of relative legality in a specific instance is a matter of interpretative proficiency: an observer able to correctly interpret the secondary rules of recognition of a legal system is qualified to identify which other normative systems count as law for the recognizing legal system.

To take the reasoning further, we shall now consider two neighboring concepts.

1.2 The Midas Principle

Let us first turn to Kelsen's take of the "Midas Principle." Here is how Kelsen put it: "Just as everything King Midas touched turned into gold, everything to which law refers becomes law."[7] Everything that a legal system wishes to "turn into" law becomes law ipso facto. This is an expression of the idea that the qualification as law is a performative statement, as we have seen a moment ago. So far, Kelsen's point and the notion of relative legality are congruent.

However, for Kelsen specifically—and this is where my argument parts from Kelsen's—it is therefore "possible for the legal order, by obliging the law-creating organs to respect or apply certain moral norms or political principles or opinions of experts to transform these norms, principles, or opinions into legal norms, and thus into sources of law."[8] Kelsen hereby contended that these other norms (which

---

[7] Hans Kelsen, *Pure Theory of Law* (University of California Press 1967) 161.
[8] Hans Kelsen, *General Theory of Law and State* (first published 1945, Harvard University Press 1949) 132.

Italian and German literature sometimes calls "rules of experience"[9]) become legal because they are *integrated* into the legal system of reference. To play with the image of King Midas, one may say that the legality-attributing factor is not the King's touch, but the fact that he takes the norm into his possession. Accordingly, a monistic conception of law is ascribed to Kelsen.[10]

Applied not to individual norms but to normative systems, this argument would lead to the situation already mentioned above: the recognized normative system would become *part of* the recognizing legal system. Kelsen's position leads to the following issue, as noted by Leslie Green: "A conflict-of-laws rule may direct a Canadian judge to apply Mexican law in a Canadian case. The *conflicts rule* is obviously part of the Canadian legal system. But the rule of Mexican law is not, for although Canadian officials can decide whether or not to apply it, they can neither change it nor repeal it, and the best explanation of its existence and content makes no reference to Canadian society or its political system."[11]

Clearly, relative legality may refer to the recognition as law of another norm, set of norms, or normative system without necessarily integrating them into the recognizing legal system. Let us here give a slightly different spin, in light of the Midas Principle (as Kelsen's construed it) and of Green's comment thereupon, to the distinction I have entered above between the two species of relative legality (recall: recognition of own legal determinations and recognition of legal determinations of another legal system). Relative legality, we may now say, is the authoritative determination by the officials of a legal system of what the system regards as law, that is: (a) what forms part of this legal system, and (b) what this legal system recognizes and enforces as legal norms without making it part of the system.

The first alternative, (a), corresponds to Kelsen's idea that the legal system of reference integrates certain norms and groups of norms, which properly form part of the system. The different rules of French law, for instance, are part of the French legal system because of the authoritative determinations of the officials of French law according to the secondary rules of recognition of the French legal system.

The second alternative, (b), corresponds to Green's comment regarding the rule of Mexican law, which is regarded as legal by the Canadian legal system, and as such is recognized and enforced through the coercive power of Canadian law, but the Mexican rule does not thereby become part of Canadian law.

In both cases, the recognizing legal system extends its own legality to the recognized norm—but it could also be a set of norms or a full normative system. The recognized element (norm, set of norms, normative system) becomes legal, in a relative sense, for the recognizing system through its recognition. The recognizing legal system can either integrate the recognized element or it may treat it as an external legal element and merely recognize and enforce its standards of conduct. (In the latter sense, law is an "open normative system," as Raz puts it, in the sense

---

[9] See the discussion in Michel van de Kerchove and François Ost, *Legal System Between Order and Disorder* (Oxford University Press 1994) 122–4.
[10] van de Kerchove and Ost, *Legal System*, 133.
[11] Leslie Green, "Legal Positivism" in Edward N. Zalta (ed), *Stanford Encyclopedia of Philosophy* (Stanford University Fall 2009 edn).

that law "contains norms the purpose of which is to give binding force within the system to norms which do not belong to it."[12]) In any event, this attributed legality is operative only for the recognizing legal system, as the recognizing legal system's determinations have no effect with regard to the application of any other legal system's rules of recognition.

The Midas Principle may be salvaged, but in a slightly different version: it is correct that a legal system turns norms, sets of norms, and normative systems into law by virtue of its secondary rules of recognition, but it does not necessarily integrate the hence legalized elements into the system; it may simply consider them external normative elements that it wishes to grant legal standing. Let us call it the pluralist Midas Principle.

1.3 The idea of relevance

To the second neighboring concept: Santi Romano's idea of "relevance," which in his words is the situation in which "an order's existence, content or efficacy meets the conditions set by another order," while irrelevance refers to the fact that "there is no relation between them."[13] It would be analytically more informative to consider that irrelevance is not really the absence of relations between the two systems, but rather, and that is more important, the denial by a legal system of another system's claim to exist as a legal system. Indeed, if we ask system A whether it recognizes system B as legal (that is, whether system B meets the conditions for existence set by system A), then "there's no relation between us" is a misleading answer that really means "no, we, A, don't recognize the legality of B."

So a more helpful expression of the concept of relevance is that it refers to this situation: an order's existence as a *legal* order meets the conditions set by the relevant secondary rules of recognition of the legal system of reference; the relevant rules of recognition are those used to recognize other legal systems and give effect to their norms.

Relevance may be considered from the discrete points of view of different legal systems of reference: for instance, order A may be relevant for B but not for C, while both B and C may be irrelevant for A. Hence, the general picture of the legality of an ensemble of normative systems is, in the words of Michel van de Kerchove and François Ost, one of "tangled relations of reciprocal recognition."[14] That is, the legality of each normative system depends on the internal point of view of the sundry legal systems that one wishes to consider and it varies according to the legal system one takes for reference. It is a picture of "general relativity," as François Rigaux puts it.[15]

---

[12] Joseph Raz, "The Institutional Nature of Law" (1975) 38 *Modern Law Review* 489, 502.
[13] Santi Romano, *L'ordinamento giuridico* (first published 1917, Sansoni 1918).
[14] van de Kerchove and Ost, *Legal System*, 110.
[15] François Rigaux, "Les situations juridiques individuelles dans un système de relativité générale" (1989) 213 *Hague Lectures* 1; François Rigaux, "Le droit au singulier et au pluriel" (1982) 9 *Revue interdisciplinaire d'études juridiques* 45, 56; François Rigaux, "La relativité générale des ordres juridiques" in Eric Wyler and Alain Papaux (eds), *L'extranéité ou le dépassement de l'ordre juridique étatique* (Pedone 1999) 75.

Now, back to the initial question: does the legality of non-state legal systems depend on the position taken on it by one or several public legal systems, or by any other normative system for that matter? The answer, clearly, is yes. But it is a qualified yes: the determinations of public legal systems clearly are decisive regarding the legal character of non-state normative systems, but only as far as those public legal systems are concerned which make those determinations. What public legal system X says about system Y is relevant for public legal system X. Nothing more and nothing less.

2. Absolute Legality

Absolute legality is something descriptively attributed to a normative system by an observer—an analytical legal philosopher for instance. It refers to the property characterizing a normative order that is regarded as law by the observer. It is determined by the wholesale account of law (recall from the preceding sub-section: it is "the account of what law, the institution, is (as opposed to other methods of governance)").

It is a matter for a point of view that is external to any legal system: what an observer considers to be an instance of the method of governance that we call law is law regardless of a hypothetical rejection of its existence as a legal system by one, several, or all other legal systems. Hence, absolute legality may also be called descriptive or analytical legality, as the qualification as law of a normative system is a simple descriptive statement; it is a matter of scientific reflection, not political determination. The qualification as law in application of the analytical framework of the observer is the necessary and sufficient condition for the examined system to be law—more precisely, it is so for all those analysts who are in accord with the definitional framework applied and the accuracy of its application in the instant case. The authority to determine the legal character of a normative system lies with legal scholars, and not with the officials of any legal system.

Arguably, to speak of "absolute" legality may be misleading if it is taken to mean that only one analytical point of view is correct. Absolute legality also has an element of relativity. Analytic legal philosophers disagree. What one analyst considers to amount to law may not accord with what another thinks. The definitional framework may also change over time. Clearly, "absolute" does not refer here to the idea that there may be one and only one right view on what qualifies as law. But the idea of legality we are dealing with deserves the adjective "absolute" insofar as such characterizations as law have a claim to universality, which may be successful or not, while relative legality is squarely within the realm of contingency. The word absolute stands in contrast to the relativity of the determinants of legality used by legal systems in their rules of recognition.

In sum, legality in its absolute meaning refers to the conclusions of an external observer; it is an analytical and descriptive position. It is what legal science and not politics says. (Assuming, arguendo, that legal science and politics do not overlap.) It is with absolute legality in mind that François Rigaux wrote that the state does in no way confer "on private orderings a legality that they would not have by themselves."[16] Similarly, it is following the same approach that Michel van de Kerchove and François Ost state that "irrelevance [in the sense given to this word by Santi Romano, which we have seen in the preceding sub-section] has no effect on the existence of a legal system or on its internal efficacy; its only consequence is that that system will be ignored as such by another system and will not produce any legal effect with respect to that other system."[17] What is meant here by the "existence of a legal system" is the existence as such of a normative system as a legal system, and not its existence from the (relative) point of view of some other legal system.

On the basis of the developments made heretofore, the following point seems to have been made plain: the question addressed in this book—whether certain arbitral non-state normative orders should be recognized as legal because they satisfactorily constitute an instance of the method of governance we call law—is a clearly distinct matter from the position taken on this question by courts, or by national legal systems generally.

Just as French law, for instance, cannot undo the existence of the English legal system (that is, its absolute legality), it cannot take away the legality of any non-state legal system. Conversely, a legal system, such as the public legal system, cannot bring another legal system into existence (absolute legality).[18] It can, however, act as if it existed (relative legality).

As a final illustration, let us imagine that Swedish law, for instance, recognized the legal character of a given private normative order and that Austrian law, for example, denies it. In that case, the legal status as such of the private normative order in question would not be made unclear by the recognition opposed to the rejection. The recognition opposed to the rejection would simply have no effect at all on the absolute legality of this order.[19] Such relations between relative and absolute legality will form the substance of the next sub-section.

3. Relations Between Relative and Absolute Legality

The relation between relative and absolute legality has recently been invoked as an important argument by Emmanuel Gaillard. To arbitration scholars and practitioners, Gaillard is as well known as the New York Convention. For other readers, it may simply be pointed out that he is one the most prominent current scholars of international arbitration and undoubtedly the one who has most strongly marked

---

[16] François Rigaux, *La loi des juges* (Odile Jacob 1997) 28.
[17] van de Kerchove and Ost, *Legal System*, 142.
[18] See also, for instance, Eric Loquin, "L'application des règles anationales dans l'arbitrage commercial international" in *L'apport de la jurisprudence arbitrale: l'arbitrage commercial international* (International Chamber of Commerce 1986) 119, 121: "l'attitude des Etats à l'égard de l'ordre anational est indifférente à son existence," where by "existence" he means existence qua *legal* order.
[19] See for instance Paul Lagarde, "Approche critique de la lex mercatoria" in *Le droit des relations économiques internationales: Études offertes à Berthold Goldman* (Litec 1982) 125, 139: "si cet ordre juridique existe... il ne tire pas son caractère juridique de la reconnaissance que l'ordre juridique étatique lui accorde, mais de lui-même. Le droit est immanent à l'organisation sociale."

today's debate on arbitration as transnational law. He is also a particularly high flying practitioner of arbitration and has close ties with a number of key policy makers in the field. In short, he is influential. It is thus important to understand his ideas. Many of them are truly novel. It is important to understand his ideas in part because it may give us a hint about where they might take the world of arbitration. His argument forms the baseline for what follows.[20]

3.1 Emmanuel Gaillard on the autonomy of arbitration

At the heart of Gaillard's relevant writings really is an intent to address the question of the "autonomy of arbitration," which he defines as the "question of the place of arbitration in the international legal ordering or, in other words, its positioning with regard to state legal orders."[21] Put differently, he considers that it is "the question of the autonomy and the relations between arbitration and one or several sovereign powers [that is, states]."[22] This point, in turn, is closely connected to the question "of the 'juridicity' of international arbitration."[23]

The details of the various concrete issues this raises in arbitration law are not important here.[24] It is enough to focus on just one part to see the general point. Under the New York Convention on the Recognition and Enforcement of Foreign Arbitral Awards of 1958, recognition or enforcement of an arbitral award made by an arbitral tribunal with seat in another state may be refused if the award has been set aside by a competent authority of the country of the seat of the arbitral tribunal. The issue this raises, well known to arbitration scholars and practitioners, is that arbitral awards set aside or annulled by the courts of the seat of the arbitration, where it was legally made, may nevertheless be recognized and enforced abroad.[25]

---

[20] Gaillard has published a number of writings in support of arbitration as transnational law. The most important ones are Emmanuel Gaillard, *Legal Theory of International Arbitration* (Martinus Nijhoff 2010); Emmanuel Gaillard, *Aspects philosophiques du droit de l'arbitrage international* (Martinus Nijhoff 2008); Emmanuel Gaillard, "The Representations of International Arbitration" (2010) 1 *Journal of International Dispute Settlement* 271; Emmanuel Gaillard, "L'ordre juridique arbitral: réalité, utilité et spécificité" (2010) 55 *McGill Law Journal* 891; Emmanuel Gaillard, "Souveraineté et autonomie: réflexions sur les représentations de l'arbitrage international" (2007) 134 *Journal du droit international* 1163.
[21] Gaillard, "Souveraineté et autonomie," 1164 (translation is mine). See also Gaillard, *Legal Theory*, 1, where he speaks of "questioning the relationship between international arbitration and national legal orders."
[22] Gaillard, "Souveraineté et autonomie," 1165 (translation is mine). See also Gaillard, *Legal Theory*, 15: "The third representation, which the author of this Course favors, is that which recognizes an autonomous character to international arbitration, viewed as having generated an authentic legal order: the arbitral legal order."
[23] Gaillard, *Legal Theory*, 2.
[24] Gaillard, *Legal Theory*, 67–149.
[25] Some classical writings on the question are (in addition to what follows in subsequent footnotes): Emmanuel Gaillard, "Anti-Suit injunctions et reconnaissance des sentences annulées au siège: une évolution remarquable de la jurisprudence" (2003) 130 *Journal du droit international* 1105; Hamid G Gharavi, *The International Effectiveness of the Annulment of an Award* (Kluwer 2002); Georgios C Petrochilos, "Enforcing Awards Annulled in Their State of Origin under the New York Convention" (1999) 48 *International and Comparative Law Quarterly* 856; Albert Jan van den Berg, "Enforcement of Annulled Awards?" (1998) 9/2 *ICC Bulletin* 15; Jan Paulsson, "Enforcing Arbitral Awards

From a black letter law perspective, the issue is pedestrian, even rather boring. But let me just briefly sketch it here, for we need it to proceed with our discussion. The Convention says "*may* be refused." The word "may" is enabling, not mandating, permissive, not mandatory.[26] The Convention either grants the enforcement state discretionary power to provide for more favorable enforcement conditions[27] or it grants the enforcement authorities themselves a discretionary power to enforce nullified awards or to refuse such enforcement. Each member state of the Convention is free to "choose the degree of liberalism that it intends to apply [to the recognition and enforcement of] foreign arbitral awards [that have been annulled in the country in which they were made]."[28] Legally, the point is clear: "There is no doubt that the enforcement judge can recognise and enforce an award which has been set aside in its state or origin... [T]he recognition [and enforcement] of an award which has been set aside is compatible with the New York Convention."[29] But can is not should. It is not because the practice of recognizing and enforcing annulled awards is allowed by the Convention that it is appropriate practice. It is, for example, a source of legal uncertainty and it creates the risk of contradicting decisions: if an award has been annulled and replaced by a new award, both the replaced and the replacing award may be enforced.[30]

So some people have sought to find limits extrinsic to the Convention on the discretionary power it grants its member states for the recognition and enforcement of nullified awards. The argument most relevant here is attributed to the realm of logical possibilities: it may well be legally possible, so the contention goes, to

---

Notwithstanding a Local Standard Annulment" (1998) 9/1 *ICC Bulletin* 14; Emmanuel Gaillard, "L'exécution des sentences annulées dans leur pays d'origine" (1998) 125 *Journal du droit international* 645; Thomas Carbonneau, "Debating the Proper Role of National Law under the New York Arbitration Convention" (1998) 6 *Tulane Journal of International & Comparative Law* 277, 281; Jean-François Poudret, "Quelle solution pour en finir avec l'affaire Hilmarton?" (1998) *Revue de l'arbitrage* 7; Sébastien Besson and Luc Pittet, "La reconnaissance à l'étranger d'une sentence annulée dans son Etat d'origine" (1998) *ASA Bulletin* 498; Philippe Fouchard, "La portée internationale de l'annulation de la sentence arbitrale dans son pays d'origine" (1997) *Revue de l'arbitrage* 329; Hamid G Gharavi, "Chromalloy: Another View" (1997) 12 *Mealeys's International Arbitration Report* 21; Gary H Sampliner, "Enforcement of Nullified Foreign Arbitral Awards—Chromalloy Revisited" (1997) 14 *Journal of International Arbitration* 141; Jan Paulsson, "The Case for Disregarding LSAS (Local Standard Annulments) under the New York Convention" (1996) 7 *American Review of International Arbitration* 99.

[26] On these semantics, see in particular Jan Paulsson, "May or Must under the New York Convention: An Exercise in Syntax and Linguistics" (1998) 14 *Arbitration International* 227.

[27] Article V(1)(e) must be read in conjunction with Article VII of the Convention, a "most favourable rights" provision that in essence mandates the court of enforcement to apply provisions in its domestic law that are more favorable than the Convention to the recognition and enforcement of the award. Article VII(1) states: "The provisions of the present Convention shall not... deprive any interested party of any right he may have to avail himself of an arbitral award in the manner and to the extent allowed by the law or the treaties of the country where such award is sought to be relied upon."

[28] Emmanuel Gaillard, comment on the *Hilmarton* case, French *Cour de Cassation*, (1994) *Revue de l'arbitrage* 327 and (1994) 121 *Journal du droit international* 701, 709.

[29] Jean-François Poudret and Sébastien Besson, *Comparative Law of International Arbitration* (2nd edn, Sweet & Maxwell 2007) 909–10.

[30] For a detailed discussion of the issues raised by this practice, see Gharavi, *International Effectiveness*, 119–38.

recognize or enforce an annulled award, but it is not logically possible to do so. The sense of logic is ascribed to the general theory of legal systems.

The argument was first made by the founding father himself of the New York Convention, Pieter Sanders, another extremely influential man in the field of international arbitration, whose arguments thus come with a veneer of principled respect. In 1959, he offered his view on the theoretical foundation of the argument that annulled awards must, despite the permissive text of the Convention, be refused recognition and enforcement. "If the award 'has been set aside'," he wrote, "there does *no longer exist* an arbitral award and enforcing a non-existing arbitral award would be an *impossibility*."[31]

Intuitively convincing, the argument is followed by the vast majority of national legal systems, which accordingly refuse to recognize and enforce foreign awards that have been annulled in their country of origin. But certain courts in a small but important minority of member states of the Convention have rejected the ground for refusal to recognize or enforce based on the setting aside abroad of the award, and have enforced nullified awards.[32] What is meaningful for the purposes of the current discussion is that at least certain of these courts grounded their choice, in the exercise of the discretion granted by the Convention, by resorting to arguments drawn from systems jurisprudence. So they did like Sanders and his followers, but with the opposite aim.

The French Court of Appeal put it very clearly in the case of *International Bechtel Co*. An arbitral award, the court held, "is not integrated into the legal order of the [state of origin or of the seat of the arbitration], so that its possible annulment by the courts of the seat does not affect its existence and does not prevent it from being recognized and enforced in other national legal systems."[33]

That is the basis of Gaillard's discussion. His purpose is to reinforce the theoretical grounding of the line of reasoning followed by the Court of Appeal, by framing arguments in language speaking of relations between legal systems. He thereby takes the argument one step further towards clarity, but also towards the underlying logical lapse made both by Sanders and the Court of Appeal.

He writes this: "*It is because* arbitration is autonomous with regard to the state of the seat *that it is possible* to recognize the validity of the award at the place of enforcement despite its annulment in the state of origin."[34] The reference to

---

[31] Pieter Sanders, "New York Convention on the Recognition and Enforcement of Foreign Arbitral Awards" (1959) 6 *Netherlands International Law Review* 43, 55 (emphasis is mine). A thorough review of the literature on this question takes place in Maxi Scherer, "Effects of Foreign Judgments Relating to International Arbitral Awards: Is the 'Judgment Route' the Wrong Road?" (2013) 4 *Journal of International Dispute Settlement* 587, fn 32.

[32] For a review of the cases and the literature, see Scherer, "Effects of Foreign Judgments," 596, fn 35.

[33] *International Bechtel Co*, Court of Appeal of Paris, September 29, 2005, n° 2004/07635 (translation is mine). Original French text: "La sentence n'est pas intégrée dans l'ordre juridique [de l'Etat d'origine] de sorte que son éventuelle annulation par le juge du siège ne porte pas atteinte à son existence en empêchant sa reconnaissance et son exécution dans d'autres ordres juridiques nationaux."

[34] Gaillard, "Souveraineté et autonomie," 1167 (translation and emphasis are mine). Similar language in Gaillard, *Legal Theory*, 139: "It is precisely because arbitration is autonomous vis-à-vis the legal order of the State of the seat that an award set aside at the seat can nonetheless be recognized in the place of enforcement." A different interpretation of his theory may follow from these two sentences,

the autonomous character of arbitration must here be read as a reference to the "autonomy" of its *legality*. The view can credibly by ascribed to him that by the "autonomy of arbitration," he means the autonomy of the legality of the arbitral award with regard to the state of the seat. This interpretation of his position follows from his description of the opposite doctrine—a classical one, put forward by traditional "Westphalian" arbitration theorists, most prominently and radically represented by FA Mann[35]—according to which arbitration is entirely grounded in and dependent on the legal order of the seat. The idea of Mann and these traditional arbitration theorists is that arbitration only exists, as a legal phenomenon, because of and by dint of the legal order of the seat. No autonomy of legality is recognized to arbitration. The classical conception of arbitration, Gaillard considers, "has the immediate consequence of making it *impossible*, in all other legal orders, to enforce awards set aside at the seat."[36] He explains the impossibility, almost using Sanders's words, by saying that "[a]n award set aside at the seat *ceases to exist*. It cannot therefore be recognized anywhere else."[37]

According to Gaillard, the autonomy of an arbitral award's legality with regard to the state of the seat is a consequence of the fact that we "can acknowledge the existence of an arbitral legal order."[38] In other words, he contends that we should adopt a pluralistic approach to law (which he labels "the transnational positivist trend" or "the arbitral legal order... [i]n its positivist vein"[39]) and recognize the existence of a transnational arbitral legal order. We should do so because such an approach is necessary to grant arbitration (at the level of act-types) and arbitral awards (at the level of act-tokens) a legality that is independent of the one conferred by the national legal system where the award was made. This independent legality is in turn necessary, in the proper logical sense of the word, to recognize or enforce arbitral awards that were annulled by the courts of the state where the award was

---

on page 136 of the same book: "the issue at stake being the recognition and enforcement of an award in a given State, it suffices that the award be detached from the legal order of the seat for it to be open to recognition elsewhere, notwithstanding its setting aside at the seat. That an award be considered as existing in the realm of the arbitral order only provides comfort to the courts of the place of enforcement that it exists autonomously, irrespective of its recognition in any national legal order, each State being free to recognize awards pursuant to conditions it determines for itself, subject only to compliance with the international obligations it has undertaken in this respect." The words "only provides comfort," taken in isolation, may lead us to think that the existence, as a legal order, of the arbitral order is only icing on the cake, as opposed to a key element in the logical construct of his theory. But the tenor of these two sentences remains somewhat elliptical in their English version reproduced here. In their French version (Emmanuel Gaillard, *Aspects philosophiques de l'arbitrage* (Martinus Nijhoff 2008) 189), their meaning is even more ambivalent, easily lending themselves to being understood as making no statement on the plane of formal logics. In addition, this idea of "comfort" is at odds with the rest of his theory, or at least would considerably water it down and make it less palatable. Let us, then, pretermit it.

[35] F A Mann, "Lex Facit Arbitrum" in *Liber Amicorum for Martin Domke* (Martinus Nijhoff 1967) 157.
[36] Gaillard, *Legal Theory*, 135 (emphasis is mine).
[37] Gaillard, *Legal Theory*, 135 (emphasis is mine).
[38] Gaillard, "Souveraineté et autonomie," 1170 (translation is mine).
[39] Gaillard, *Legal Theory*, 45.

made. Indeed, such awards can no longer derive any existence as law from the legal system of the state of the arbitral tribunal's seat. So goes Gaillard's argument.

And, at a first glance, he seems to have a point. If the arbitral award derives its legal character from a non-state legal system, then the national legal system of the seat of the arbitration cannot undo this legality. Annulment by the courts of the seat of the arbitration would have no consequence on the legal existence of the award itself and, it would seem to follow, an annulled award could thus be recognized and enforced elsewhere. Annulment would merely amount to a refusal by the legal system of the seat to recognize the award within the territory of the legal system where it was made. Annulment would, per se, in fact have no consequence for any legal system other than the national legal system that has annulled the award. That is an application of the idea of relative legality, more precisely of the species of relative legality that refers to a legal system's recognition of a norm or decision as one of its own laws or legal determinations. When legal system A says "no, X (the award) is not one of my legal determinations," this does not prevent system B from saying "well, it is one of mine: X is one of my legal determinations." So far, Gaillard is correct, and this appears to be a meaningful argument to make.

3.2 Absolute legality as a determinant of relative legality

There is an issue in the logical link between Gaillard's two propositions. It is correct that a state can recognize and enforce annulled foreign awards. And it certainly appears admissible to argue that arbitral awards draw their legal status from a non-state legal system, at least in certain cases.

But the former proposition is correct not because scholars admit, *ex hypothesi*, the existence of a non-state arbitral legal order. It is not because legal scholars see a non-state arbitral order in the landscape of legal systems that national courts *can* recognize awards that have been annulled in their state of origin. The reason for the lack of a relationship of entailment between these two propositions emerges with greater clarity if we consider the distinction between absolute and relative legality.

One author, Georgios Petrochilos, pointed to the heart of the matter, albeit not entirely with the right shade of grey. He wrote this: "The only way out of the [permissive provisions of the New York Convention] would be to say that there is no award to enforce, it having been annulled *ab initio*. The argument is, however, a *petitio principii*: it assumes that there exists no award, whereas the forum's law clearly says the contrary, since it takes no account of the annulment."[40]

Petrochilos is right when asserting that it is meaningful for the legal status of the award that "the forum's law clearly says the contrary, since it takes no account of the annulment." Nothing prevents a legal system from giving effect to a decision or any other norm that was, up to that point, unable to derive a legal nature from any legal system at all. To give effect to an award is to extend to it the recognizing legal

---

[40] Petrochilos, "Enforcing Awards," 862.

system's legality; it is the acceptance of the recognizing system to regard the decision as an external legal element (but not its integration or absorption properly speaking into the system, for the reasons laid out by Green above[41]). The recognized external element (here the award) *becomes* legal *for the recognizing legal system* (hence in the sense of relative legality) by virtue of its recognition by the system.

The recognition is the necessary and sufficient condition of (relative) legality: the external element becomes legal regardless of its status prior to its recognition and regardless of the status it is being granted or denied by any other legal system. Such are the workings of relative legality and the pluralist Midas Principle, as we have pondered above.

Indeed, just as rules of experience[42] acquire a legal nature for the recognizing legal system merely because they are recognized, any other originally non-legal norm may become legal if a legal system recognizes it. Recall Kelsen: "Just as everything King Midas touched turned into gold, everything to which law refers becomes law":[43] everything that a legal system wishes to "turn into" law *becomes* law, regardless of its past nature. A legal system can regard and treat as legal an isolated norm or a norm (for instance a decision) pertaining to a normative system that, *arguendo*, does not amount to a legal order by any standard and give it effect, thereby to all intents and purposes recognizing and enforcing it as a legal element.

In other words, relative legality does not require absolute legality. A legal system can recognize something as law that jurisprudence would typically not describe as law. A legal system can extend its legality (Midas Principle) to every norm it cares to consider legal. For instance, nothing would prevent state X from recognizing a court decision from state Y, even if the decision has been annulled in state Y. (Such a position, it may be pointed out, is unrelated to the question of the international responsibility that state X may incur for such a recognition. But this is a different matter, and a matter that does not raise an issue with regard to the present situation, as the New York Convention only sets a threshold above which foreign awards must be recognized and enforced, and no threshold below which they must be refused recognition and enforcement.)

Expressed in jurisprudential terms, secondary rules of recognition have no limitation as to what they may consider to be law as far as the legal system of reference is concerned. Whether any such recognition is practically sensible is a distinct question, and it is beyond the scope of analytic jurisprudence.

Now, given these clarifications, it is inaccurate to say that it is *because* an award derives its legal nature from a non-state legal order (a legal nature, this part is correct, that the legal system of the seat of the arbitration cannot undo) that it can be recognized and enforced in the forum state. It further is inaccurate to maintain that the legal invalidity of the award in its country of origin (put differently, its lack

---

[41] Section 1.2 "The Midas Principle," above.
[42] See van de Kerchove and Ost, *Legal System*, 22–4 and discussion in Section 1.2 "The Midas Principle," above.
[43] Kelsen, *Pure Theory of Law*, 161.

of legal existence in this legal system) prevents its recognition or enforcement by another legal system or on grounds drawn from the general theory of legal systems.

The only limitation applicable to the recognition or enforcement of nullified awards, beyond pragmatical considerations, is the principle of comity: respect for and non-interference in the work of foreign legal institutions.[44] Is the recognition and enforcement, by a court of country X, a breach of the comity it owes to the court of country Y, which had clearly said a given arbitral award ought not to live? Perhaps.[45] The particulars of the case would go a long way towards deciding that point. But there is no categorical legal obligation here, or any compulsion, pressure, or logical impossibility to be derived from the general theory of legal systems.

It is not that the general theory of legal systems squarely sits on the fence in the debate between Gaillard and the classical arbitration theorists à la Sanders. Gaillard's underlying argument against classical arbitration theorists, namely that no logical impossibility attaches to the recognition and enforcement of foreign annulled awards, is supported by the general theory of legal systems. But his argument is correct not because of his invocation of absolute legality (the argument that there is such a thing as a non-state arbitral legal system). It is correct because of the workings of relative legality and the Midas Principle.

Pace Gaillard, we should clearly discern two functions. On the one hand, we have the function of officials of legal systems, who make law through the Midas Principle, which extends the recognizing system's (relative) legality to the recognized norms or sets of norms. On the other hand, there is the function of analytic legal philosophers, who merely describe and analyze and set for their own discipline the conditions of (absolute) legality and their application in particular instances. They have, as scholars, no power to *make* law. Determinants of absolute legality are no determinants of relative legality—except, of course, if the secondary rules of recognition of a legal system designate the determinations of certain legal scholars acting in this capacity as sources of law, in which case these legal scholars become officials of the legal system in question.

Gaillard's reference to absolute legality in the determination of relative legality, however, yields some important insights into the rhetorical consequences of legality. National legal systems, and more precisely courts, would seem to be typically more willing to recognize as legal (relative legality) and grant the corresponding deference to norms that legal scholars consider to be legal (absolute legality). For

---

[44] Nigel Blackaby, Constantine Partasides, with Alan Redfern and Martin Hunter, *Redfern and Hunter on International Arbitration* (Oxford University Press 2009) 650: "If, for example, an award has been set aside in Switzerland, it will be unenforceable in that country; and it might be expected that, if only as a matter of international comity, the courts of other States would regard the award as unenforceable also. This is not necessarily so, however. Courts in other countries may take the view (and indeed, as will be described, in some countries they have taken the view) that they will enforce an arbitral award even if it has been set aside by the courts of the seat of the arbitration."

[45] On the principle of comity, Adrian Briggs, "The Principle of Comity in Private International Law" (2011) 354 *Hague Lectures* 65; Thomas Schultz and David Holloway, "Retour sur la comity I: les origines de la comity au carrefour du droit international privé et du droit international public" (2011) 138 *Journal du droit international* 864; Thomas Schultz and David Holloway, "Retour sur la comity II: La comity dans l'histoire du droit international privé" (2012) 138 *Journal du droit international* 571.

example, there seems to have been a temporal correlation between, on the one hand, the emergence of academic theories that conceived of the lex mercatoria as a non-state legal system and, on the other hand, the recognition by national arbitration laws that the lex mercatoria could validly be the applicable law in an arbitration. Absolute legality appears in such situations to constitute a live factor influencing the determination of relative legality.

One may surmise that the reason for such influence is that once a group of norms enters the realm of scholarly-attributed legality (absolute legality), it will be thought by the officials of many legal systems to *deserve* to be treated as legal (relative legality). It would deserve to receive preferential treatment by being treated as law because of the underlying assumption that law is something valuable, that the qualification of legality entails a judgment on the regulative quality of the hence legalized normative order. In sum, although there is no logical relationship of entailment between absolute and relative legality, there often is a rhetorical connection between these two forms of legality, absolute legality appearing to exert some influence on the practice of relative legality in instant cases.

3.3 Relative legality as a determinant of absolute legality

I have argued that relative legality does not *require* absolute legality. The reverse relationship must now be pondered. Its exposition will remain relatively brief, as the foregoing developments have allowed us to elucidate the salient aspects of the distinction and the interactions between these two forms of legality. The question to be addressed now is whether a determination of relative legality is a necessary and/or a sufficient condition for the determination of absolute legality.

One basic contrast is germane. It relates to the discussion entered into above in connection with Kelsen's Midas Principle, and his monist conception of law, and Green's subsequent comment thereupon.[46] It is informed by a distinction we have encountered earlier on: on the one hand, norms that form part of a legal system; on the other hand, norms that a legal system enforces qua legal norms without making them part of the system. The contrast I want to focus on here also builds on an underlying argument made by Gaillard we have not properly broached yet.

Consider, first, norms forming part of a legal system. If we, as external analytical observers, consider a normative system to qualify as a legal system (absolute legality), then this qualification extends to each of its constitutive or integral parts: we would consider every part of the system to be legal in nature. If we admit that the German legal system, for example, partakes of the characteristics of a legal system, then we would inevitably be led to consider that all those norms that form part of the German legal system are law. The secondary rules of recognition of the German legal system determine what forms part of German law—they identify the building blocks of the Kelsenian pyramid of German law, if you will. Hence, these secondary rules of recognition, because the normative system to which they

---

[46] See Section 1.2 "The Midas Principle," above.

belong is considered legal, constitute authoritative formulations not only of relative legality but, in the end effect, also of absolute legality. With regard to absolute legality, such secondary rules admit of no false positives (every norm they designate as part of the system is a legal norm in the absolute sense) but of a very large number of false negatives, namely all those norms that are not part of German law but nevertheless are legal in nature because of their belonging to another legal system. Hence, when we speak of the relative legality of the integral or constitutive normative elements of what has analytically been recognized as a legal system, relative legality is a sufficient but not necessary condition of absolute legality.

Consider, then, norms that a legal system takes over and enforces qua legal norms without making them part of the system. That which one, several, or even all legal systems recognize and treat as legal in the specific sense of an external, non-integrated element does not authoritatively become legal for the analytical observer by dint of this recognition. Suppose that the legal system of country X features a conflicts rule that provides that in certain situations the applicable law is Y, a set of divine scriptures and the therein contained commands. These religious norms do not form part of the legal system of country X, because, to echo Green's argument, the officials of the legal system of country X "can neither change [Y] nor repeal it" (this indeed partakes of the authority of the relevant god).[47] To quote another passage from Green, the "legal organs [of X] have applicative but not creative power over them":[48] if the legal organs of X do not have full authority over the set of norms Y, then this implies that the rules Y belong to another normative system, which has created them and can modify and abolish them. This other normative system, in the instant case a hypothetical religious order, is a distinct system with normative autonomy whose legality must be assessed distinctly. Whether Y and the religious order constitute law in and of themselves is a question for the analyst, not for the officials of system X. The officials can only decide what to do with these norms for the purposes of system X, that is whether and with which status they wish to recognize and apply them.

The following example might help: suppose that a number of legal systems consider a given normative system to be law despite its extreme procedural iniquity. Because of its procedural inequity, it would *ex hypothesi* tragically depart from, for instance, the Fullerian principles of legality.[49] This normative system does not, *ex hypothesi*, amount to law for the scholar of analytical jurisprudence. The realpolitik preceding World War II, for example, does not bind the hands of the external observer who seeks to gauge whether the rules of the Nazi regime deserve to be called law or not.

Now, to Gaillard's argument. His "transnational positivist conception of arbitration" usefully illustrates the ideas entered heretofore, at least in one understanding of his work. As that understanding is not entirely obvious, two lengthy quotations are warranted here, both taken from sections entitled "Transnational Positivist Trend/Conception." In his article published in 2007, he writes this:

---

[47] See Section 1.2 "The Midas Principle," above.
[48] Green, "Legal Positivism."   [49] See Chapter 8, below.

[A]rbitrators draw their power from all the *national legal systems that are willing to recognize*, under certain conditions, the validity of the arbitration agreement that created their mandate and are willing to recognize the existing or future award made on the basis of this arbitration agreement, so long as it meets certain minimal conditions. The *convergence of national legal systems in recognizing*, on certain minimal conditions on which a very broad consensus exists, the validity of arbitration agreements and arbitral awards is sufficient to *justify the autonomy of international arbitration*. No legal system, even the law of the seat, has exclusive authority over the arbitration.[50]

In his book *Legal Theory of International Arbitration*, published in 2010, he writes this:

The notion of an *arbitral legal order* accounts for the fact that, in practice, *States broadly agree on the conditions that an arbitration must meet* in order for it to be considered a binding method of dispute resolution, the result of which, the award, deserves their sanction in the form of legal enforcement. As arbitrators' power to adjudicate rests on the *ultimate recognition* of their awards *by States*, this approach remains in keeping with positivist thinking. As no State alone holds a monopoly over such recognition, this representation of international arbitration accepts the idea that a *system rising above each national legal system taken in isolation can be brought about by the convergence of all laws*.[51]

Elsewhere in the book, he further speaks of the "[e]ndorsement of the majoritarian principle," which is associated with the idea that "the arbitral legal order is based on national legal orders."[52] He also devotes seven pages to reporting evidence of "The Recognition of the Existence of an Arbitral Legal Order by National Legal Orders."[53] It seems meant to substantiate the existence of a transnational arbitral legal order.

Admittedly, his words are slightly elliptical from the point of view of legal theory. We may nevertheless recall from the outset of the discussion of his theory that the "autonomy of arbitration" is meant as legal autonomy, or the autonomy of arbitration as a legal phenomenon. It thus essentially stands for the existence of an autonomous arbitral non-state legal order.[54]

Hence, we seem entitled to ascribe the following argument to Gaillard: the fact that the vast majority of courts recognize arbitration agreements and awards in the overwhelming majority of cases, with only minimal conditions posed, "justifies arbitral autonomy"; it "justifies" that we conceive of the existence of a non-state arbitral system.

In jurisprudential terms, this would seem to translate as follows: It is because national legal systems recognize the legal phenomenon of arbitration as a normative order requiring only minimal control (that is the so-called "transnational positivist concept of arbitration") that this normative order should indeed by considered to partake of the characteristics of legality. Relative legality, in other words, would determine our assessment of absolute legality. This line of reasoning seems to be

---

[50] Gaillard, "Souveraineté et autonomie," 1172–3 (translation and emphasis are mine).
[51] Gaillard, *Legal Theory*, 46 (emphasis added).
[52] Gaillard, *Legal Theory*, 48.   [53] Gaillard, *Legal Theory*, 60–6.
[54] See Section 3.1 "Emmanuel Gaillard on the autonomy of arbitration," above.

based on the idea that arbitration really is meant to form a discrete, "autonomous" order, not a sub-order part of any national legal system. This precisely appears to be the point of his argument according to which national legal systems cannot repeal this order's norms, and in particular arbitral awards.

And herein lies the issue: as we have seen above, the attribution of relative legality by national legal systems to non-integrated, external normative elements is not a determinant for the analytical external observer. The "transnational positivist conception of arbitration" yields no authoritative conclusion for the analytical legal scholar as to the proper existence, in and of itself, of one or several arbitral legal orders. The determinations made by the courts of national legal systems would only have such an effect if they considered that the arbitral legal order was part of any such national legal system, which precisely is the point he seeks to avoid.

6
Why Think in Terms of Legal Systems

I have repeatedly said, and will say it again many more times throughout this book, that for something to qualify as law it needs to amount to a legal system or to be part of one. In other words, I think in terms of legal systems. I define legality by focusing on legal systems, thereby taking an approach grounded in legal positivism. There is no law outside of legal systems. But why? And how does international arbitration illustrate that point? These are the questions for this chapter.

At this juncture, we must indeed probe certain relationships between the concept of a legal system and non-state law. We should not yet enter here into the discussion of what should be understood by the concept of a legal system, nor define the minimal conditions upon which a non-state normative system deserves the label of law. These are the tasks for the next chapters. We first have to entertain the question why the former (the concept of a legal system) is useful and even necessary for the second (the definition of non-state law) and address one immediate consequence that follows from this.

The first main section of this chapter discusses the point in the abstract. The second illustrates the point by referring to the lex mercatoria, as the forerunner of the current theories on arbitration as transnational law.

1. Law Obtains as Systems

The only approach to legality that truly is workable in practice for the identification of non-state law—which is also the one that corresponds to the dominant view of what law is—is legal positivism. I mean positivism here not in the classical conception of legal positivism inherited from Bentham and Austin that sees law only in states (an approach that is unduly restrictive be it only because there is historical evidence as to the existence of law before the emergence of states[1]), but merely in the sense of the separability of law and morality.[2] The separability thesis means, as Hart puts it, "the simple contention that it is in no sense a necessary truth that laws reproduce or satisfy certain demands of morality, though in fact they have

---

[1] Harold J Berman, *Law and Revolution: The Formation of the Western Legal Tradition* (Harvard University Press 1983) 333–56; Andrei Marmor, *Positive Law & Objective Values* (Oxford 2001) 40.
[2] See for instance Matthew H Kramer, *Where Law and Morality Meet* (Oxford University Press 2008), ch 7; Jules L Coleman, "Negative and Positive Positivism" (1982) 11 *Journal of Legal Studies* 139 and HLA Hart, "Positivism and the Separation of Law and Morals" (1958) 71 *Harvard Law Review* 593.

often done so."[3] This means that, from an external point of view and without prejudice to the specific rules of recognition set for itself by any given legal system, morality is not a condition of legality. In other words, legality is in this approach independent from the substance of the norms and can be obtained regardless of the just or moral character of the solutions that the norms provide, unless the legal system in question sets as a condition of validity the norms' conformity with certain moral ideals.[4]

Such an approach appears to be the only workable one because, if we do take the substantive contents of a regulation into consideration to determine its legality, one of two issues arises.

The first issue occurs if we take, as a condition of legality, the substance of the norms in an inconspicuous acceptation. This would for instance be the case if we retained very light substantive requirements that norms must satisfy as a sufficient condition to deserve the label of "law."

Let me try an example. In *The Concept of Law*, Hart wrote a comparatively little known passage on what he called "the minimum content of natural law."[5] He contended that there are certain minimal substantive conditions that must be met for law to exist. (In his case, the conditions are necessary, not sufficient, but the argument remains the same, *mutatis mutandis*.) A legal system must necessarily, he maintained, include certain contents in order to effectively operate, and thus to exist as a properly legal phenomenon. He had in mind prohibitions regarding the use of force in general and the aggression of the defenceless in particular, rules imposing not more than a limited altruism on the part of its addressees, rules allocating resources, and sanctions as instruments for the effectiveness of all other rules against those people who do not understand the necessity of the aforementioned rules or do not have the strength of will to follow them. If a normative system does not contain these universally recognized principles of conduct, which are indispensable for at least minimal human flourishing, and which can be derived from "truisms" about human nature and their predicament, then it cannot form a legal system and should not be granted the label of law.

The issue that arises is simply one of uselessness for our purposes: no arbitral regime I know of is even remotely in breach of these minimalist requirements.

The second issue arises if we set the threshold higher. If indeed we take a higher standard of morality or substantive justice as a condition of legality, we expose ourselves to what normative positivism, in the sense that Jeremy Waldron gives to this term, precisely sought to avoid.[6] Normative positivism is legal positivism as a

---

[3] HLA Hart, *The Concept of Law* (2nd edn, Clarendon Press 1994) 185–6.

[4] Accordingly, my general analytical position can be ascribed to inclusive positivism, namely that "It is not necessarily the case that there is a connection between law and morality," which can be opposed to exclusive positivism, where "It is necessarily the case that there is no connection between law and morality": see Leslie Green, "Legal Positivism" in Edward N Zalta (ed), *Stanford Encyclopedia of Philosophy* (Stanford University Fall 2009 edn) and Wilfrid J Waluchow, *Inclusive Legal Positivism* (Clarendon Press 1994).

[5] Hart, *Concept of Law*, 193–200.

[6] Normative positivism may also refer to the conception that law can be identified with norms. It is in this sense sometimes also simply called "normativism". See Deryck Beyleveld and Roger

normative thesis: it is normative insofar as it rests on the idea that we ought to avoid the "evils that might be expected to afflict societies whose members were unable to disentangle their judgments about what was required or permitted by the law of their society from their individual judgments about justice and morality."[7] This is an idea to be found, for instance, in the positivist philosophies of Thomas Hobbes and Jeremy Bentham. Put differently, to use Waldron's words again, normative positivism seeks to "separate our understanding of law from our commitment (or anyone's commitment) to particular controversial moral and political ideals". The point is to ensure that "the debate about the nature of law [is] not...held hostage to political, moral, and ideological controversy."[8] What applies to the nature of law in and of itself also should apply to specific incarnations of it: the substantive regulative quality of a normative system (that is, its substantive justice or its merits) should not be taken into consideration to determine whether it deserves the label of law, lest we enter into endless debates on different conceptions of substantive justice (that is to say, debates on the proper allocation of resources).

So we have made the argument that legal positivism, in its aforementioned guise, forms the proper approach to apprehend the question whether non-state normative regimes deserve the label of law. We must now entertain the question of how this position entails that the analysis should be conducted in terms of systems.

If a non-positivist, merits-based approach might allow us to say that one norm, taken in isolation, is law because it is considered to be just by its addresses, as for example Bronislaw Malinowski[9] or Jean-François Perrin[10] would contend, the same is not possible in legal positivism. Indeed, if we do not define law with regard to its substance, we must define it according to its form. And taken in isolation, a legal norm cannot be distinguished, by its formal aspect, from a social norm. What allows to make the distinction is its pedigree, its relation to other norms. While the individual form of a norm does not allow to set it apart from a social norm, its collective form does. The links and interactions of a norm with other norms enable the discrimination of social from legal norms. As Brian Tamanaha puts it, the difference between social norms and legal norms is based on the "degree of differentiation in the institutionalized identification and enforcement of norms."[11] To use

---

Brownsword, "Normative Positivism: The Mirage of the Middle Way" (1989) 9 *Oxford Journal of Legal Studies* 462 and Pascale Deumier, *Le droit spontané* (Economica 2002) 298–302.

[7] Jeremy Waldron, "Normative (or Ethical) Positivism" in Jules Coleman (ed), *Hart's Postscript: Essays on the Postscript to The Concept of Law* (Oxford University Press 2001) 412–13.

[8] Waldron, "Normative (or Ethical) Positivism," 415.

[9] Bronislaw Malinowski, *Crime and Custom in Savage Society* (first published 1926, Littlefield Adams 1985) 55: "The rules of law stand out from the rest in that they are felt and regarded as the obligations of one person and the *rightful* claims of another" (emphasis is mine).

[10] Jean-François Perrin, *Sociologie empirique du droit* (Helbing & Lichtenhahn 1997) 30: "*C'est cette reconnaissance du caractère juste d'un rapport de droit et de devoir qui signe, selon nous, la juridicité d'une assertion normative. La norme en question est donc juridique, c'est-à-dire juste dans ce groupe et pour ce groupe. Cette définition mobilise l'idée de justice, prise dans son acception la plus usuelle. Un rapport de droit est juste lorsqu'il est établie conformément à une règle qui attribue à chacun ce qui lui est dû (suum cuique tribuere)*."

[11] Brian Z Tamanaha, "The Folly of the 'Social Scientific' Concept of Legal Pluralism" (1993) 20 *Journal of Law and Society* 192, 206.

Hans Kelsen's words, "Law is not, as it is sometimes said, a rule. It is a set of rules having the kind of unity we understand by a system."[12]

What matters for legality in legal positivism is what has been posited (or, in Tamanaha's words, what has been institutionally identified and enforced) and this positivization necessarily presupposes the presence of institutions and other norms, which interrelate and thereby form a system. Even if we used a distinctly "casual" form of legal positivism—the Austininan conception that law is a command of the sovereign, backed up by the threat of a sanction—it would require a plurality of interrelated norms and institutions, and therefore a system.[13] As François Ewald has put it, convincingly though a bit awkwardly in terms of analytic jurisprudence, "The idea of a single legal norm has no meaning."[14] Norms become legal when they are recognized by a legal system, which confers legality to these rules.

The same conclusion can be reached on the basis of the primary function of law, which is to direct behavior and organize the collective life of its addressees. Law is a specific form of social ordering.[15] Hence, as Jacques Chevallier explains, the operativeness of its function depends on the achievement of order, and this element of order therefore necessarily also imbues the internal organization of law, which must take the form of a system.[16] The goal of law can only be achieved if, on the one hand, there is more than one norm and if, on the other hand, this plurality of norms operates with a certain degree of internal harmony, that is logical consistency and coherence, which precisely is the characteristic of a *system* of norms.[17]

In other words, in the legal positivist approach, legality necessarily requires a legal *system* and, regardless of the approach, law must be organized as a system in order to be fully operative. In sum, there cannot be law without a legal system; legality necessarily finds its source in a legal system. What makes a norm or set of norms legal is their belonging to a legal system, their pedigree, which is the core argument of legal positivism.[18] Hence, to investigate the legality of a normative phenomenon, one must think in terms of systems.[19]

---

[12] Kelsen, *General Theory of Law and State*, 3.

[13] The term "casual positivism" is borrowed from Jeremy Waldron, "The Concept and the Rule of Law" (2008) 43 *Georgia Law Review* 1.

[14] François Ewald, "The Law of Law" in Gunther Teubner (ed), *Autopoietic Law: A New Approach to Law and Society* (de Gruyter 1988) 36.

[15] See, eg, Evgeny Pashukanis, *Law and Marxism: A General Theory* (first published 1929, Ink Links 1978).

[16] Jacques Chevallier, "L'ordre juridique" in Jacques Chevallier and Danièle Loschak (eds), *Le droit en procès* (Presses Universitaires de France 1983) 8.

[17] Chevallier, "L'ordre juridique," 14–15.

[18] On the variety of strands of legal positivism, see for example Hart, "Positivism and the Separation," 601–2; Norberto Bobbio, *Il positivismo giuridico* (Giappichelli 1961); Norberto Bobbio, *Teoria dell'ordinamento giuridico* (Giappichelli 1960). More specifically on the criteria of belonging to a legal system, Michel Virally, *La pensée juridique* (LGDJ 1960) vii and Roger A Shiner, *Norm and Nature: The Movement of Legal Thought* (Oxford University Press 1992) 19. The unawareness of this variety of meanings of "legal positivism" is what led Bruno Oppetit to this awkward statement: "les négateurs de la *lex mercatoria*—il suffirait de dire: les positivistes": Bruno Oppetit, "Le droit international privé, droit savant" (1992) 234 *Hague Lectures* 331.

[19] Similarly but for different reasons Bobbio, *Teoria dell'ordinamento*, 7, Michel Troper, "Système juridique et Etat" (1986) 30 *Archives de philosophie du droit* 2, 30; François Ost and Michel van de Kerchove, *De la pyramide au réseau ? Pour une théorie dialectique du droit* (Publication des Facultés universitaires Saint-Louis 2002) 284–5.

2. Can the Lex Mercatoria Not be a System?

When the lex mercatoria came in for criticism as a credible instantiation of what we understand to be a legal system, a number of authors sought to find alternative ways to salvage its legality. They sought to explain how it could be law without amounting to a legal system. I think these attempts invariably fail in analytic jurisprudence. I want to show why by focusing on the two main alternative ways to represent the lex mercatoria as law without being a legal system: the lex mercatoria as a method of decision-making and the lex mercatoria as a set of legal rules.

2.1 The lex mercatoria as a secondary rule of recognition

What does it exactly mean to maintain that the lex mercatoria is a "method of decision-making"?[20] Fouchard, Gaillard, and Goldman point the way. Their reasoning starts here: "it cannot be too strongly emphasized," they say, "that applying transnational rules involves understanding and implementing a method, rather than drawing up a list of the general principles of international commercial law."[21] They claim that this method for the selection of rules is the "true test of the effectiveness of lex mercatoria as an instrument for resolving disputes in international trade."[22] In substance, the idea is that the conduct that the lex mercatoria commands may not be identifiable *in abstracto* by scholars, but will certainly be recognized by the arbitrator when he or she has to apply it, which thus makes it effective. The lex mercatoria is, then, not viewed as a defined and readily available list of norms, but as a method used to identify those norms. Brutally simplified, it is a way to say: "we don't know what these norms are, but the arbitrators will when they have to apply them."

This comes across even more clearly in another work of Emmanuel Gaillard, where he writes that "the transnational rules [of the lex mercatoria] do not result from a list but from a method."[23] Notice this: the rules *result* from the method. He then specifies what this method consists of in the following words: "in the absence of determinations on the method by the parties themselves, the counsels and arbitrators must make a comparative law analysis so as to identify the applicable

---

[20] Emmanuel Gaillard, "Transnational Law: A Legal System of a Method of Decision Making?" (2001) 17 *Arbitration International* 59, 64: "This understanding of transnational law [as a method of decision-making] presents a distinct advantage over the view which reduces it to a list, for it eliminates the criticism based on the alleged paucity of the list."

[21] Emmanuel Gaillard and John Savage (eds), *Fouchard, Gaillard, Goldman on International Commercial Arbitration* (Kluwer 1999) § 1455.

[22] Gaillard and Savage, *Fouchard, Gaillard, Goldman*, § 1455

[23] Emmanuel Gaillard, "Thirty Years of Lex Mercatoria: Towards the Selective Application of Transnational Rules" (1995) 10 *ICSID Review* 208, 224: "transnational rules are a method, not a list". See also Gaillard, "Transnational Law," 62: "The other approach to defining the contents of transnational law is to view transnational law as a method of decision-making, rather than as a list."

rule or rules."[24] "Whatever the level of detail of the question posed," he goes on, "the method is capable of providing a solution, in the same way that a national law would."[25]

Along the same lines, Andreas Lowenfeld argued that the lex mercatoria is "a source of law made up of custom, convention, precedent, and many national laws... [It is] an alternative to a conflict of laws search."[26] It is thus meant to be equivalent to a rule of private international law, at least in certain respects. He seems indeed to consider that the lex mercatoria is a normative mechanism that allows us to identify or recognize the applicable norms—like a set of conflicts of law rules.

Ole Lando, too, takes a similar position, maintaining that the lex mercatoria "has the advantage that it does away with the choice-of-law process which many lawyers abhor."[27] It is here conceived of as a process of norm selection that replaces choice of law rules.[28]

Again, clearly: the lex mercatoria is understood here as a normative process towards the selection of norms. If one is to apply the lex mercatoria, one is to identify rules and principles by means of a certain method.

What implications does this have for the examination of the lex mercatoria's legal character? Before we address this question, two germane points must be made. First, the lex mercatoria, even as a method, is meant to be a legal phenomenon, and not the manifestation of a mere social ordering of the *societas mercatorum*. As Lord Mustill puts it, the lex mercatoria is not meant to be an "expedient for deciding according to 'non-law'."[29] For Lowenfeld, "[i]t is important to emphasize that lex mercatoria is not *amiable composition*."[30]

---

[24] Gaillard, "Thirty Years," 226: "Failing a clear indication by the parties as to how the applicable transnational rules are to be determined,... the process [of the *lex mercatoria*] involves counsel and arbitrators carrying out an analysis of comparative law in order to establish the relevant rule or rules." See also Gaillard, "Transnational Law," 62–3: "This approach consists, in any given case, of deriving the substantive solution to the legal issue at hand not from a particular law selected by a traditional choice-of-law process, but from a comparative law analysis which will enable the arbitrators to apply the rule which is the most widely accepted, as opposed to a rule which may be peculiar to a legal system or less widely recognized."

[25] Gaillard, "Thirty Years," 226: "However detailed the question at issue, the transnational rules method will produce a solution, in the same way as national laws."

[26] Andreas F Lowenfeld, "Lex Mercatoria: An Arbitrator's View" (1990) 6 *Arbitration International* 133, 143.

[27] Ole Lando, "The Lex Mercatoria in International Commercial Arbitration" (1985) 34 *International and Comparative Law Quarterly* 747, 754.

[28] Lowenfeld and Lando disagree on the point whether the lex mercatoria replaces or displaces the choice of law process: see Lowenfeld, "Lex Mercatoria," 145: "[The lex mercatoria] is, in other words, an additional option in the search for the applicable law, not an alternative to that search." This debate has no implication on the fact that the lex mercatoria is understood as a method for the selection of norms and the difference between the positions of the two authors is thus one that does not make a difference for the purposes of the present study.

[29] Michael Mustill "The New Lex Mercatoria: The First Twenty-Five Years" (1988) 4 *Arbitration International* 86, 92.

[30] Lowenfeld, "Lex Mercatoria," 141.

Second, the lex mercatoria, even as a method, is considered to be, in a manner of speaking, something more than the sum of its constitutive parts.[31] This may sound elliptical. Let me clarify. When an arbitrator is required to apply the lex mercatoria, he or she would fail in the task by doing the following: After having made the comparative law analysis or followed any other relevant norm-identification process, he or she applies, strictly speaking, rule X of national legal system A, plus rule Y of national system B, plus rule Z of national legal C, and so on, where X, Y, and Z have in substance the same content, which content is thus given a transnational character. Instead, he or she must distill the norm by following the relevant method[32] (recall: the transnational rules *result* from the method) and apply the result as a norm *of its own*, as a new norm.[33] That new norm does not draw its legal character from one of the national legal systems within which it exists, but from somewhere else.

If the lex mercatoria is meant to be a method for the identification of a set of legal norms in application of which the dispute will be resolved, where does the legal character of these norms come from?

One may consider, a priori, that this legal character, this legality, comes from the different national legal systems and international law.[34] But in the light of the

---

[31] Emmanuel Gaillard, "La distinction des principes généraux du droit et des usages du commerce international" in *Études offertes à Pierre Bellet* (Litec 1991) 203, 205: "[O]n tiendra provisoirement pour acquis qu'il est possible en pratique de dégager de telles règles d'une analyse de droit comparé ou de diverses sources internationales et que ces règles ne se limitent pas à des principes si généraux qu'ils se retrouvent dans tous les droits... ce qui les priverait de tout intérêt." See also Andreas Bucher and Pierre-Yves Tschanz, *International Arbitration in Switzerland* (Helbing & Lichtenhahn 1988) 105, referring to the "application of rules of law which are recognized in international trade independently from their enactment by any given state." See also Jean-François Poudret and Sébastien Besson, *Comparative Law of International Arbitration* (2nd edn, Sweet & Maxwell 2007) §§ 696–7: "although they claim to refer to an autonomous legal order, adherents of the *lex mercatoria* do not hesitate to use rules derived from other legal systems... The generality of these principles does... have the advantage of constituting a reservoir into which arbitrators may dip in order to infer particular or new rules applicable to the case at hand. To this extent this source overlaps with arbitral practice ['jurisprudence arbitrale' in the original French version of that book], which is a sort of modern praetorian law... In short, we have seen that the *lex mercatoria* draws its norms from heterogeneous sources of unequal value derived from various legal systems."

[32] Mustill "The New Lex Mercatoria," 92: "Although the essence of the lex mercatoria is its detachment from national legal systems, it is quite clear from the literature that some, at least, of its rules are to be ascertained by a process of distilling several national laws."

[33] Whether the resulting norm is considered to have been crafted, discovered, or identified by the arbitrator is irrelevant. What matters is that it is the result of an application of the method of the lex mercatoria, that the norm has been "imported", whatever its origin, into the lex mercatoria in application of its method. Further on the "reception" of a norm in the "transnational order", see Philippe Kahn, "Les principes généraux du droit devant les arbitres du commerce international" (1989) 116 *Journal du droit international* 305, 326–7.

[34] Based specifically on international law, their legality would, according to this view (which I do not share), stem from treaty and customary law as generalized through the concept of general principles of law (Art 38(1)(c) ICJ Statute): Peter Malanczuk, *Akehurst's Modern Introduction to International Law* (7th edn, Routledge 1997) 48–9: "general principles of international law... are not so much a source of law as a method of using existing sources—extending existing rules by analogy, inferring the existence of broad principles from more specific rules by means of inductive reasoning, and so on." In other words, the lex mercatoria would be a method referring to a method (the general principles of international law) referring to treaty and customary law.

immediately preceding discussion, the idea does not fly. When an award is made as a result of applying the lex mercatoria, it is meant to be binding not because rules X, Y, and Z, belonging to discrete national legal systems, international conventions, customary international law, or other sources, command the legal solution embodied in the award. It is meant to be binding because a transnational rule (selected in application of the lex mercatoria method, effectively resulting from it) commands it.[35] Lord Mustill says this clearly: "the rules of the lex mercatoria have a normative value which is independent of any one national legal system."[36] Ole Lando concurs: "the binding force of the lex mercatoria does not depend on the fact that it is made and promulgated by state authorities but that it is recognized as an autonomous norm system by the business community and by state authorities."[37] Or again, Andreas Bucher and Pierre-Yves Tschanz: "International contracts and awards often refer to principles or rules the binding force of which does not result from any national rule of law."[38] The same position is also implicit in the arguments of many authors who focus not on the source of legality but on the inventory of the norms that constitute the lex mercatoria.[39]

Let us make a parallel. We are dealing here with the same idea as when a national court relies on a comparative law analysis to reach a decision. In that case, the normative value of the rule according to which the decision is made, its legality really, results from the court's own national legal system (by dint of judicial law-making), not from those legal systems where the solution was found.[40]

Arbitrators applying the lex mercatoria distill rules and principles from various national legal systems, and possibly from international law as a legal system or a set of legal systems. Then they assemble and combine these rules and principles, and possibly reinterpret them to better fit the particulars of international commerce.[41] The norms are then applied in their new identity. In the process, as the sundry quotations above explain, these rules and principles are uncoupled from

---

[35] Malanczuk, *Akehurst's Introduction*, 50: "In the case of 'internationalized contracts' between a state and foreign companies, the purpose of referring to general principles... is primarily... to prefer to trust the arbitrator's (s') discretion to discover relevant rules of law creatively, rather than being at the mercy of the contracting state's national legislation."

[36] Mustill "The New Lex Mercatoria," 88. See also Gaillard and Savage, *Fouchard, Gaillard, Goldman*, § 1447: "To denote rules other than those of a given jurisdiction, we shall use the generic expression lex mercatoria."

[37] Lando, "The Lex Mercatoria," 752.

[38] Bucher and Tschanz, *International Arbitration*, 105.

[39] Paul Lagarde, "Approche critique de la lex mercatoria" in Philippe Fouchard, Philippe Kahn, and Antoine Lyon-Caen (eds), *Le droit des relations économiques internationales—Études offertes à Berthold Goldman* (Litec 1982) 125, 128: "Un inventaire scrupuleux des normes de la *lex mercatoria* doit exclure les règles de droit matériel international de nature étatique ou interétatique. Le critère ici doit être formel et non matériel... L'originalité de la *lex mercatoria* est d'être du droit [adopté sans contrainte de l'Etat], créé par la *societas mercatorum*, et c'est donc en dehors des sources étatiques qu'il faut en chercher les manifestations."

[40] Mads Andenas and Duncan Fairgrieve, "Finding a Common Language for Open Legal Systems" in Guy Canivet, Mads Andenas, and Duncan Fairgrieve (eds), *Comparative Law Before the Courts* (British Institute of International and Comparative Law 2004) xxviii.

[41] Thomas Carbonneau, "Arbitral Law-Making" (2004) 25 *Michigan Journal of International Law* 1183, 1203–4: "The content of the governing *lex*, however chosen, is quite malleable then, with the degree of malleability being determined by the arbitrator's ingenuity."

their original source of legality, namely the relevant national and international legal systems.

Let us look at this from a slightly different angle. The foregoing implies that when an arbitrator applies the lex mercatoria, he or she applies *a law* and not merely *law*. That contention may be in contradiction with those legal provisions (introduced for instance in France, the Netherlands, and Switzerland in order to circumvent the question of the lex mercatoria's nature as a legal system) that allow arbitrators to apply "rules of law," as opposed to "the law" or "a law."[42] But recall from Chapter 5: what legal provisions provide, that is what certain legal systems say (relative legality), has no bearing on an analytical examination of what is law (absolute legality).

I mean "a law" here in the sense that it is a given instantiation of "law," marked by an element of cohesion to which I will return in a moment, and more extensively in the next chapter. "Law" can refer to a disparate collection of rules belonging to discrete legal systems (for instance national legal systems). These rules would, here, obtain their legality from these different legal systems. Consider an arbitrator applying the (national) law of country A to the validity of the arbitration agreement, the law of country B as the law governing the arbitration, and the law of country C to the merits of the dispute. This arbitrator would be applying law (or laws), but not *a law*. Or consider the situation called "*dépeçage*": if the parties elect several national laws that apply each to one specific legal question, for instance to contractual versus non-contractual liability, to the validity of a patent versus the validity of a license, and so on.[43] "A law," by contrast, is an organic totality, thus characterized by an element of cohesion, which has a single source of legality.

Brutally simplifying for the sake of clarity, the idea is that the lex mercatoria is, in the current approach, understood as being the result of combining an array of national legal systems and using the resulting product as a new, separate normative entity.

These points inform the answer to the question asked above: what is a method of selection of rules within the arsenal of conceptual instruments available to examine or assess the legal character of a normative phenomenon? Or rephrase the question: what is something that determines which norms belong to a law? One simple answer offers itself convincingly: Hart's distinction between primary and secondary rules.[44] (Recall: primary rules are rules of conduct, providing what the addressees are required and permitted and empowered to do. Secondary rules determine, among other things, the pedigree that primary rules must have in order to belong

---

[42] The question, which reflects the second main view of the lex mercatoria (namely that it is a set of rules), will be examined in further detail in the following main section. See also Gaillard, "Transnational Law," 62–3: "one may be tempted to conclude that, where the relevant arbitration rules or arbitration statute mandates the arbitrators to select the 'law' applicable to the dispute, as opposed to mere 'rules of law', it is nonetheless open to them to select . . . transnational rules as 'the law' applicable to the dispute."

[43] Klaus Peter Berger, *International Economic Arbitration* (Kluwer 1993) 492–3; Gaillard and Savage, *Fouchard, Gaillard, Goldman*, § 1436.

[44] Hart, *Concept of Law*, 91ff.

to the same legal system as the secondary rule. Secondary rules that do just that are more specifically called secondary rules of recognition. Secondary rules create the "element of cohesion" adumbrated above when distinguishing between law and a law.)

To the implications that follow. First, let us see that a method of rule selection is a norm, since a norm is a statement that contains prescriptions or imperatives.[45] Second, and more precisely, a method of rule selection is nothing more and nothing less than a norm of recognition of other norms: a secondary rule of recognition. Gaillard himself suggests as much when he writes that "lex mercatoria should be defined today by its sources . . . as opposed to its content."[46] Indeed, a "definition according to sources" is a definition according to the object of secondary rules of recognition: a secondary rule defines the pedigree that a norm must have, where it comes from, or again, what its recognized sources are. A national legal system, for instance, is typically "defined by its sources," by what the officials of the legal system in question say belongs to the system and what does not. It is generally not defined by any content of any rule. A non-legal normative system, on the other hand—more specifically one that does not have secondary rules of recognition—cannot be defined by its sources, as the sources are left undefined by the lack of secondary rules.

The lex mercatoria as a method of rule selection really fits quite neatly under a more elaborate and precise definition of the rule of recognition than the one I have just given. As Matthew Kramer writes, "the Rule of Recognition in any legal system exists as a set of normative pre-suppositions that underlie and structure the law-ascertaining behavior of the system's officials. It is an array of norms on the basis of which the officials determine what counts as legally binding and what does not."[47] Indeed, the lex mercatoria as a method of rule selection underlies and structures the law-ascertaining behavior of arbitrators when they decide a case in application of the lex mercatoria. The lex mercatoria as a method determines what will count as legally binding and what will not.

Now, the presence of such secondary norms—regardless how specific or vague they are—is precisely, at least in the dominant Hartian approach, what distinguishes a legal system from a social normative system.[48] This implies that the view according to which the lex mercatoria is a method for the selection of rules to generate a law which is independently of a legal character necessarily relies, at its most foundational level, on the implicit idea that the lex mercatoria is in fact a legal system. The arbitrator is the official of the lex mercatoria's legal system. He or she

---

[45] See for instance Matthew H Kramer, *In Defense of Legal Positivism: Law Without Trimmings* (Oxford University Press 1999) 80.

[46] Gaillard, "Transnational Law," 62.

[47] Matthew H Kramer, "Of Final Things: Morality as One of The Ultimate Determinants of Legal Validity" (2005) 24 *Law and Philosophy* 47, 57.

[48] Hart, *Concept of Law*, 91ff; Norberto Bobbio, "Ancora sulle norme primarie e norme secondarie" (1968) 1 *Rivista di filosofia* 35; Paul Bohannan, "The Differing Realms of the Law" (1965) 67 *American Anthropologist* 33, 34–7; Michel van de Kerchove and François Ost, *Legal System Between Order and Disorder* (Oxford University Press 1994) 110.

determines, in application of the secondary rule of recognition that is the method, which norms belong to the system.[49]

A brief recap. We have seen that the lex mercatoria must be a law, even in the approach that considers it to be merely a method. This has led us to the conclusion, by logical inference from the dominant Hartian approach to law, that the lex mercatoria must rely on the assumption that it is a legal system of its own.[50]

2.2 The lex mercatoria as just rules

If the lex mercatoria is not a method of decision-making, can it be a set or repertoire of legal rules without amounting to a legal system? I think it cannot, and the following explains why.

The idea that the lex mercatoria is a set of legal rules is not necessarily divorced in practice from the idea that it is a method of decision-making. But it can and should nonetheless be distinguished analytically. The main conceptual difference resides in the obliqueness, in the preceding approach (method) as opposed to the current one (repertoire), of the reliance on readily identifiable rules. It took place in the preceding approach through the intermediary step of the "method." Here it happens directly. This difference sheds some additional light on the general question of the nature of the lex mercatoria, as will become plain in the subsequent discussion.

That the lex mercatoria is a set of legal rules but not a legal system was the conventional wisdom before the publication of Berthold Goldman's first article on

---

[49] Ibrahim Fadlallah, "Le projet de convention sur la vente de marchandises" (1979) 106 *Journal du droit international* 764, 766: "La *lex mercatoria* peut être conçue restrictivement, si on ne la renvoie pas au néant, comme limitée aux normes propres spontanément sécrétées par le commerce international. Mais un système ne se réduit pas à ce qu'il a inventé. Reconnu, il s'étend à l'ensemble des règles et pratiques qu'il intègre, quelle qu'en soit la provenance"; Eric Loquin, "Où en est la lex mercatoria?" in Charles Leben, Eric Loquin, and Mahmoud Salem (eds), *Souveraineté étatique et marchés internationaux à la fin du 20e siècle—Mélanges en l'honneur de Philippe Kahn* (Litec 2000) 25–6, who explains Emmanuel Gaillard's position in the following terms: "Cette méthode relève de ce que l'on pourrait appeler 'un darwinisme juridique'. Il s'agit de sélectionner, à travers toutes les sources du droit, les règles qui sont les plus aptes à satisfaire les besoins du commerce international. C'est l'appropriation de la règle à ces besoins qui explique sa *réception* dans la *lex mercatoria*" (emphasis is mine). See also Gunther Teubner, "Breaking Frames: The Global Interplay of Legal and Social Systems" (1997) 45 *American Journal of Comparative Law* 149, 151, who asks the question: "What are the secondary rules which would recognize the primary rules of *Lex mercatoria* and distinguish them from mere professional norms?" For theoretical developments on how the arbitrator can be the criterion of legality, see for instance the parallel in Michel van de Kerchove and François Ost, *Le droit ou les paradoxes du jeu* (Presses universitaires de France 1992) 179 ("L'intervention du juge est à la fois l'indice et l'opérateur principal de la juridicité").

[50] The following progression in Emmanuel Gaillard's argumentation is interesting in this regard: he first asks how "the transnational rules methodology compares with the application of a fully fledged legal order" (Gaillard, "Transnational Law," 65), which means that he assumes that the lex mercatoria is not a fully fledged legal order (one does not compare A and B if one assumes that A is an instance of B). He then lists four features that he argues are necessary and sufficient for a normative system to be a legal system and applies these features to the lex mercatoria as a method. He concludes that "if not a genuine legal order, transnational rules do perform, in actual practice, a function strikingly similar to that of a genuine legal order" (71).

the lex mercatoria.[51] (That article started the "trench warfare"[52] or "war of faith"[53] that characterized the subsequent discussions of the lex mercatoria.[54]) It is also the conception of certain more contemporary authors, more or less explicitly.[55] In essence, the position can in fact be attributed to all those who evoke and recognize the existence of "principles and rules of transnational law"[56] in the realm of international trade and commerce, while denying that they amount to a legal system.[57] It is also the position taken by those legal texts that have introduced the language "rules of law" instead of (or in addition to) "the law" or "a law"[58]— such as certain national arbitration laws,[59] institutional arbitration rules,[60] the UNCITRAL Model Law on International Commercial Arbitration,[61] and the

---

[51] Berthold Goldman, "Frontières du droit et lex mercatoria" (1964) 9 *Archives de philosophie du droit* 177. The second main article by Goldman on this matter is Bertold Goldman, "La Lex Mercatoria dans les contrats et l'arbitrage internationaux: réalité et perspectives" (1979) 106 *Journal du droit international* 475.

[52] Lagarde, "Approche critique," 125.

[53] Teubner, "Breaking Frames," 150.

[54] For representative writings reflecting the dominant position before Goldman, see for example Philip C Jessup, *Transnational Law* (Yale University Press 1956) 2: "I shall use, instead of 'international law' the term 'transnational law' to include all law which regulates actions or events that transcend national frontiers. Both public and private international law are included, as are other rules which do not wholly fit into such standard categories" and the comments on it by Georges Abi-Saab, "Cours général de droit international public" (1987) 207 *Hague Lectures* 1, 123; Clive M Schmitthoff, "International Business Law: A New Law Merchant" (1961) *Current Law and Social Problems* 129 ("autonomous body of law"). A few years later, Schmitthoff characterized the lex mercatoria as a legal field ("Rechtsgebiet"), which even more clearly reflects the idea of a collection of legal rules which do not form, together, a legal system: Clive M Schmitthoff, "Das neue Recht des Welthandels" (1964) 28 *Rabel Journal of Comparative and International Private Law* 47, 48.

[55] Jan Paulsson, "La Lex Mercatoria dans l'arbitrage CCI" (1990) *Revue de l'arbitrage* 55; Lowenfeld, "Lex Mercatoria," 144; Norbert Horn, "Uniformity and Diversity in the Law of International Commercial Contracts" in Nobert Horn and Clive M Schmitthoff (eds), *The Transnational Law of International Commercial Transactions* (Kluwer 1982) 14; Eric Loquin, "Où en est la lex mercatoria?", 25: "une *collection* de règles d'origine variable rassemblées sur le *seul* fondement de leur adéquation aux besoins du commerce international" (emphasis is mine).

[56] Bucher and Tschanz, *International Arbitration*, 198.

[57] Admittedly, many writings reveal a certain hesitation or confusion through the adjunction, in their rejection of the lex mercatoria as a legal system, of adjectives such as "complete," "self-sufficient," "autonomous," "real," or "genuine." For an analysis of such language, in related contexts, see Simon Roberts, "After Government? On Representing Law Without the State" (2005) 68 *Modern Law Review* 1, 19–20.

[58] Gaillard, "Transnational Law," 65: "this language ('rules of law')...was in fact specifically intended to bypass the issue of whether lex mercatoria or general principles qualify as a genuine legal order." Nigel Blackaby, Constantine Partasides, with Alan Redfern and Martin Hunter, *Redfern and Hunter on International Arbitration* (Oxford University Press 2009) 227: "The reference to 'rules of law', rather than to 'law' or 'a system of law' is a coded reference to the applicability of appropriate legal rules, even though these may fall short of being an established and autonomous system of law."

[59] For instance the laws of Germany (§ 1051 ZPO), Italy (Art 834 al 1 CPCI), the Netherlands (Art 1054 WBR), France (Art 1511 Code of Civil Procedure, Decree No 2011–48 of January 13, 2011), Switzerland (Art 187 PIL Act).

[60] For instance the ICC Arbitration Rules (Art 21), LCIA Rules (Art 22.3), International Arbitration Rules of the AAA (Art 28.1), the WIPO Arbitration Rules (Art 59.1).

[61] Art 28.1: "The arbitral tribunal shall decide the dispute in accordance with such rules of law as are chosen by the parties as applicable to the substance of the dispute."

Convention on the Settlement of Investment Disputes between States and Nationals of Other States (ICSID Convention).[62]

It is uncontroversial that a repertoire of rules "recognized in international trade independently from their enactment by any given state"[63] does indeed exist.[64] It is further uncontentious that there have been "countless applications of transnational rules by international arbitrators since far before the debate over the concept [of lex mercatoria] even began."[65] We are also on safe ground when saying that there is a "discrete body of transnational commercial norms,"[66] that transnational commercial rules can effectively be uncovered, being "drawn from international arbitral and contract practice, backed up by comprehensive comparative references."[67] Klaus Peter Berger, among others, has satisfactorily established the existence of such rules by empirical studies.[68] It seems fair to say, as he does, that the lex mercatoria is consequently "capable of being codified in norm-like principles and rules together with commentary-like explanations, thus providing international legal practitioners with a means to apply the lex mercatoria in everyday legal practice."[69] Or, as Harold Berman and Felix Dasser argue, whatever our theoretical framework is, it "should not stop us from seeing what is right in front of our noses," namely "the factual existence" of rules and principles that are applied in practice.[70]

In sum, the question of whether the lex mercatoria exists as a set of rules seems to deserve a clean positive answer.

(Notice that this says nothing about the ascertainability of such rules by commercial actors, or their usefulness or substantive completeness. These are distinct questions. Briefly on the completeness argument, since it is raised occasionally in relation to the lex mercatoria: clearly, the substantive completeness of a normative system is not a necessary feature of legality. It is not because a normative system's official, while applying the norms of that system, determines that he or she has to regularly pronounce a non liquet that the entire system should be denied its legal character.

---

[62] Art 42: "The Tribunal shall decide a dispute in accordance with such rules of law as may be agreed by the parties."
[63] Bucher and Tschanz, *International Arbitration*, 105.
[64] See Filip JM de Ly, "Emerging New Perspectives Regarding Lex Mercatoria in an Era of Increasing Globalization" in Klaus Peter Berger et al, *Festschrift für Otto Sandrock* (Recht und Wirtschaft 2000) 182. See also Paul Bowden, "L'interdiction de se contredire au détriment d'autrui (estoppel) as a Substantive Transnational Rule in International Commercial Arbitration" in Emmanuel Gaillard (ed), *Transnational Rules in International Commercial Arbitration* (ICC 1993) 125, 127: "The [International Law Association] Committee's approach in its continuing study of transnational law has been to step back from the highly contentious issues that arise from any theoretical consideration of transnational law, or *lex mercatoria*, as a discrete body of principles and to examine, in a pragmatic way, the application of individual identifiable principles at least as a phenomenon of international commercial arbitration, which it undoubtedly is."
[65] Gaillard, "Transnational Law," 59.
[66] Yves Fortier, "The New, New Lex Mercatoria, or Back to the Future" (2001) 17 *Arbitration International* 121, 127.
[67] Fortier, "The New, New Lex Mercatoria," 127.
[68] Klaus Peter Berger, *The Creeping Codification of the Lex Mercatoria* (Kluwer 1999) 278–311.
[69] Berger, *The Creeping Codification*, 3.
[70] Harold J Berman and Felix Dasser, "The 'New' Law Merchant and the 'Old': Sources, Content, and Legitimacy" in Thomas Carbonneau (ed), *Lex Mercatoria and Arbitration: A Discussion of the New Law Merchant* (rev edn, Juris and Kluwer 1998) 64.

A very incomplete system would merely be quite meaningless. In any event, it is not because a normative system is not composed of very many norms that the system is necessary incomplete. Interpretative proficiency goes a long way towards applying a small number of norms to a very large number of situations. That question has often been discussed in the field of general international law, where it is not considered a matter of the system's legality.[71] In jurisprudence, and this is a problem of jurisprudence, the proper question here is whether the lex mercatoria is virtually comprehensive, which is a clearly distinct question. But again we should not be concerned and move on, for virtual comprehensiveness should be abandoned as a feature of legality, as we have seen in Chapter 4.)

Now, would it be safe for lex mercatorists to simply back down one step and argue that, granted, the lex mercatoria may not exist as a legal system, but it is a repertoire of *legal* rules? Clearly, they may say, it is not a mere "doctrinal creation":[72] look at the empirical studies, it is used in practice. Can they end the controversy by saying that the lex mercatoria is simply a set of "rules of law," and not a legal system? A priori, one would be tempted to grant them that.

But wait and consider this. These "rules of law," clearly, are applied not as norms of one or several specific national legal systems. That would have made the rules rules of *law* because they would be ascribed to those legal systems. No, these rules are meant to be legal for another reason. What would this reason be?

Or again, if it seems quite agreeable that there are transnational commercial rules, why would they be legal, of a legal nature? What is it that would make such rules *legal* rules?

One theoretical construct, meant to provide an answer to the question of the source of the legality of the lex mercatoria as a set of legal rules but not a legal system, can be found in a natural law approach. Thomas Carbonneau, for instance, considers that the lex mercatoria, which he maintains "includes natural law principles," is simply "part of the bargain in international contracts."[73] The lex mercatoria, in that sense, would intrinsically be part of international commerce as a social phenomenon. International commercial actors would have rights flowing directly from their commercial activity, regardless of the particulars of the transaction, the will of the parties and what any rule of black letter law provides. These

---

[71] Admittedly, in international law one will not find a "clear and specific rule readily applicable to every international situation, but... every international situation is capable of being determined as a matter of law": so Robert Jennings and Arthur Watts (eds), *Oppenheim's International Law*, vol 1 (9th edn, Longman 1992) 13. See also Joost Pauwelyn, *Conflict of Norms in Public International Law* (Cambridge University Press 2003) 150ff. For a similar argument with regard to the lex mercatoria: Hans-Joachim Mertens, "Das lex mercatoria-Problem" in Reinhard Böttcher et al (eds), *Festschrift für Walter Odersky* (de Gruyter 1996) 857. The question of the completeness of the lex mercatoria is discussed in Berger, *Creeping Codification*, 93ff.

[72] Géraud de la Pradelle, "La justice privée" in Habib Gherari and Sandra Szurek (eds), *L'émergence de la société civile internationale: vers la privatisation du droit international?* (Pedone 2003) 134.

[73] Thomas Carbonneau, "A Definition of and Perspective Upon the Lex Mercatoria Debate" in Thomas Carbonneau (ed), *Lex Mercatoria and Arbitration: A Discussion of the New Law Merchant* (rev edn, Juris and Kluwer 1998) 11, 16.

rules would simply flow from values that pre-exist human normative decisions and are independent of them.[74]

Incidentally, this natural law approach led Carbonneau to argue that the lex mercatoria is hierarchically superior to national laws and trumps them. This is indeed consistent with the idea of natural law: individuals have certain inherent rights by the mere fact that they are human beings; the relevant rights are those pertaining to the field of activity in question (for instance: commercial rights for commercial activities).[75]

In such an approach, the determinant criterion of legality is the legitimacy of a rule, that is its moral estimableness or conformity with some higher moral order.[76] For example, the reasoning would be that we consider certain rights to be fundamentally legitimate (in other words morally indispensable) and that, therefore, they form part of "natural" human rights or the "natural" regulation of international commerce. Principles such as *pacta sunt servanda*, therefore, would typically be a legal principle, not because it may be found in any or every national legal system, but because it is intrinsically legitimate and morally laudable.

Such an approach faces three issues. First and most importantly, it would hardly be workable, as what constitutes a profoundly legitimate right or what is a profoundly legitimate rule is open to much controversy, and thus hardly predictable. When hardly predictable rules trump the much more predictable rules of national legal systems, the result can barely be welcome. Can businesspeople sit down and wait until moral philosophers agree on what is really morally estimable in their commercial relations? That does not make sense.

Second, it would produce only very few norms for international commerce. Many rules necessary for the smooth operations of international commerce are not particularly estimable from a moral point of view and simply serve to coordinate behavior (consider the decisive time for the transfer of risks in a sale of goods, for instance).

Third, morality is simply not a convincing necessary element of law: there have been legal regimes in history that were clearly evil but were nonetheless generally recognized as legal regimes.[77] A natural law approach to the lex mercatoria appears unsatisfactory and inappropriate.

The second theoretical construct that may be called in to ground the legality of the lex mercatoria as a set of legal rules requires to take an approach inspired by legal realism.[78] In substance, the idea is to focus on effectiveness: a legal rule is a rule of

---

[74] See for instance Michel Villey, "Law in Things" in Paul Amselek and Neil McCormick (eds), *Controversies About Law's Ontology* (Edinburgh University Press 1991) 2.
[75] Norberto Bobbio, *Giusnaturalismo e positivismo giuridico* (Edizioni di Comunita 1965) 135ff.
[76] François Ost, "Validité" in André-Jean Arnaud (ed), *Dictionnaire encyclopédique de théorie et de sociologie juridique* (LGDJ and Story-Scientia 1988) 433. See also Waldron, "Normative (or Ethical) Positivism," 415ff.
[77] See for instance Kramer, *In Defense*, 177–82, discussing Dworkin's opposite view.
[78] For example, see Rodolfo Sacco, "Mute Law" (1995) 43 *American Journal of Comparative Law* 455, 459–60, 465: "Law may live, and lived, even without a lawgiver... When the Homo Habilis produced the first pebble tools, the dichotomy between law and enforcement did not exist... Adherence to the rule implied its existence and validity... the law was mute, except for yelling accompanying

conduct that is effective, one that is followed in practice.[79] If such an approach were adopted, the rules of the lex mercatoria would be those norms that are followed in practice by international commercial actors. We might initially be content with such a proposition. But a moment's thought leaves us with a sense of weariness, when we realize that we are losing all sense of what law is.[80] Indeed, is brushing one's teeth in the morning—a norm undoubtedly followed by international commercial actors—a legal norm? Is shaking hands when a deal is done a legal norm? How many people have to follow a rule before it becomes legal? For how long? What if a practice widely spread in certain circles (think of dodging taxes) is clearly in violation of black letter law rules? Where is the distinction to be drawn between legal norms and social norms?

As I have said in the opening lines of this chapter's first main section, the only approach to legality that truly is workable in practice for the identification of non-state law is legal positivism. Again, I do not mean positivism in the classical conception of legal positivism that sees law only in states. There would be no point there in trying to think of stateless law. I mean it in the sense of the formal criterion of a norm's belonging to a legal system.

This means that, using Hartian terminology, the norm must succeed in the test set by a secondary rule of recognition. A social norm becomes legal if it is endorsed by an institution of the legal system, if it is reinstitutionalized or restated in such institutions, if it is recognized by an official of the legal system to which it then belongs (the arbitrator, in the case of the lex mercatoria). Such endorsement or reinstitutionalization or recognition must occur according to the applicable rule of recognition (the "method" in the language used earlier in this chapter). To apply a rule of recognition is to verify authoritatively that a norm has been taken over into the system through the operation of some acceptance by officials of the system in question.[81]

Again: the legality of a norm follows from its belonging to a legal system, which is determined in application of secondary rules. Thus there must be a secondary rule of recognition in the first place. But are there really rules of recognition in the system or systems of international arbitration? How do they operate? Is it enough for a legal system just to have secondary rules of recognition? These will be questions for the next chapter.

For the time being, we should remember that rules not part of any legal order are not legal. The UNIDROIT principles are not, per se, legal rules.[82] (Just to be clear

---

ceremonies and self help. Sources were mute. Acts were mute." See also Giorgio del Vecchio, "Sulla statualità del diritto" (1929) 9 *Rivista internazionale di filosofia del diritto* 1, 19 and Leopold J Pospisil, *Anthropology of Law: A Comparative* Theory (Harper & Row 1971) 96.

[79] Ost, "Validité," 433.   [80] Roberts, "After Government," 24.

[81] Hart, *Concept of Law*, 90ff; Bobbio, "Ancora sulle norme"; Kramer, "Final Things," 50; Joseph Raz, *The Concept of a Legal System: An Introduction to the Theory of Legal System* (2nd edn, Clarendon Press 1980) 200; Kent Greenawalt, "The Rule of Recognition and the Constitution" (1986) 85 *Michigan Law Review* 621, 634–7; Bohannan, "Differing Realms"; Ost and van de Kerchove, *De la pyramide au réseau*, 369.

[82] Jean-Michel Jacquet, Philippe Delebecque, and Sabine Corneloup, *Droit du commerce international* (2nd edn, Dalloz 2010) 63: "Les règles transnationales élaborées par des organismes plus ou

to those who tune in now and have missed the first part of this book: "legal" does not mean, here, "relating to the field of law," as in "legal thinking" or "legal tradition." Such an understanding of the word "legal"—in which sense the UNIDROIT principles are straightforwardly legal—is entirely unrelated to the current discussion.) General principles of law too, as any other set of rules, cannot be legal in isolation.[83]

In sum: the question whether the lex mercatoria exists as a set of rules seems clearly to deserve a positive answer. The question whether such rules are legal in nature, in the absence of the lex mercatoria being a legal system, yields an answer that is just as clear, though negative. Legality obtains only within a legal system; what does not belong to a legal system is not law. Put differently, the question of the nature of the lex mercatoria always boils down to this: is the lex mercatoria a legal system or not? There is no way around it.

---

moins liés au milieu des opérateurs échappent à tout contrôle de validité. Mais elles n'échappent pas à un contrôle de positivité qui, pour être plus diffus n'en est pas moins redoutable: il convient en effet que les contractants et les arbitres s'y réfèrent sans quoi elles demeureront lettre morte. Tel est le test de vérité des règles transnationales." For an overview, see Friedrich Blase, *Die Grundregeln des europäischen Vertragsrechts als Recht grenzüberschreitender Verträge* (Quadis 2001) 192–242. The UNIDROIT principles are further discussed in Section 1.3 "Substantive Matters" in Chapter 7.

[83] On the different meanings of the term "general principles of law," see Gaillard, "Transnational Law," 67.

7
The External Identity of a Stateless Legal System

Let us put on a blue overall and pretend to be a mechanic for a moment. Walk up to a legal system and look at it as if it were the engine of a car we have not seen before. When we lift the hood, the first thing we see is the engine's external aspect: the black and grey parts, the wires, the connectors. We can understand what the purpose of these parts is. We do not yet know how each part was designed and made and whether the engine thus really fulfills its purpose. But at least the external identity of these parts taken together seem to be that of an engine.

We can see that what we have before us seems able to achieve its overall aim: propel the car forward or backward. The thing before us has the parts that allow us to identify most engines, though perhaps not all engines, as engines. It may occasionally, but only rarely, lead us to call something an engine that would not deserve it. But we can reasonably call the thing an engine, on the authority we have as a mechanic, without fooling the customer to whom the car is intended to be sold—with the reservation that the parts we have identified were indeed properly designed and made.

Back in the house, now in the obligatory corduroy and tweed, what can we make of legal systems? What do they look like from the outside? What is their external, structural identity? Hart would argue, stated here with the utmost terseness, that a distinctive feature of legal systems is that they display secondary rules in addition to primary rules. Well then, how do arbitration regimes perform in this regard? Can we identify secondary rules that are proper to arbitration regimes? It seems indeed that we can, for instance, when we look at social conventions among arbitrators. This will be the story for the first main section of this chapter.

The subsequent sections of this chapter will then probe the more general idea of secondarity as a determinant of legality. We will see that the secondarity of rules—secondary rules of recognition, sanction, and change having emerged in the development of a legal system next to primary rules of conduct—is only one part of the secondarity of a legal system. It must be accompanied, for instance, by the secondarity of powers. But let us now start with simple things.

1. International Arbitration's Own Secondary Rules

International arbitration practitioners throughout the world form a global community:[1] a "very small world" or a "band apart" as Thomas Clay would say (he is one of them).[2] Arbitrators, counsels in arbitration, representatives of arbitration institutions, and to a certain extent arbitration scholars, are in frequent contact, with geographical distances representing only a very minor limiting factor. This has a number of consequences, one of which is of particular interest to us here: the development of rules specific to that community.

1.1 Social conventions among adjudicators

Common-sense empirical observations suggest that it is a universal and inevitable phenomenon that norms emerge when a group is formed and remains formed for a certain period of time. Wherever there is a community, there is some sort of ordering, and ordering is inevitably achieved through norms. To make this observation, however, is not to subscribe to Ulpian's adage *ubi societas, ibi ius*: not every social ordering can be considered to be law, as certain legal anthropologists, legal sociologists, and legal philosophers might contend,[3] lest we lose sense of what specifics define law.[4] Rather, in such Latin terms, the observation would read *ubi societas, ibi regula*. In other words, wherever there is a community, there are social rules or norms, but these rules do not necessarily qualify as legal rules.

Let us turn to the function of these social norms. A definition of the concept of a norm gives us a good start, merely by elucidating what is obvious. Here is how Matthew Kramer puts it: "A norm is any general directive that lays down a standard with which conformity is required and against which people's conduct can be assessed... It can be a rule, a principle, a doctrine, a regulation, a broad decree, or some other sort of touchstone for guiding and appraising human conduct— conduct which the norm is designed to channel by rendering certain acts or omissions mandatory."[5]

Accordingly, social norms serve to assess what is right or desirable, and what is wrong or contemptible. They serve to gauge the behavior of the members of the

---

[1] See Yves Dezalay and Bryant G. Garth, *Dealing in Virtue: International Commercial Arbitration and the Construction of a Transnational Legal Order* (University of Chicago Press 1996).

[2] Thomas Clay, "Qui sont les arbitres internationaux? Approche sociologique" in José Rodell (ed), *Les arbitres internationaux* (Éditions de la société de législation comparée 2005) 13.

[3] See for instance Rodolfo Sacco, "Mute Law" (1995) 43 *American Journal of Comparative Law* 455; Giorgio del Vecchio, "Sulla statualità del diritto" (1929) 9 *Rivista internazionale di filosofia del diritto* 1; Giorgio del Vecchio, "On the Statuality of Law" (1937) 19 *Journal of Comparative Legislation and International Law* 1, 4 ("Every time a society, by spontaneous efforts, tends to form itself, it tends to form within itself a law"), and Leopold J Pospisil, *Anthropology of Law: A Comparative* Theory (Harper & Row 1971).

[4] Simon Roberts, "After Government? On Representing Law Without the State" (2005) 68 *Modern Law Review* 1.

[5] Matthew H Kramer, *In Defense of Legal Positivism: Law Without Trimmings* (Oxford University Press 1999) 80.

group and thereby they guide and direct the behavior of the group. Hence, social norms shape the way in which members of the group carry out the tasks relevant to the group. So far, the argument is rather uncontentious.

But if we apply this reasoning to the behavior of a community of legal decision-makers—adjudicators, judges, arbitrators—we may see a less trivial consideration emerge. What becomes apparent is that the tasks they carry out and that are relevant to the community are influenced by social norms, for instance, when making legal decisions or deciding cases.

Let us take a simple example. In a group, a belief or a custom emerges and forms a social norm. The norm provides that certain legal rules ought to be interpreted in a certain way. Then, the application and thus the meaning of these legal rules change, shaped in their implementation by the social norm.

In sum, the basic contention is this: social norms that are specific to a community of decision-makers influence the contents of the law that these decision-makers apply (or make, depending on the view and the circumstances).

Similar considerations have already been applied to the judicial function. For instance, Anne-Marie Slaughter developed a theory on the transnationalization of law through the global social networking of judges. By meeting repeatedly, the argument goes in substance, national judges from different countries gradually form a community. This community in turns develops common interpretive policies regarding common problems that require an internationally harmonized solution, such as problems related to forum shopping. These policies translate into transnational rules, which are specific to this community of judges and remain social in nature. These rules contribute to shaping the meaning that national judges will give to their own domestic law provisions.[6]

The international judicial function shows comparable developments. Useful insights are provided by Daniel Terris, Cesare Romano, and Leigh Swigart in a thorough sociological study of the role of the judges of international courts and tribunals. In their study, they found that "[a] shared understanding of the judicial function, and what it entails, binds [international judges] together. And a common commitment to the aims of international justice animates their growing sense of belonging to a single professional group. Their shared outlook, cutting across many different courts, has led to mutual respect and deference, and has made judges and courts more predictable and the interpretation of law more stable than it might otherwise be."[7] In short, the global judicial dialogue between judges of international courts and tribunals helps avoid the fragmentation of international law, to wit, the diverging interpretations by different international courts and tribunals of the same rule of general international law. To be clear: the interpretation of

---

[6] Anne-Marie Slaughter, *A New World Order* (Princeton University Press 2004) ch 2; Anne-Marie Slaughter, "International Law in a World of Liberal States" (1995) 6 *European Journal of International Law* 503, 534–5, 537.

[7] Daniel Terris, Cesare PR Romano, and Leigh Swigart, "Toward a Community of International Judges" (2008) 30 *Loyola of Los Angeles International and Comparative Law Review* 419, 419–20.

general international law gains in consistency through the *social* community formed by international judges.[8]

The essence of these considerations is captured by the social thesis of legal positivism. As Andrei Marmor explains, Hart's secondary rules[9] are ultimately social conventions, practiced by officials, that have a normative force similar to customs.[10] What the law is in a given legal system ultimately depends on *social* conventions that develop among the decision-makers of the system in question. If the members of a community of adjudicators globally share convictions about what shall be treated as binding reasons for a decision, then these convictions will form the relevant social conventions for their decisions. These are the social conventions "to which they *actually* appeal in arguments about what standards they are bound to apply"—a phrase by which Leslie Green defines the social, Weberian foundation of the authority of secondary rules of recognition.[11]

Put more bluntly, legal decisions are rendered in application of legal rules shaped by social conventions. Secondary rules of recognition identify primary rules of conduct. Thus, according to the social thesis, social conventions take part in the determination of the contents of the applicable law.

This theory appears to find application in the field of arbitration. As was sketched at the outset of this section, the global arbitration world forms what international relations scholars call an "epistemic community," that is, a "network of professionals with recognized expertise and competence in a particular domain and an authoritative claim to policy-relevant knowledge within that domain or issue-area."[12] Regular interactions of members of an epistemic community, despite their different backgrounds, lead to cross-fertilization and homogenization of their views on the issues relevant to their field—in our case aspects of the practice of arbitration.[13]

---

[8] On international judges forming a global community, Anne-Marie Slaughter, "A Global Community of Courts" (2003) 44 *Harvard International Law Journal* 191; Laurence R Helfer and Anne-Marie Slaughter, "Toward a Theory of Effective Supranational Adjudication" (2003) 107 *Yale Law Journal* 273; Jenny S Martinez, "Toward an International Judicial System" (2003) 56 *Stanford Law Review* 429. See also, on the circulation of information among judges of different international courts and tribunals, René Provost, "Judging in Splendid Isolation" (2008) 56 *American Journal of Comparative Law* 125.

[9] HLA Hart, *The Concept of Law* (2nd edn, Clarendon Press 1994), ch 5. Recall: secondary rules are rules that regulate the recognition, change, and adjudication of the primary rules, which are rules of conduct.

[10] Andrei Marmor, *Law in the Age of Pluralism* (Oxford University Press 2007) 129: "In every society there are certain social rules that determine what the law is, how it is to be identified, created and modified, and those social rules basically determine what the law in that society is." See further Andrei Marmor, *Positive Law and Objective Values* (Oxford University Press 2001) chs 1–2; Jules L Coleman, *The Practice of Principle* (Oxford University Press 2001); Leslie Green, "Positivism and Conventionalism" (1999) 12 *Canadian Journal of Law and Jurisprudence* 35; and Leslie Green, "The Concept of Law Revisited" (1994) 94 *Michigan Law Review* 1687.

[11] Leslie Green, "Legal Positivism" in Edward N Zalta (ed), *Stanford Encyclopedia of Philosophy* (Stanford University Fall 2009 edn) (the emphasis is mine).

[12] Peter M Haas, "Epistemic Communities and International Policy Coordination" (1992) 46 *International Organization* 1, 3.

[13] Haas, "Epistemic Communities," 3.

They share, to a certain extent, a common sociological paradigm, as Thomas Kuhn would have it, namely "an entire constellation of beliefs, values, techniques, and so on shared by members of a given community" which "governs ... a group of practitioners."[14]

1.2 Procedural matters

In the field of arbitration, these shared principled beliefs, relating to the most appropriate ways to deal with certain aspects of certain types of disputes, have in part found expression in a process that may broadly be called codification, or in more jurisprudential terms "formal positivization." The beliefs have translated into formal amendments or creations of regulations—model laws, institutional procedural rules and revisions of national arbitration laws. The result is a global harmonization of the practice of arbitration. Arbitrators today conduct arbitrations in quite the same way in different countries irrespective of the applicable legislation, so long as the parties have kindred procedural demands.[15]

The development of principled beliefs has also led to the global harmonization of arbitral practice in another way, which is less acknowledged though perhaps more important. Think of the "infusion of new ideas and information leading to new *patterns of behavior*."[16] This is now an "unpositivized" or uncodified sort of social convention. Elaborating on the source of such common patterns of behavior, William Park, one of the leading arbitration scholars, speaks of a constant intellectual cross-pollination leading to "homogenization, hybrids, and amalgam" and a global legal culture (in the singular) that "may appear more *non*-national than *inter*-national."[17] Bruno Oppetit, one of the architects of the French school of international arbitration, described the same phenomenon in the following words: "before things have changed in national laws and international treaties, *ideas, practices and decisions* have progressively converged, through osmosis ... towards a consensus on very similar principles of organization and conduct of proceedings."[18] More pragmatically, as suits British scholarship in this field, Lord Mustill calls these social conventions in the arbitration community the "unwritten procedural code of international arbitration."[19]

---

[14] Thomas S Kuhn, *The Structure of Scientific Revolution* (2nd edn, University of Chicago Press 1970) 175, 180.

[15] Stacie I Strong, "Why is Harmonization of Common Law and Civil Law Procedures Possible in Arbitration but Not Litigation?" in Mónica María Bustamante Rúa (ed), *Cultura y Proceso* (Universidad de Medellín 2013); Julian DM Lew and Laurence Shore, "International Commercial Arbitration: Harmonizing Cultural Differences" in *AAA/ICDR Handbook on International Arbitration and ADR* (2nd edn, Juris 2010) ch 1.

[16] Katherine Lynch, *The Forces of Economic Globalization* (Kluwer 2003) 95.

[17] William W Park, *Arbitration of International Business Disputes* (2nd edn, Oxford University Press 2012) 121.

[18] Bruno Oppetit, *Théorie de l'arbitrage* (Presses Universitaires de France 1998) 113–14: "par osmose, les *idées, les pratiques, les jurisprudences*, avant même les législations nationales et les conventions internationales, ont progressivement convergé ... vers un consensus sur des principes, souvent très proches, d'organisation et de fonctionnement" (the emphasis is mine).

[19] Michael Mustill, "The History of International Commercial Arbitration—A Sketch" in Lawrence W Newman and Richard D Hill (eds), *The Leading Arbitrators' Guide to International Arbitration* (Juris 2004) 1, 23.

The gist of these observations is this: unwritten social norms have spontaneously emerged within the arbitration community, which express beliefs about the proper way to conduct an arbitration. In the language used above, these norms form "touchstones for guiding and appraising"[20] the conduct of arbitrations and thereby shape the proceedings. This explains in part why arbitrators conduct procedures almost in the same way in different countries irrespective of the applicable legislation, regardless of the formal legal room for interpretation they enjoy.

1.3 Substantive matters

These social conventions regulate not only the conduct of the procedure in its technical sense of procedural law matters. They also extend to questions of substantive law, such as the proper interpretation of the law applicable to the merits.

A first example is provided by an experienced international arbitrator, writing on how contractual provisions are actually interpreted in practice. She contends that we can see an "inclination to transnationalize" in the way that arbitrators color the applicable law when interpreting a contract.[21] Where an arbitral tribunal should, according to proper legal orthodoxy, merely apply a given national law to interpret a contract and decide on the merits of a case, what in fact happens is quite frequently the following: either the tribunal applies the national law in question and supplements it with general principles of law considered to be transnational, found for instance in the UNIDROIT Principles for International Commercial Contracts.[22] Or, going one step further, arbitral tribunals "emend what the applicable national law in principle provides,"[23] in order to "avoid the consequences, deemed inadequate or unjust, of a contractual provision or a rule of the applicable national law."[24] Such inadequateness or unjustness of the consequences arises from their "not be[ing] in accord with the common usages of international commerce."[25] The

---

[20] See Section 1.1 Social conventions among adjudicators.
[21] Gabrielle Kaufmann-Kohler, "Arbitral Precedent: Dream, Necessity, or Excuse?" (2007) 23 *Arbitration International* 357, 364.
[22] The UNIDROIT Principles are: "To put it very briefly, ... a set of some 120 articles, covering the general part of contract law. In this stage, they are not meant to become binding law, but they may inspire national legislators; they may provide guidance to courts when interpreting existing uniform law and to arbitrators when deciding disputes over international commercial contracts; and they will stimulate together with the Principles of European Contract Law the discussion on a uniform contract law for Europe": Arthur Hartkamp, "The UNIDROIT Principles For International Commercial Contracts and the United Nations Convention on Contracts for the International Sale of Goods" in Katharina Boele-Woelki et al (eds), *Comparability and Evaluation: Essays on Comparative Law, Private International Law, and International Commercial Arbitration, in Honour of Dimitra Kokkini-Iatridou* (Martinus Nijhoff 1994) 85.
[23] Gabrielle Kaufmann-Kohler, "Le contrat et son droit devant l'arbitre international" in François Bellanger et al (eds), *Le contrat dans tous ses états* (Stämpfli 2004) 361, 367: "les arbitres ... corrigent le résultat du droit national applicable."
[24] Kaufmann-Kohler, "Arbitral Precedent," 367: "il s'agit d'éviter les conséquences jugées inadéquates ou injustes d'une disposition contractuelle ou d'une règle du droit national applicable."
[25] Kaufmann-Kohler, "Arbitral Precedent," 368: "les arbitres écartent ouvertement la solution que leur imposerait le droit applicable. Ils invoquent alors [que] la règle du droit applicable n'est pas conforme aux usages du commerce international généralement acceptés."

conclusion is that in arbitration generally one should wonder if "the arbitrators of international commerce are not progressively introducing a corrective function of national law based on *lex mercatoria*."[26] This corrective function would be reminiscent of the way in which international law is used in certain forms of investor-state arbitration to correct provisions of national law that do not comport with international law.[27]

Given as much, it appears that it is nowadays considered to be good practice in international arbitration—in other words, it is in accordance with social conventions specific to the global arbitration community—to "transnationalize" the law applicable to the merits: the applicable law is specifically interpreted in a somewhat different manner than it would be by a national court.

The directives of the applicable law are interpreted differently in international arbitration because the members of the arbitration community share a social convention according to which it is desirable to interpret them differently. The purpose of that social convention is to remove the dispute from the ambit of the idiosyncrasies of a possibly inadequate national law. An arbitrator who does not resort to such transnationalization, it would seem to follow, would be considered by the arbitration community not to have excelled in his or her functions. This means a risk of criticism or perhaps even slating, disparagement, or ostracism—which form the normal sanctions for violations of social norms. In the field of arbitration, disparagement may easily translate into professional and economic sanctions—crudely speaking, fewer appointments.

Let me probe a second example: statistics of current practice, academic conclusions reached by scholars in their writings, and opinions expressed by practitioners proffering their take on the job all signal that today it is good practice to follow "precedents in arbitration," at least in certain areas of arbitration.[28] An increasing number of people seem to believe that it is an adequate, even desirable thing to do.

Accordingly, one might venture to say that here too a social convention has developed or is developing, according to which an arbitrator should at least show to have researched prior similar cases.

To be sure, there is no legal obligation to follow prior arbitration cases and no award can be set aside or refused enforcement for being in contradiction with the yet elusive notion of arbitral jurisprudence. Yet prior awards are increasingly frequently followed, leading to what is sometimes called a de facto doctrine of stare decisis.[29] An empirical study suggests that it has become increasingly "improper" to make an award without proper references to prior cases in the fields

---

[26] Kaufmann-Kohler, "Arbitral Precedent," 369: "il faut se demander si, même en l'absence d'un texte comparable à l'article 42 de la Convention CIRDI, les arbitres du commerce international n'introduisent pas progressivement une fonction correctrice du droit national fondée sur la lex mercatoria."
[27] See Art 42 Convention on the Settlement of Investment Disputes between States and Nationals of Other States of 1966 (ICSID Convention).
[28] See generally Emmanuel Gaillard and Yas Banifatemi (eds), *Precedent in International Arbitration* (Juris 2008).
[29] On this concept, though in a different context, eg, Raj Bhala, "The Myth About Stare Decisis and International Trade Law" (1999) 14 *American University International Law Review* 845, 940–2.

of investment arbitration, sports arbitration, and in internet domain name dispute resolution[30] (which is, roughly speaking, arbitration-like).[31] This does not apply, however, to international commercial arbitration.[32] So in many fields other than international commercial arbitration, it is against social conventions not to refer to prior cases, but not against any formal, black letter legal norm.

A secondary rule of recognition seems thus to have developed that mandates arbitrators, in certain areas of arbitration, to consider prior cases as reasons for their decision. In these areas, prior cases have come within the purview of the regimes' secondary rules of recognition and have become sources of law, regardless of the fact that no formal legal rule compels arbitrators to do so, regardless of the fact that these precedents are not precedents, legally speaking.[33]

A recap may be in order at this juncture. Secondary rules, in other words the rules defining the sources of law or what the law is in a given situation, are not necessarily rules formally laid down. They can be, and always will be in part, rules developing spontaneously within the community of decision-makers, that is, non-positivized social conventions.

The social conventions developing within the arbitration community shape the global, transnational or, in William Park's words mentioned above, the non-national culture or regime of arbitration. The law produced by arbitrators through their awards is partly determined by the social conventions that develop within their community.

Transnationalization of the law applicable to the merits and a certain doctrine of precedents have thus become part of the global law of arbitration. It is part of the bargain when parties refer to arbitration, even though no formal legal rule provides for it. Frankly, treatises on international arbitration should today bear a sub-chapter on such social conventions as part of the law applicable to international arbitration. But that is not going to happen for quite some time, because of the epistemological obstacle that attaches to the black letter law approach, which, like all epistemological obstacles, prevents us from seeing part of reality.

1.4 On the road to legalization

The development of secondary rules specific to a group of adjudicators may be considered to be the sign that the norms produced by these adjudicators increasingly become an autonomous normative system of its own. This would for instance be in keeping with HLA Hart and Norberto Bobbio.[34] The normative system

---

[30] ICANN's Uniform Domain Name Dispute Resolution Policy, which is not legally speaking arbitration but functions in a way similar enough for it to shine a relevant light on arbitration. This system is discussed below, see Section 4 Powers to Prescribe.
[31] Kaufmann-Kohler, "Arbitral Precedent," 365–73.
[32] Kaufmann-Kohler, "Arbitral Precedent," 362–5.
[33] Florian Grisel, "Sources of Investment Law" in Zachary Douglas, Joost Pauwelyn, and Jorge Viñuales (eds), *The Conceptual Foundations of International Investment Law: Bridging Theory into Practice* (Oxford University Press 2014, forthcoming).
[34] Hart, *Concept of Law*, ch 5; Norberto Bobbio, "Ancora sulle norme primarie e norme secondarie" (1968) 1 *Rivista di filosofia* 35.

would in addition become more sophisticated in its organization and accordingly tend towards becoming a legal system, as opposed to a mere social normative system.

Now following Gunther Teubner, one might accordingly expect that the emerging legal system evolves towards normative densification (more rules), through increasing self-reference and with the objective to further its autonomy from other legal systems. Gunther Teubner would say that a nascent legal system typically tends towards increasing self-regulation.[35]

Such a development precisely is what one may observe in the field of arbitration. On the one hand, a de-legalization movement has taken place, meaning that more liberal national arbitration laws have been introduced.[36] But this has not resulted in fewer rules.

Indeed, on the other hand, the private actors of the global arbitration community have introduced an important amount of extensive and detailed procedural rules and guidelines, which led to a so-called "proceduralization" of arbitration.[37] Private regulation is replacing public regulation. The source of regulation has shifted from state law (essentially national laws, but also international conventions) to sources that are specific to the arbitration community.[38]

The proceduralization of arbitration by dint of private regulations appears to have been a consequence of the room left by the states, in other words the liberalization of arbitration by national laws. Regulatory voids typically have been filled with new norms: Anthropological observations suggest that parties, actual and potential, typically seek to increase the predictability of the regulatory framework that governs their dispute settlement processes.[39]

But the proceduralization of arbitration likely also was a *cause* for the enactment of liberal national laws: as we have seen in Chapter 1, a private field that is more fully self-regulated, that looks more like what we usually recognize as a legal system, more easily triggers a state policy of laissez-faire.

---

[35] Gunther Teubner, *Law as an Autopoietic System* (Blackwell 1993).

[36] Park, *Arbitration of International Business Disputes*, 129; Dezalay and Garth, *Dealing in Virtue*, 34; Lynch, *The Forces of Economic Globalization*, 121; Berthold Goldman, "Instance judiciaire et instance arbitrale internationale" in *Etudes offertes à Pierre Bellet* (Litec 1991) 219.

[37] Philippe Fouchard, "Alternative dispute resolution et arbitrage" in Charles Leben et al (eds), *Souveraineté étatique et marchés internationaux à la fin du 20e siècle: à propos de 30 ans de recherche du CREDIMI: Mélanges en l'honneur de Philippe Kahn* (Litec 2000) 95, 112; Philippe Fouchard, "Où va l'arbitrage international?" (1989) 34 *McGill Law Journal* 435, 450; Pierre Lalive, "Avantages et inconvénients de l'arbitrage 'ad hoc'" in *Etudes offertes à Pierre Bellet* (Litec 1991) 301, 315; Pierre Lalive, "Arbitration—The Civilized Solution?" (1998) 16 *ASA Bulletin* 483; Alan S Rau, "Contracting Out of the Arbitration Act" (1997) 8 *American Review of International Arbitration* 225, 259.

[38] Goldman, "Instance judiciaire," 225; Lalive, "Avantages," 315; Rau, "Contracting Out," 259; Pierre Lalive, "Nouveaux regards sur le droit international privé, aujourd'hui et demain" (1994) 1 *Revue suisse de droit international et européen* 3, 13.

[39] Jerold S Auerbach, *Justice Without Law?* (Oxford University Press 1983) 15. For similar contentions made by legal philosophers, see for instance François Ost, "Le rôle du juge. Vers de nouvelles loyautés?" in *Le rôle du juge dans la cité* (Bruylant 2002) 15. See also Serge Guinchard, "L'évitement du juge civil" in Jean Clam and Gilles Martin (eds), *Les transformations de la régulation juridique* (LGDJ 1998) 221, 225.

2. A Broader Idea of Secondarity

Let us resume our exploration of the structural or external aspects of law as legal systems, instead of, for instance, considering specific characteristics of norms considered in isolation. Norberto Bobbio used to consider examinations of the latter sort to amount to "looking at the tree and not the forest."[40] I want to delve further into this idea of secondarity.[41]

Secondarity, as we have seen, is a matter of the distinction between social normative orders and legal systems. But let us now consider this: secondarity is based on the idea that normative systems sometimes evolve and follow a series of identifiable steps, from a relatively loose array of norms of conduct to a formalized system of rules roughly akin to the public legal system. In the process, the social normative system turns into a legal system. The system of norms becomes legal. Social norms become legal norms.[42]

Recall: as the name suggests, the concept of secondarity is about secondary rules, as opposed to primary rules. The starting point of the theory is Hart's tenet that an essential element of the distinction between a legal system and other normative systems is the fact that a legal system results from a combination of primary rules of conduct and secondary rules, which regulate the recognition, change, and adjudication of the primary rules. Other, non-legal normative orderings typically only have primary rules of conduct.

In social orderings, for instance, there are no rules that bestow on certain people or institutions the powers to identify the relevant social rules, to change them, and to decide when they have been violated and what the reaction should be.

When that changes, when such powers are specifically conferred on specific people or institutions, the social ordering in question may become a legal system. This requires the secondarization of the norms, as we have seen, but it also implies the secondarization of the institutions and the people of the normative system. If you already see the point, good for you. If you do not, let me try to show you. To do that, I want to start by presenting the ideas of two of the principal individuals who have thought up the concept of secondarization: Norberto Bobbio and Paul Bohannan.

2.1 Norberto Bobbio on the evolution of normative systems

Norberto Bobbio was a prominent Italian philosopher of law and political science and a historian of political thought. He produced some key insights on the various relationships that may exist between primary and secondary norms.[43] He for

---

[40] Norberto Bobbio, *Teoria dell'ordinamento giuridico* (Giappichelli 1960) 7.
[41] See also the discussion of the concept of secondarity in François Ost and Michel van de Kerchove, *De la pyramide au réseau? Pour une théorie dialectique du droit* (Publication des Facultés universitaires Saint-Louis 2002) 368–71.
[42] On legal norms emerging from social norms, see Julius Stone, *Social Dimensions of Law and Justice* (Stanford University Press 1966). See also Michel van de Kerchove and François Ost, *Legal System Between Order and Disorder* (Oxford University Press 1994) 110.
[43] Bobbio, "Ancora sulle norme."

instance remarked that the very semantics of the word "secondary," in secondary rules, suggest a chronological order. Primary rules of conduct come first, he said, and they are in certain cases later followed by the meta-level of secondary norms—rules on other rules, or adjectival law as opposed to substantive law. The emergence of secondary rules, if it occurs, is not anodyne. It bespeaks, not as a symptom but rather as an integral part of the phenomenon, a normative system evolving from what Bobbio calls a "primitive or pre-legal ordering composed only of primary norms"[44] to, first, a simple system, then a semi-complex system, and finally a complex normative system. A legal system is a typical instance of a complex normative system.

These evolutionary stages (simple, semi-complex, and complex system) are defined as follows. A simple system is one composed essentially of primary norms. But it also contains at least some sort of a basic rule of recognition that identifies the norms belonging together: without this element of cohesion, the use of the word "system" would be improper. Semi-complex systems have in addition either rules of creation (or change) or of sanction (or adjudication), but not both. Complex systems are those including all these different types of norms: primary rules as well as the three categories of secondary rules identified by Hart (recognition, change, and adjudication). It is a system where rules regulating conduct are themselves regulated comprehensively by other norms.

What drives this evolution from loose orderings of rules of conduct to complex normative systems are attempts to reach or maintain what Bobbio calls a state of dynamic equilibrium. Such an equilibrium, Bobbio explains, is achieved through secondary rules guaranteeing the conservation and transformation of the primary rules.[45]

Conservation means in this case the avoidance of breaches of primary rules at a rate that would threaten the entire system of dissolution by inefficacy. Or again, it means attaining a high level of efficacy through clear, predictable, and effective sanctions. Diffuse and spontaneous social blame is replaced by an institutionalized and formally regulated system of responses to violations of rules of conduct.

Ensuring transformation is to overcome the relative stasis inherent to slow customary adjustments operating by repeated practice over long periods and desuetude.[46] Quicker and more flexible transformations of the primary rules are made possible by the institutionalization of the creation of norms, by the introduction of a formal mechanism of elaboration and change of rules. This allows, on the one hand, increased adaptation to social changes and, on the other hand, deliberate impulses of social change by the proactive introduction of new primary rules.

So far we have still focused on the introduction of secondary rules—that is to say, on the transition from one layer to two layers of rules. We have considered how they mark the difference between, on the one hand, a simple system of rules corresponding to a "primitive" society as in the theory of the state of nature, and,

---

[44] Bobbio, "Ancora sulle norme," 39. [45] Bobbio, "Ancora sulle norme," 47–51.
[46] Ost and van de Kerchove, *De la pyramide au réseau*, 368; Hart, *Concept of Law*, 90.

on the other hand, a complex normative system whose epitome is probably the law of modern states.[47]

But the introduction of secondary rules also implies the development of specific institutions. According to Bobbio, in a simple normative system, specific institutions for the conservation and transformation of the system are missing. The subsequent development towards a more complex system is dependent on the development of clearly identified judicial and legislative powers.[48]

The judicial power, Bobbio maintains, typically appears first. Judges have at that stage a double role: responding to sanctions (conservation) and creating the rules they will apply (transformation). In a second step, judges are joined by a parliament or another specifically legislative institution.

The emergence of secondary rules goes hand in hand with the evolution of these formal institutions: the rules attribute certain powers to specific institutions, which in return give effect to these rules by responding formally to a violation of a primary rule or by creating a new rule following a predefined procedure. Secondary rules have no efficacy without formal institutions and formal institutions cannot exist without well-developed secondary rules.[49]

2.2 Paul Bohannan on the reinstitutionalization of norms

Further clarification on the concept of secondarity, relating more specifically to the role of institutions, is found in the work of Paul Bohannan, a prominent American anthropologist. Bohannan's main contribution to the idea of secondarity is his notion of "double institutionalization" or "reinstitutionalization."[50]

To see his point, we first need to consider the coexistence, within a single social field, of social norms and legal norms. The development of a legal system does not do away with the underlying social normative order.[51]

Metaphorically, we may think of the emergence of a legal system as taking place in a way similar to biological cell reproduction: the social normative system progressively creates a new normative system, which is built initially from the same material but subsequently develops on its own. A legal system is in this sense an offspring of a social normative system, progressively detaching itself from its parental system. After this detachment, the legal system becomes, as François Ost and Michel van de Kerchove put it, a "specialized system of creation of legal rules and of sanction of breaches of these legal rules," which is "superposed and

---

[47] Bobbio, "Ancora sulle norme," 46; Hart, *Concept of Law*, 89.
[48] Bobbio, "Ancora sulle norme," 51.
[49] See also Santi Romano, *L'ordinamento giuridico* (first published 1917, Sansoni 1918). Romano essentially contends that a legal system is composed of, on the one hand, primary rules of conduct and, on the other hand, institutions.
[50] Paul Bohannan, "The Differing Realms of the Law" (1965) 67 *American Anthropologist* 33, 34–7.
[51] See for instance Georges Gurvitch, *Sociology of Law* (first published 1940 in French and 1942 in English, Transaction Publishers 2001) 52ff, 203ff; van de Kerchove and Ost, *Legal System*, 110; Jacques Chevallier, "L'ordre juridique" in Jacques Chevallier and Danièle Loschak (eds), *Le droit en procès* (Presses universitaires de France 1983) 7, 21.

disconnected from the underlying social system, to the point of creating the illusion that it operates in a vacuum, autopoietically, cut free from the ponderousness of its social bases."[52] But it is only, precisely, an illusion. For such a degree of autopoiesis, of disconnection, is of course never completely attained. To be sure, as Eugen Ehrlich for instance pointed out, a legal system is never closed entirely to its normative environment.[53]

And it is precisely on the interaction between the underlying social normative system and the legal system that Bohannan's focus lies. He explains that this interaction takes the form of a double institutionalization: norms are first instituted informally in the social system and then, if they are to become legal, reinstitutionalized in the legal institutions. The "salient difference," Bohannan argues, between social and legal norms is that "law is specifically recreated, by agents of society, in a narrower and recognizable context—that is, in the context of the institutions that are legal in character and, to some degree at least, discrete from all others."[54] Social norms are reinstitutionalized or restated "in such a way that they can be 'applied' by an institution designed (or, at least, utilized) specifically for that purpose."[55] Primary (social) norms are restated in accordance with secondary rules and thereby acquire their legal character. The institutions now follow a "regularized way to interfere."[56]

2.3 Secondarity of norms, people, and institutions

So the general point is the following: the concept of secondarity encapsulates the view that the progression from social to legal norms relies on a phenomenon of duplication or secondarization of (1) norms, (2) individuals, and (3) institutions. Here are these three components explained:

(1) Secondarity of norms: as soon as a group of individuals is formed, norms will emerge—we have already seen the slightly but decisively amended maxim: *ubi societas, ibi regula*.[57] At first, the norms will be purely substantive as they regulate conduct. Then, in a second stage, adjectival law or procedural rules will develop, which grant certain individuals certain powers.

(2) Secondarity of individuals: by being granted these powers, the individuals concerned become agents of their group, and thus now have two roles—they are *members* of the group and *agents* of the group.

(3) Secondarity of institutions: informal institutions (such as Councils of the elders) are replaced by formal institutions (such as parliaments and courts), which are regulated by the procedural rules and manned by the individuals to whom the special powers have been granted.

---

[52] Ost and van de Kerchove, *De la pyramide au réseau*, 369.
[53] See for instance Eugen Ehrlich, *Fundamental Principles of the Sociology of Law* (first published 1913, Transaction Publishers 2001), on his concept of "living law."
[54] Bohannan, "Differing Realms," 34.   [55] Bohannan, "Differing Realms," 36.
[56] Bohannan, "Differing Realms," 35.
[57] See Section 1.1 "Social conventions among adjudicators."

Or again, the idea of secondarization is that, progressively, there is a doubling up of members of a group and its norms: people start to have two hats (they become both members of the group and officials of law formulation and application); these people sit in formal institutions and their action is conducted in the context of these institutions; and the identification of these people and their powers, and how they are to exert their powers within the formal institutions, becomes regulated by specific, clearly identified rules. At some stage of this development, which cannot be pinned down very precisely, the normative system shifts into being a legal system.

3. Powers of Reinstitutionalization

In the foregoing I have sketched the idea that for a norm to be a legal norm, for it to be transformed from a social norm into a legal norm, it needs to be restated (or "reinstitutionalized") in the formal institutions of the legal system, by the officials or agents of the legal system. Recall that quote on the preceding page: norms must be "restated in such a way that they can be 'applied' by an institution designed (or, at least, utilized) specifically for that purpose."[58]

Now let me put this differently: the restatement of a norm boils down to passing the test set by a secondary rule of recognition. Restatement amounts to recognition—note that we sometimes speak of the "adoption" of a rule. A social norm becomes legal if it is endorsed (restated, reinstitutionalized, recognized) by an institution of the legal system and such endorsement occurs according to the applicable rule of recognition. To apply a rule of recognition is to verify if a norm that does not yet belong to the system should be taken over into the system by operation of its restatement in institutions "designed specifically for that purpose."

3.1. Dissensions among officials of a legal system

Given as much, we must now grapple with the obvious fact that these institutions may not, and frequently do not, act in perfect harmony. Dissension normally exists between different officials of a single legal system. When such dissension concerns the production of law, this means that the law-ascertaining behavior of different officials may not make reference to exactly the same rules.[59]

When we use Hart's phrase "the Rule of Recognition," we actually speak of *rules* of recognition, in the plural, of an "overarching array" of rules.[60] They are plural not only in the sense that one rule cannot govern all facets of the validation of a norm as law, but also in the sense that different legal authorities apply different

---

[58] Bohannan, "Differing Realms," 36.
[59] See for instance Matthew H Kramer, "Of Final Things: Morality as One of the Ultimate Determinants of Legal Validity" (2005) 24 *Law and Philosophy* 47, 50.
[60] Kramer, "Of Final Things," 49, 51.

rules of recognition.[61] What is declared to be law—to be legally valid—by the legislative branch is for instance not necessarily recognized by the judiciary. In other words, the institutions of a legal system do not restate norms under exactly the same conditions: "there are various rules of recognition," as Joseph Raz puts it, "each addressed to a different kind of officials."[62]

The degree of variance among these rules of recognition is certainly limited. As Matthew Kramer puts it, a "bewilderingly higgledy-piggledy array of contrary signals and interventions"[63]—fundamental and highly recurrent contradictions between the decisions of officials of a system—would simply not be law. What would be lacking is what Michel van de Kerchove and François Ost refer to as the "principle of unity binding different elements together so as to make them into a system."[64] But variance nonetheless typically exists.

What follows from the plurality of rules of recognition is that a given norm may be restated, and thus granted legality, by a higher or lower number of institutions or officials within a single system.[65] The legality of a norm typically is clearer if it is recognized by a higher number of officials. If all the conditions of all officials are met, the norm in question most clearly will be law, as the integration of the norm into the system will have taken place to the greatest extent. There are different levels of completeness in the reinstitutionalization (or the restatement, or the recognition).

3.2 Formulation, application, enforcement

The reinstitutionalization takes place at three main stages: the formulation of the norm, its application, and its enforcement. The reinstitutionalization of a norm is most complete (and consequently the norm in question is legal to the highest degree of clarity allowed by the system) when the norm passes the tests set by the three slightly differing rules of recognition corresponding to these different stages. A norm that passes these three tests is most clearly law.

Let us take this example: first, a norm is formulated. It may be enacted or reinstitutionalized by dint of the praetorian power of the judiciary, through case law. Consider the prohibition of smoking: it develops as a social rule, and different facets of it are reinstitutionalized in a given legal system by enactment of anti-smoking laws. Second, the norm is then applied in the adjudication of concrete cases, or else it has the character of a paper rule. Admittedly, when the norm is formulated by the judiciary itself, it may be difficult to distinguish these two stages of reinstitutionalization in practice, but they can nonetheless be distinguished analytically. In my example of smoking, this means that the anti-smoking laws are effectively applied in court. Finally, the norm needs to be enforced in practice,

---

[61] See for instance Joseph Raz, *The Concept of a Legal System* (2nd edn, Clarendon 1980) 200.
[62] Raz, *The Concept of a Legal System*, 200.   [63] Kramer, *In Defense*, 142–6.
[64] van de Kerchove and Ost, *Legal System*, 135.
[65] In this sense, there is not one supreme criterion of legality, prevailing over all others, as opposed to the position defended, in not so different a context, by Kent Greenawalt, "The Rule of Recognition and the Constitution" (1986) 85 *Michigan Law Review* 621, 634–7.

or else it still has the character of a paper rule, though to a lesser extent than if it is not even applied in court. In my example of smoking, this means, for instance, that the police intervene to actually prohibit smoking.

These three main stages of reinstitutionalization constitute what John Locke saw as the three principal reasons for a community to leave the state of nature and form what came to be called, more than a century after Locke, a *Rechtsstaat* (a government subject to the rule of law). Locke writes that, in the state of nature "[t]here wants an established, settled, known law, received and allowed," "a known and indifferent judge," and "power to back and support the sentence when right, and to give it due execution."[66]

3.3 Autonomy for identity

In order to make it possible for these acts of reinstitutionalization to actually occur (and to achieve the Lockean goals of a community leaving the state of nature), the normative system needs institutions that have these powers of formulation, application, and enforcement. These institutions make the reinstitutionalization of norms possible, which means to detach the legal system from its underlying social normative system, so as to achieve the duplication of the normative system that lies at the heart of the concept of secondarity. This is also to say that the legal system, by virtue of these institutions, gains some degree of autonomy from the underpinning social system. This autonomy may be considered from a vertical angle, as we just did. The legal system so to speak hovers over (that is the idea of verticality) the social system. But this autonomy may also be considered from a horizontal angle. The institutions discussed here are also necessary to give expression to the system's own rules of recognition so as to be autonomous from other systems of the same nature (that is the idea of horizontality): other legal systems.

To see the point about a legal system's autonomy from other legal systems, and why it is a requirement for anything to qualify as a legal system, it helps to envision a normative system that would be radically non-autonomous.

Imagine a system whose normative content would be *formulated* in institutions not belonging to it, in the sense that both the recognition of the norms as part of the system and the admissible ways of modifying them would be beyond the system's control. Let us further imagine that the *application* of these norms— which are imposed, recall, from outside the system—would also be beyond the control of the system. This means that the administration and adjudication of these norms, for instance the determination of sanctions in cases of violations, would be operated by someone or something outside the system. To complete the picture, add to this scenario the hypothesis that the *enforcement* of the system's norms would depend on the collaboration of institutions outside the system. The system's norms could possibly be denied actual effect by an entity external to the system.

---

[66] John Locke, *Second Treatise on Civil Government* (first published 1690, Prometheus 1986) ch IX, §§ 124–6.

Such a normative system would certainly strike one as barely having any proper identity. It would be indistinguishable from its environment as an operative normative system. Hence, it could not be a distinct legal system, but merely a collection of norms drawn together from different legal systems and obeying these other systems' rules of recognition, change, and application. Such a collection of norms, because of its lack of autonomy, would have no "power of self-organization," as Charles Rousseau puts it.[67] It would be unable to form a legal system of its own, though it could of course be part of another, broader legal system.[68]

This criterion of autonomy from other legal systems is expressed by van de Kerchove and Ost when they write that "[t]he minimal condition on which a legal system possesses an identity *in relation to another* is that it is composed not only of rules of behavior, but also of a rule of recognition *peculiar to it* and making it possible for it to identify those rules as its own."[69] Yet it is not hard to see why it is not sufficient for a legal system to be equipped simply with secondary rules of recognition. In addition, these rules of recognition must be efficacious, so that the legal system may effectively decide upon its borders. It must effectively be able, in the words of Hans Kelsen, to "regulat[e] its own creation and application,"[70] without which one may not speak properly of a system of norms of its own.[71] The operations of the rules of recognition can only be efficacious—there can only be self-organization or autonomy—if the legal system in question has its own institutions to implement them. (Consider the famous quote by Oliver Wendell Holmes: "the prophecies of what the courts will do in fact, and nothing more pretentious, are what I mean by the law."[72] That is in fact essentially a question relating to the efficacy of rules of recognition, in that it means that the only rule of recognition that is really efficacious is the rule used by courts.)

Let me restate: the tests of recognition, implied by the acts of formulation, application, and enforcement, can operate effectively only if the normative system has institutions with these powers of formulation, application, and enforcement. As François Rigaux would say, the legal system must thus have its own powers of prescription, adjudication, and enforcement, which provide it with the capacity to formulate, apply, and enforce its own norms.[73] If a normative system displays

---

[67] Charles Rousseau, *Droit international public* (Sirey 1970) 407.
[68] See also van de Kerchove and Ost, *Legal System*, 139–42.
[69] van de Kerchove and Ost, *Legal System*, 141 (my emphasis).
[70] Hans Kelsen, *Pure Theory of Law* (University of California Press 1967) 71; this is an essential feature of law in Kelsen's approach.
[71] van de Kerchove and Ost, *Legal System*, 139–42.
[72] Oliver W Holmes, "The Path of the Law" (1897) 10 *Harvard Law Review* 457, 461.
[73] François Rigaux, "Les situations juridiques individuelles dans un système de relativité générale" (1989) 213 *Hague Lectures* 1, 28: "un ordre juridique se définit par ses institutions, auxquelles sont attribuées trois compétences..., la compétence législative (*jurisdiction to prescribe*), la compétence juridictionnelle (*jurisdiction to adjudicate*) et la compétence d'exécution (*jurisdiction to enforce*)... une proposition normative n'acquiert cette nature que si elle émane d'un pouvoir institué, et à la double condition que les contestations que peut faire naître son application soient soumises à une autorité apte à les trancher et que la décision rendue soit exécutoire, le cas échéant par la contrainte." See also François Rigaux, "Souveraineté des États et arbitrage transnational" in Philippe Fouchard, Philippe Kahn, and Antoine Lyon-Caen (eds), *Le droit des relations économiques internationales—Études offertes à*

the institutions in question here, which provide for system-specific formulation, application, and enforcement of norms, it has prescriptive, adjudicative, and enforcement jurisdiction. I mean jurisdiction here in the sense of power,[74] rather than a right or an authority as is commonly[75] used in international law when states are granted these rights.[76] Jurisdiction is here an issue of efficacy: the normative system shows its capacity to formulate, apply, and enforce its norms.

Now reverse the argument. If a given normative system has prescriptive, adjudicative, and enforcement jurisdiction, if it has institutions that adopt rules, apply those rules in their own dispute resolution mechanisms, and enforce them, then the system has institutions that allow it to be autonomous from other systems. It shows that the system has the ability to effectively reinstitutionalize norms to the greatest clarity of legality. Such a system would thus be able to produce law with a high level of clarity regarding its legality and be itself a legal system in a very clear fashion.

When I point to enforcement by a system's own institutions, I mean it in the sense that the norms do not, in order to obtain a reasonable degree of compliance, need to resort to another system's coercive system or to any external mechanism of enforcement. "External" implies here that the mechanism lends its coercive arm on conditions that are not determined by the normative system under examination. An example would be the enforcement procedure of the public legal system for an arbitral award. The award, in order to gain access to coercive might, must meet the requirements set by a public legal system. This condition of enforcement power is particularly important: on the one hand because of the central role of coercive might in the concept of law—as has been maintained by authors as diverse as Immanuel Kant,[77] John Austin,[78] Rudolf von Jhering,[79] Max Weber,[80] Hans

---

Berthold Goldman (Litec 1982) 261, 279: "pour mériter la qualification d'ordre juridique, un système de relations sociales [doit] se composer de trois séries d'éléments: des règles de conduite observées par leurs destinataires, des règles de décision appliquées par un juge, des mécanismes de contrainte qui assurent l'effectivité du système."

[74] Robert Paul Wolff defines power as "the ability to compel compliance, either through the use or the threat of force," in Robert P Wolff, *In Defense of Anarchism* (Harper & Row 1970) 4. The term force must here be taken in a very broad sense, over and above mere physical force and encompassing all means of coercion; this will be clarified later on.

[75] Authority being understood here as "the right to command and correlatively the right to be obeyed": Wolff, *In Defense*, 4. See also Chapter 1, Section 7.4 "Prudential vs moral reasons-for-action," above.

[76] See the classical work of Michael Akehurst, "Jurisdiction in International Law" (1974) 46 *British Year Book of International Law* 145.

[77] Immanuel Kant, *The Metaphysics of Morals* (first published 1797, Cambridge University Press 1996) 25 (Section "Introduction to the Doctrine of Right," § D. "Right is Connected with an Authorization to Use Coercion").

[78] John Austin, *The Province of Jurisprudence Determined* (first published 1832, Hackett 1998) 13–14.

[79] Rudolf von Jhering, *Law as a Means to an End* (first published 1877–83, Boston Books 1913) 231: "The State is society as the bearer of the regulated and disciplined coercive force. The sum total of principles according to which it thus functions by a discipline of coercion, is Law."

[80] Max Weber, *Economy and Society: An Outline of Interpretive Sociology*, vol 1 (first published 1925, University of California Press 1978) 313, 332: "The term 'guaranteed law' shall be understood to mean that there exists a coercive apparatus" and "'Valid' legal norms, which are guaranteed by the coercive apparatus of the political authority."

Kelsen,[81] and John Rawls[82]—and, on the other hand, because it is precisely what is lacking in most contemporary allegations of the existence of stateless legal systems.

4. Powers to Prescribe

It is not hard to see that arbitration regimes have powers to prescribe (generally speaking, and the idea of this entire book, which is hopefully plain by now, is not to go into the details of the current setups of sundry arbitration systems but rather to make points in principle). As we have seen near the outset of this chapter, not only can arbitrators disconnect their interpretation of the law applicable to the merits from the interpretation a court would make of the same norms, but they also actually do so.

Recall: we have called this the idea of transnationalizing the applicable rules, which is a way to craft and mold new norms that are specific to the respective arbitration regimes.[83] Put bluntly, the law is different there. As a matter of general principle, barely anything could lead an arbitral award to be annulled for reasons relating to its substantive directives—this matters because such annulment would cause its effectiveness to decrease or even disappear. Little stands in the way of what an arbitration regime, through an award, may command the parties to do, from a substantive, not procedural point of view. (I only consider here, of course, the realm of activities that normally relate to arbitration, not social and individual life in general.[84] I do not mean that an arbitration regime can command parties to commit murder, to divorce, or to go for a walk. So much should be evident.)

It should also be clear that the idea of prescriptive powers, or prescriptive jurisdiction, does not require the system's norms to entirely differ from the norms of another legal system. An arbitration regime's own prescribed norms do not have to be different from the norms of any other system, much less dramatically different, for the regime to display prescriptive jurisdiction. After all, the Swiss law of contracts, for instance, is remarkably similar to the French law of contracts, in some respects, and to the German law of contracts, in other respects. That does not mean that the Swiss legal system is somehow unable to prescribe its own norms. Autonomy does not necessarily mean difference. Difference, on the other hand, likely signals autonomous powers.

Empirical studies in two areas, in addition to the research I mentioned on the transnationalization of the applicable rules in commercial arbitration, can help

---

[81] Kelsen, *Pure Theory*, 320: a normative order is "'law' if it is a coercive order, that is to say, a set of norms regulating human behaviour by attaching certain coercive acts (sanctions) as consequences to certain facts." See also Hans Kelsen, *General Theory of Law and State* (first published 1945, Harvard University Press 1949) 61.

[82] John Rawls, *A Theory of Justice* (Harvard University Press 1971) 235: "A legal system is a coercive order of public rules addressed to rational persons for the purpose of regulating their conduct and providing the framework for social cooperation."

[83] See Section 1.3 "Substantive matters," above.

[84] On the point of a regime regulating, or not, virtually all aspects of social and individual life, see Chapter 4, Section 1 "Comprehensiveness, exclusiveness, supremacy," above.

us see how such prescriptive autonomy or prescriptive power may play out. The studies relate to regimes that come close to, and for our purposes may be assimilated to, arbitration regimes, though they do not legally amount to arbitration.

4.1 Domain names

The first set of studies relates to a dispute resolution regime for internet domain names. I first need to provide some background about the system, and then point to the manifestation of its prescriptive powers.

Domain names are the identifying names for internet addresses, such as nytimes.com. They are the identifying names, and not the addresses themselves, because the latter are made up of numbers, called IP addresses. When a domain name is entered into a web browser, the browser obtains the corresponding IP addresses from a database and then connects to the corresponding server, on which the contents of the website in question are hosted. Without this conversion of the domain name into the IP address, the browser is unable to access the website. This conversion database was first controlled by a single man, Jon Postel, one of the fathers of the internet itself. He regulated the attribution of domain names quite informally, on the basis of "rough consensus," in global accordance with the internet community's general understandings of how regulation should be done. Due to the increasing complexity and quantitative importance of the management of the domain name system, most of it was later transferred to a private non-profit corporation based in California, called the Internet Corporation for Assigned Names and Numbers (ICANN).[85] In 1999, ICANN introduced a specific dispute resolution mechanism, applicable to all the domain names it controls: the Uniform Domain Name Dispute Resolution Policy (UDRP). The main objective of the UDRP was to fight cybersquatting—the practice of registering a domain name very similar to a trademark for the purpose of subsequently offering it to the trademark holder at an extortionary price. The UDRP sought to introduce a low-cost, effective, and simple procedure for disputes between trademark holders and domain name holders. On the basis of the UDRP, a trademark owner can challenge a purportedly infringing domain name, regardless where the trademark is registered.

To obtain the transfer of the domain name or its cancellation, the trademark holder must show that certain conditions defined in the UDRP are met, namely that the domain name is identical or confusingly similar to the complainant's trademark, that the domain name holder has no rights or legitimate interests in the domain name, and that the domain name was registered and is used in bad faith.[86] If the complainant successfully shows that these conditions are met, the dispute resolution panel in principle will order the domain name to be either transferred to the complainant or, in exceptional cases, cancelled.

---

[85] See for instance Jack L Goldsmith and Tim Wu, *Who Controls the Internet? Illusions of a Borderless World* (Oxford University Press 2006) 33–46, 168–71.

[86] UDRP, para 4(a) and UDRP Rules, para 3(b)(ix).

The decision is implemented by technological means by the registrar of the domain name in question—a company, approved by ICANN, contracting with clients to register their domain name in a central database. (To implement the decision, the registrar changes the association between the domain name and the IP address, which prevents the domain name from connecting to the original IP address. Instead of connecting to the server hosting the contents of the respondent's website, web browsers connect to the server hosting the complainant's website. The respondent's website effectively becomes invisible.) Only on one condition is the decision in application of the UDRP not implemented by the registrar: the respondent must show, within ten days after the UDRP decision is handed down, that he has commenced a lawsuit in certain jurisdictions.[87] But this almost never happens. In almost all cases, disputes submitted to the UDRP are resolved by an ICANN-approved panel applying rules of the ICANN-adopted UDRP, and the decision is enforced by an ICANN-approved domain-name registrar.

The prescriptive jurisdictional power of this regime manifests itself in the fact that the law applicable to the merits (and, incidentally, to the procedure) is the UDRP, which has been promulgated by ICANN itself. The UDRP determines both how the merits of the case are assessed and how the procedure is conducted. Admittedly, the UDRP provides that decisions on the merits of a case shall be in accordance with the UDRP as well as "any rules and principles of law that it deems applicable."[88] In spite of this, an empirical study has shown that by far the most dominant normative source is the UDRP itself.[89] The provisions setting the conditions on which a domain name will be transferred or cancelled are essentially ICANN's own provisions, with only limited and inconsistent reference made to national laws as extra-systemic sources of interpretation for the UDRP. The UDRP effectively trumps national trademark laws. In fact, further empirical studies show that it grants trademark owners substantially more protection than most national laws.[90]

The mere promulgation of the UDRP by ICANN was already considered to be a "glaring example of... policymaking."[91] Since then, the effects of the UDRP have grown further, because of the rising practice of a doctrine of de facto stare decisis, as was adumbrated above.[92] This practice excludes national law even further because interpretation tends to become more intra-systemic: there is increasingly less need to look to national laws to find rules to resolve a case. The regime becomes normatively denser as precedents become more numerous. This trend was supported by institutional developments: in order to reduce certain inconsistencies

---

[87] UDRP, para 4(k).   [88] UDRP Rules, para 15(a).
[89] Thomas H Webster, "Domain Name Proceedings and International Dispute Resolution" (2001) 2 *Business Law International* 215, 236.
[90] Alexandre Cruquenaire, *Le règlement extrajudiciaire des litiges relatifs aux noms de domaine* (Bruylant 2002); Keith Blackman, "The Uniform Domain Name Dispute Resolution Policy: A Cheaper Way to Hijack Domain Names and Suppress Critics" (2001) 15 *Harvard Journal of Law & Technology* 211, 233–6; Milton Mueller, *Ruling the Root: Internet Governance and the Taming of Cyberspace* (MIT Press 2004) 231.
[91] A Michael Froomkin, "Wrong Turn in Cyberspace: Using ICANN to Route Around the APA and the Constitution" (2000) 50 *Duke Law Journal* 17, 96.
[92] See Section 1.3 "Substantive matters," above.

among decisions rendered under the UDRP, more easily accessible databases, search engines for prior decisions, and other informational tools have been developed.[93] With such simplified recourse to precedents, reference to public legal systems has decreased even further, be it only for reasons of convenience and work efficiency.

One may either praise such an evolution, because of its increased predictability, or criticize it, for its troublesome democratic legitimacy as it is moving away from state law. But this is not the purpose of my contention here. I only mean to point to the idea that this normative system is moving towards increasing normative autonomy from other legal systems.

4.2 eBay

The second relevant empirical study relates to a dispute resolution regime that was used primarily for eBay. Here again, let me provide some background before I point to the regime's prescriptive powers. Note that what I describe here is meant as a historical example, to illustrate my general point, not as a description of the current situation on eBay. The situation has changed in a number of ways, big and small, in May 2008, and much less data is available on what currently happens than on what used to be. The point here, again, is to illustrate an idea, not to provide a news-driven up-to-date account of certain facts.

The common knowledge first: eBay is an online marketplace displaying millions of items for sale at any given time, worldwide. Sales take place between two eBay members; eBay itself only provides the venue for trading. Inevitably, some of these sales give rise to disputes. This would happen in any context in which transactions are concluded. But on the internet, this gives rise to a particular challenge. On the one hand, the parties involved are largely remote and anonymous traders who in principle engage only in one-shot transactions; this makes control through word of mouth—spreading the word about poor business practices—radically less efficient, if at all possible.[94] On the other hand, the average value of transactions on online auction sites is low, while the costs of dispute resolution would typically be higher than for offline transactions of the same amount, for reasons related to geographic distances, jurisdictional ambiguity, the need for translation, and other similar factors. This had the effect of making the costs of access to justice prohibitive and leaving the parties with no practicable options of dispute resolution.[95]

At the start, a loose social order emerged spontaneously, with members establishing vague standards of conduct, commenting on each other's behavior by email and on bulletin boards, and socially excluding those members who were found to be repeatedly non-compliant. Then a group of six members called *The Posse*

---

[93] See for instance Ethan Katsh, "Online Dispute Resolution: Some Implications for the Emergence of Law in Cyberspace" (2006) 10 *Lex Electronica*, at 10.
[94] On the eBay community, see for instance David P Baron, "Private Ordering on the Internet: The eBay Community of Traders" (2002) 4 *Business and Politics* 245.
[95] For further detail, see Thomas Schultz, 'Private Legal Systems: What Cyberspace Might Teach Legal Theorists' (2007) 10 *Yale Journal of Law & Technology* 151, 159–161.

developed. It started policing the marketplace by closely monitoring and authoritatively damaging the reputation of those who breached the informal norms that had developed.[96] But as the eBay community grew, this loose ordering became insufficient. Something more predictable and thus more formalized was needed. This was provided in several steps, by addressing three aspects of the problem. First, eBay gradually introduced user policies, which became increasingly dense, detailed, and formalized. Second, it introduced a reputation management system. Third, it put in place a dispute resolution mechanism.[97]

The eBay user policies—the norms of conduct formulated by eBay—have become a well-developed set of rules that regulate a large portion of the members' behavior on the marketplace. They were updated regularly on the basis of new social practices on eBay.[98] This was achieved either by simply looking at how behavior changes on the marketplace, or by directly discussing with selected representatives of the eBay "civil society" (its community of traders), some of these representatives being nominated directly by the community itself.[99] In what looks like codifying customs, these eBay user policies thus transcribed—or "positivized" in the sense of posited norms—observed member habits, which themselves expressed spontaneous social rules.

The reputation management system was built on two elements. The first element was a link between the online profile of an eBay member and his or her real identity. A relatively thorough identity check was run when an online profile was created, using for instance credit card details. Those who had an online profile and switched to a new identity were in principle clearly marked out. The second element was feedback, on the other party's contractual behavior, left after the conclusion of each transaction by each party. (Since May 2008 only the buyer can rate the seller.) Feedback could be positive, negative, or neutral, and it became permanently part of the assessed party's online profile and was displayed to every future potential contracting partners. Negative feedback could in principle only be removed by mutual agreement. This reputation management system created a history of transactions by integrating over time the assessments of contracting partners—which is how commercial reputation usually works.

The dispute resolution mechanism was a two-tiered process of computer-assisted negotiation followed by mediation. Both stages of the process took place entirely on the internet—a form of online dispute resolution. The management of the process was the task of a company, called SquareTrade, which used to provide online dispute resolution services in various contexts, but primarily for eBay. (SquareTrade operated as described here, with a few incremental changes, from 1999 to

---

[96] Baron, "Private Ordering," 246–7.
[97] For an overview of regulations on eBay, see for instance Federica Casarosa, "Transnational Private Regulation of the Internet: Different Models of Enforcement" in Fabrizio Cafaggi (ed), *Enforcement of Transnational Regulation. Ensuring Compliance in a Global World* (Elgar 2012) 279, 289ff.
[98] Gralf-Peter Calliess, "Transnational Consumer Law: Co-Regulation of B2C E-Commerce" in Olaf Dilling, Martin Herberg, and Gerd Winter (eds), *Responsible Business: Self-Governance and Law in Transnational Economic Transactions* (Hart 2008) 225.
[99] Baron, "Private Ordering."

June 2008, after which it was replaced by somewhat different dispute resolution services directly provided by eBay and by PayPal.) In the first stage of the procedure, the two parties would negotiate using an interactive system on the internet. The system suggested typical issues that the parties might be facing, thereby helping them identify and understand their own issue. It then recommended typical settlement agreements that were statistically likely to be accepted in the situation described by the parties. (It was based on a simple form of artificial intelligence, constantly learning from prior cases to guess what the parties' issues and agreeable solutions were likely to be—an "expert system," in IT jargon.) Were the system to fail by not achieving a voluntary resolution of the case, the parties had the possibility to request the intervention of a mediator. He or she would then replace the computer in its attempt to bring the parties to an agreement, typically by suggesting what their issues and acceptable solutions may be.[100]

Clearly, this was not arbitration. It is nevertheless relevant here. Consider that negotiation does not take place in a legal vacuum. There is almost always reference, implicit or explicit, conscious or unconscious, to some legal system, or at least to some normative order, which the parties believe is germane to their rights and obligations. This is called the effect of the shadow of the law.[101] The law's shadow is stronger when a third party intervenes in the negotiation and reminds the parties of their rights and obligations under that law. The third party typically is a mediator, but could also be a computer, as was the case here: the parties' aggregated understandings of their rights and obligations were reflected in the issues and solutions suggested by the computer. The key question, for the purposes of our discussion, was then to know under the shadow of which law eBay dispute resolution took place. An empirical study showed that, at least in 1999 and there is no reason to believe it subsequently changed, it was not the domestic law of the habitual residence of any of the parties. It rather was "eBay law."[102] The norms that eBay members considered the relevant rules of conduct, on which they took bearing in their negotiations, were the body of eBay user policies—"eBay law"—rather than any of the national laws that would have been applicable in court.[103]

---

[100] On this process, Steve Abernethy, "Building Large-Scale Online Dispute Resolution and Trustmark Systems" in Proceedings of the UNECE Forum on ODR 2003, <http://www.mediate.com/Integrating/docs/Abernethy.pdf>.

[101] Robert H Mnookin and Lewis Kornhauser, "Bargaining in the Shadow of the Law: The Case of Divorce" (1979) 88 *Yale Law Journal* 950, 968; Robert Cooter, Stephen Marks, and Robert Mnookin, "Bargaining in the Shadow of the Law: A Testable Model of Strategic Behavior" (1982) 11 *Journal of Legal Studies* 225. See also Pierre Bourdieu, "Les rites comme actes d'institution" (1982) 43 *Actes de recherche en sciences sociales* 59.

[102] Ethan Katsh, Janet Rifkin, and Alan Gaitenby, "E-Commerce, E-Dispute, and E-Dispute Resolution: In the Shadow of 'eBay Law'" (2000) 15 *Ohio State Journal on Dispute Resolution* 705, 728.

[103] See also Ethan Katsh, "Adding Trust Systems to Transaction Systems: The Role of Online Dispute Resolution" in Proceedings of the UNECE Forum on ODR 2002, <http://www.ombuds.org/un/unece_june2002.doc>. Katsh considers that such a phenomenon is due to the fact that recourse to national courts is an unrealistic option.

Reputation and dispute resolution were linked in several ways in this system, thereby creating what Gralf-Peter Calliess and Peer Zumbansen call "socio-legal bonds" between eBay members and the system.[104] A party refusing to participate in the dispute resolution procedure or subsequently to comply with the outcome would run the risk of suffering reputation-damaging feedback left by the other party. If negative feedback had already been given, it could be removed either by the parties or the mediator, if a settlement agreement was reached. It could also be removed by eBay if the party who had left negative feedback refused to subsequently participate in the dispute resolution process. In addition, there was an icon that traders could display on their offerings. The icon, generically called a trustmark, certified that the trader had pledged to submit to the dispute resolution process and had shown to comply with the pledge. This had significant economic impact: an eBay trader displaying this trustmark would see the number of bids for his items increase by about 15 percent and the average selling price go up by 20 percent.[105]

Now to eBay's prescriptive jurisdictional power. It manifested itself in eBay's user policies. Recall: they were adopted formally by eBay based on the practices emerging in the eBay community. The same policies, with only minor alterations, were applicable throughout eBay's entire marketplace, in all countries. They were, in other words, transnationally applicable. Conversely, the substance of the provisions that would have been applicable if an eBay dispute went to court—including mandatory consumer protection laws that cannot legally be contracted out of—would have varied from one national law to another. Almost inevitably, certain disputes received different treatment when resolved in such a forum, referring only to eBay policies, than they would have in a court applying mandatory provisions of a national law.[106]

5. Powers to Adjudicate

Arbitration regimes have powers to adjudicate. They have the institutions to provide for system-specific norm application: the arbitral tribunals themselves. A regulatory regime based primarily on an adjudicative dispute resolution mechanism almost by definition has adjudicative jurisdiction. This is fairly straightforward and need not occupy us any longer.

But ICANN's regime, to continue with the example started above, is a bit less straightforward. It deserves some examination. The adjudicative powers of ICANN's normative system manifest themselves in the dispute resolution institutions that ICANN has accredited, which apply the UDRP. A trademark owner who

---

[104] Gralf-Peter Calliess and Peer Zumbansen, *Rough Consensus and Running Code. A Theory of Transnational Private Law* (Hart 2010) 160.
[105] Steve Abernethy, interview reproduced in annex to Gabrielle Kaufmann-Kholer and Thomas Schultz, *Online Dispute Resolution: Challenges for Comtemporary Justice*, 328 (Kluwer 2004).
[106] See Calliess, "Transnational Consumer Law," examining such differences between German law and the eBay policies.

wishes to challenge a domain name may start UDRP proceedings by filing a complaint with one of the four such institutions.[107] The institution to which the complaint has been referred then appoints a dispute resolution panel, which resolves the dispute by issuing a decision applying the UDRP. The respondent (the domain-name holder) has no choice but to participate in the procedure. This is so because of a contractual structure that forces anyone wishing to register a domain name controlled by ICANN to subscribe to a certain dispute resolution agreement. (ICANN does not control *all* domain names, in particular not many national ones, but it does control almost all international ones.) ICANN includes, in all contracts with registrars by which it grants them access to its database resolving domain names into IP addresses, a clause stipulating that contracts between those registrars and registrants (people wishing to register domain names) must contain a given third-party beneficiary clause. The registrars are forced to enter into this accreditation contract with ICANN if they want to be technically able to register names. The third-party clause obliges the domain-name holder to submit to the UDRP procedure if anyone, anywhere, initiates such a procedure. By agreeing to this clause, the domain-name holder grants the registrar with whom he or she has registered her domain name the right to transfer or cancel the name in accordance with the decision of the dispute resolution panel. These contracts have the effect of making it impossible to hold an ICANN-controlled domain name without submitting to the jurisdiction of the dispute resolution institutions that ICANN selects.

The UDRP does not technically qualify as arbitration. Whereas arbitral proceedings produce awards that have a binding character similar to that of a court decision and are recognized and enforced by courts with only very limited possibilities of resistance, UDRP decisions are not granted any weight, or at least any binding character, by courts.[108] For courts, a UDRP procedure barely has any legal existence. If it were possible to appeal UDRP decisions in national courts so that they review the way in which the UDRP is interpreted, one may have argued that the rule of recognition of ICANN's normative system is submitted to the rule of recognition of the relevant public legal system and that it is not autonomous. However, the reality is that courts never (to the best of my knowledge) tell UDRP panels how the UDRP should be interpreted. The public trademark regime and the private ICANN system simply run in parallel, each of them applying their own set of primary rules.

Since the UDRP is not arbitration, in case of a conflict between a UDRP decision and a court decision on the same matter, the latter has precedence, simply because it has more force: ICANN, as a corporation, may be forced by the public legal system to comply with a court decision.

---

[107] The list of such institutions is available at <http://www.icann.org/en/help/dndr/udrp/providers>. Currently, these institutions are the Asian Domain Name Dispute Resolution Centre, the National Arbitration Forum, the Arbitration and Mediation Centre of the World Intellectual Property Organization, and the Czech Arbitration Court Arbitration Center for Internet Disputes.

[108] Kaufmann-Kohler and Schultz, *Online Dispute Resolution*, 38–9.

But this does not prevent ICANN's regime from having adjudicative power. First, the number of such conflicts of decisions is statistically negligible (in the area of one percent of the cases).[109] Second, it is not the determination of the substance of ICANN's normative system that is submitted to the public legal system. The question here is only a matter of the general effectiveness of the system. In case of a conflict with the public legal system (which, again, almost never occurs), ICANN's system is simply ineffective.

This ineffectiveness is unrelated to the determination of what ICANN's system effectively recognizes to be its normative contents at the stage of adjudication. ICANN's rule of recognition applied by its adjudicative bodies remains intact. ICANN's normative system still regulates its own creation and application, even if the end result is on a rare occasion not enforced.

To eBay: a more complex case that deserves closer attention. Its adjudicative power manifested itself in its online dispute resolution mechanism, which I have discussed above. As we have seen, the parties had a clear incentive to participate in this dispute resolution mechanism: the threat of damage to their reputation. Were a party to refuse participation, he or she would likely be sanctioned by negative feedback, which would have shown on his or her profile. If negative feedback had already been given, it was the best chance to see it removed that was at stake. If a party was bearing a trustmark, thereby increasing his or her competitiveness as a seller, non-participation would have created the risk of its forfeiture.

Admittedly, this adjudicative power is not very strong, since it is not adjudication: the dispute resolution process consists of mediation and computer-assisted negotiation. A third party does not resolve the dispute by authoritatively applying rules so as to reach a final and binding disposition. Still, this does not mean that this dispute resolution procedure is not the place where eBay's rules come to be applied. The application of rules need not take place in an authoritative way in order to be effective. Rules need not be thrust upon their addressees in order to take effect. Law's normativity may also simply follow from what Marc Galanter calls "information transfer,"[110] which in essence is the communication of the substance of primary rules, accompanied by repeated reminders thereof. Such a creation of legal awareness, if met with a certain degree of orientation according to those rules by the addressees, amounts to a form of application of law. This is precisely what the phenomenon of negotiating in the shadow of the law is about. It is "regulation accomplished by the flow of information rather than directly by authoritative decision": information transfer.[111] Now concretely, we have seen that the law whose shadow the parties seem to negotiate under is the body of eBay's own user

---

[109] In 2000, the precise figure seems to be somewhere between 0.5 and 1 percent: Elizabeth G Thornburg, "Going Private: Technology, Due Process, and Internet Dispute Resolution" (2000) 34 *University of California at Davis Law Review* 151, 224. There is no reason to believe the figure has dramatically changed since then, for instance because the economic barrier created by the costs of taking such a dispute to court has largely remained the same.
[110] Marc Galanter, "The Legal Malaise: Or, Justice Observed" (1985) 19 *Law & Society Review* 537, 545.
[111] Galanter, "The Legal Malaise," 545.

policies, which emerge from the eBay community and have been "reinstitutionalized," in Bohannan speak, by eBay itself.

In sum, both ICANN and eBay's normative systems are, or were, equipped with institutions able to apply, directly or indirectly, the systems' norms autonomously. Hence, they have, or had, their own powers to adjudicate.

6. Powers to Enforce

Enforcement jurisdiction, in the sense of a normative system displaying the power to enforce its norms itself, is clearly the trickiest part for stateless orders. A commercial arbitral award, in order to gain access to coercive might, must meet the requirements set by the public legal system. The commercial arbitration regime, then, lacks an important element of autonomy, as it needs to rely on national courts for enforcement.[112] As Simon Roberts would say, its "legality is routinely secured from underneath, 'downwards' into the State, as it were."[113] The regime can only have as effective contents what national courts allow it to have.[114] Assuming again that only effective rules matter, the final and decisive rule of recognition is in the hands of national courts. It is controlled by the public legal system. Because of this need to rely on enforcement in state courts, the public legal system is sovereign over what may be submitted to arbitration and how its norms actually bite.[115] Even Berthold Goldman admitted that the lex mercatoria as a legal system, for this reason, is an "incomplete system."[116] Notice, however, that this does not imply a necessary failure of arbitral regimes as stateless legal regimes, since the test discussed here concerns the *clarity* with which a normative system can be law. I shall briefly return to this question in the next chapter, when speaking of the opportunities to challenge arbitral awards and oppose their enforcement.

Does this mean that no dispute resolution system could ever display enforcement powers and thus accede to legality in its clearest form? It does not. And my assertion is that the two regimes I have used as examples in the foregoing exhibit this missing element. This allows them—provided the conditions discussed in the next chapter are also fulfilled—to be legal systems to a particularly high degree of clarity in

---

[112] See for instance Bruno Oppetit, *Théorie de l'arbitrage* (Presses universitaires de France 1998) 87. See also W Laurence Craig, William W Park, and Jan Paulsson, *International Chamber of Commerce Arbitration* (3rd edn, Oceana 2000) 495; Lawrence M Friedman, "One World: Notes on the Emerging Legal Order" in Michael Likosky (ed), *Transnational Legal Processes. Globalisation and Power Disparities* (Butterworths 2002) 31, 33.

[113] Roberts, "After Government," 18.

[114] Christian von Bar and Peter Mankowski, *Internationales Privatrecht* (2nd edn, Beck 2003) 81.

[115] See for instance Paul Lagarde, "Approche critique de la lex mercatoria" in Philippe Fouchard, Philippe Kahn, and Antoine Lyon-Caen (eds), *Le droit des relations économiques internationales—Études offertes à Berthold Goldman* (Litec 1982) 125, 147ff; Jan Paulsson, "La Lex Mercatoria dans l'arbitrage CCI" (1990) *Revue de l'arbitrage* 55, 63 and Jean-Michel Jacquet, Philippe Delebecque, and Sabine Corneloup, *Droit du commerce international* (2nd edn, Dalloz 2010) 59–61.

[116] Berthold Goldman, "Nouvelles réflexions sur la lex mercatoria" in Christian Dominicé (ed), *Études de droit international en l'honneur de Pierre Lalive* (Helbing & Lichtenhahn 1993) 241, 249: "cet ordre juridique n'est pas, ou n'est pas encore, complet."

comparison to most other private legal systems. Their enforcement power manifests itself in the fact that these systems do not need to rely on the coercive might of the state. They are equipped with what may be called self-enforcement mechanisms.

The main role of the coercive system of the state is to create prudential reasons to obey the law. As we have seen in Chapter 1, prudential reasons-for-action are opposed to moral reasons-for-action, in that the former, and not the latter, are dependent on the actor's own interests. People act in a certain way for prudential reasons if they believe that it is in their interest to do so, that they would be better off, for reasons that do not include having a good or bad conscience. People act in a certain way for moral reasons if they believe it furthers the interests of someone else. To achieve compliance based on prudential reasons—as opposed to compliance because of the morality of certain norms—a normative system must in principle create reasons to be obeyed that are dependent on the interests of the addressees. Such reasons typically are created by the threat of a sanction, a sanction being understood, following John Rawls for instance, as the deprivation of some of the normal advantages of a member of the group on the ground that he or she has breached a norm.[117] In the case of the public legal system, sanctions are made possible primarily by the coercive arm of the state.

The sanction of last resort of the coercive arm of the state, which consequently corresponds to the most fundamental reason to obey the law, is the use of physical force, as in forcefully taking away assets or imprisonment. This led to the belief that physical force is an essential element of law, and thus produced the classical legal positivists' monistic construction of law (recall: law as the exclusive product of the modern state), because the control of physical force ultimately rests in the hands of the state.[118]

However, as Raz for instance points out, the threat of physical force is not the only interest-dependent reason for compliance that a normative system may create or the only vector of sanctions that norms may rely on.[119] A normative system, as Matthew Kramer puts it, may rely on any "pattern of incentives that will secure [its] efficacious functioning."[120] Such incentives essentially operate, in Rawls's words, by "altering the prices one has to pay for the performance of actions, [which] supplies a motive for avoiding some actions and doing others."[121] These prices may be of a very different nature: they may be of a nature that can be controlled by physical force (liberty, possession), but they may also be of a nature that can be controlled by social forces (reputation) or market forces (financial gains and losses). To use Lawrence Lessig's terminology, law can resort to different modalities of constraint.[122]

---

[117] John Rawls, "Two Concepts of Rules" (1955) 64 *Philosophical Review* 5, 10: "[being] deprived of some of the normal rights of a citizen on the ground he has violated a rule of law."
[118] Kelsen, *Pure Theory*, 333; Bobbio, *Teoria*, 186; Lon L Fuller, *The Morality of Law* (rev edn, Yale University Press 1969) 109–10; François Rigaux,"Les situations juridiques individuelles dans un système de relativité générale" (1989) 213 *Hague Lectures* 1, 31.
[119] Joseph Raz, *Practical Reason and Norms* (Oxford University Press 1999) 150; Matthew H Kramer, *Objectivity and the Rule of Law* (Cambridge University Press 2007) 157.
[120] Kramer, *In Defense*, 91. [121] Rawls, "Two Concepts," 107.
[122] Lawrence Lessig, "The New Chicago School" (1998) 27 *Journal of Legal Studies* 661.

Law may not only step in to supplement a community's failing reputation or a market's failing economic sanctions.[123] It may also *create* and *use* social or economic constraints. When is this possible? Matthew Kramer explains that imperatives are "products of the overwhelming superiority... of the addressors over the addressees."[124] To create such a situation of overwhelming superiority, a normative system (as the addressor) needs to control certain resources that matter for the addressees.[125] These resources, again, can be liberty or possession, but they can also be reputation or financial advantages, which may easily be controlled by non-state actors.[126] In sum, other mechanisms, which may be controlled privately, can create prudential reasons to obey a private legal system, thereby playing the same role as the coercive system plays through physical force for the public legal system. This is the first part of what the concept of self-enforcement stands for: a private mechanism that creates, by the threat of a sanction relying on the private control of valuable resources, prudential reasons to comply with the norms of the system to which the self-enforcement mechanism belongs. It is self-enforcement in the sense that the private legal system does not have to rely on the coercive arm of the state to secure the enforcement of its norms.

As I have suggested above, prudential reasons typically are created by the threat of a sanction. However, law may also create prudential reasons in another way: by virtue of a modification of the feasibility of certain actions. The feasibility of an action creates prudential reasons-for-action, or more precisely reasons for abstaining from acting, in the sense that if an action is impossible or very difficult to perform then typically a person has a strong prudential reason not to perform it. The feasibility of an action can be influenced, if not determined, by law. Examples would be locked doors that enforce a prohibition to enter into given rooms or narrow bollards enforcing width restriction to prevent trucks from passing through residential areas. (A cherished example is in a cozy street called Storey's Way near Churchill College in Cambridge and not too far from the Lauterpacht Centre for International Law: there are narrow bollards there that undoubtedly help see law's modalities and, given the patchwork of paint on them, they must help hear and feel it too sometimes.) In the specific context of the internet, the contention has a particular importance. Technology, there, plays the role of the laws of nature, making possible or impossible certain actions, or more generally making them difficult (and thus less frequent) or easy (and thus more frequent).[127] The control of technology, which is available to rule-makers and is not used infrequently, allows compliance to be obtained. This is the second part of what self-enforcement stands for: the implementation of norms by direct manipulation of the environment

---

[123] Marmor, *Positive Law*, 44–5.   [124] Kramer, *In Defense*, 85.
[125] I have elaborated on this idea of "resource control" as a basis for constraint in Thomas Schultz, *Réguler le commerce électronique par la résolution des litiges en ligne. Une approche critique* (Bruylant 2005) 327–30.
[126] The resources can also be of another nature, for instance the announcement of a future divine punishment in a theocratic society: see Fuller, *Morality*, 109–10.
[127] Lawrence Lessig, *Code: Version 2.0* (2nd edn, Basic Books 2006) 9–28, 120–37.

in which certain actions take place, again without recourse to the state's coercive might.

ICANN's legal system for domain names uses technology to enforce its norms. Its control of certain technological operations is its enforcement power. It uses technology to enforce norms that do not a have a simple structure of permission/prohibition, but relate to the distribution of resources, namely domain names. As has been mentioned above, a decision rendered under the UDRP, by one of ICANN's accredited dispute resolution institutions, is self-enforced by changing an entry in the database that makes domain names visible on the internet. This has the result of re-attributing to the prevailing party the resource that the domain name represents. Such a self-enforcement mechanism is made possible by ICANN's control over this database and thus over the visibility of domain names, which is the resource that matters for the parties.

In principle, the enforcement by this mechanism can be warded off easily, by initiating proceedings in certain courts, within ten days of the UDRP decision.[128] In other words, the domain-name holder can decide to opt out of ICANN's legal system—which, it may be recalled, she had been forced to enter in order to be able to register her domain name. If she decides to do so, ICANN's legal system will give way, it will not use its power to enforce the decision (transfer or cancel the domain name).[129] However, as we have seen in the previous section, this almost never occurs in practice. There seem to be two main reasons for this. First, there are the costs of court proceedings, which often will be in disproportion to the value of the domain name, especially because of the likelihood that the dispute will have an international character, which generates additional costs. These costs act as an economic barrier to access the public legal system. Second, the brevity of the time-limit within which the court proceedings must be initiated (ten days) also makes it practically difficult to trigger the intervention of the public legal system.[130] The end result is that ICANN's legal system is equipped with its own enforcement mechanism, which effectively handles the vast majority of cases. ICANN virtually always carries out its own enforcement of its own norms.

eBay's enforcement power lay in its control of the reputation of its members. If an eBay member refused to comply with the outcome of eBay's dispute resolution procedure, he did so at the price of his reputation. He either was given negative feedback or, if that had already happened, it was not removed. In addition, he ran the risk of losing his trustmark. These were important factors of his economic well-being, since a damaged reputation, determined by negative feedback and the loss of

---

[128] UDRP, para 4(k). These courts are in principle either the court of the registrar of the domain name or of the domain-name holder.

[129] UDRP, para 4(k): "[W]e will not implement the Administrative Panel's decision, and we will take no further action, until we receive (i) evidence satisfactory to us of a resolution between the parties; (ii) evidence satisfactory to us that your lawsuit has been dismissed or withdrawn; or (iii) a copy of an order from such court dismissing your lawsuit or ordering that you do not have the right to continue to use your domain name."

[130] Keith Blackman, "The Uniform Domain Name Dispute Resolution Policy: A Cheaper Way to Hijack Domain Names and Suppress Critics" (2001) 15 *Harvard Journal of Law & Technology* 211, 233–6.

the trustmark, meant a decrease of both the number of potential transactions and the average value of bids placed to conclude the transactions.

As was quickly sketched above, Andrei Marmor explains that a legal system usually intervenes in a market, using public coercive might, because the reputation sanctions the market provides do not operate effectively, due to a lack of circulation of information.[131] The eBay legal system, however, worked by resolving this information problem, so that reputation sanctions became operative. It used the market's own constraining mechanisms. To express this in terms used above, the price for an eBay member not to conform to the outcome of the dispute resolution procedure was her standing in the eBay community of traders (social forces), and consequently her capacity to make profitable transactions (market forces). That this price was high enough to constitute a real constraint and an effective enforcement mechanism is suggested by the fact that the outcomes of the dispute resolution procedure reportedly were being complied with in 98 percent of the cases.[132] Here again, the economic barrier to access courts certainly was as real as it is in the context of ICANN's legal system. This closed off eBay's private legal system from the public legal system. It is not that the public legal system did not seek to apply to eBay transactions, but in the vast majority of cases it effectively did not intervene because the parties did not initiate court proceedings, which in that kind of dispute is an essential element of the application of the rules of the public legal system.

---

[131] Marmor, *Positive Law*, 45.
[132] Gralf-Peter Calliess, "Online Dispute Resolution: Consumer Redress in a Global Marketplace" (2006) 7 *German Law Journal* 647, 653.

8

The Internal Identity of a Stateless Legal System

In the previous chapter, we considered what stateless law may look like from the outside, as it were. We have explored the essential features of law from a systemic perspective. We have examined certain architectural features, certain building blocks. Their absence either prevents a normative system from being a legal system, or prevents it from clearly being law, from achieving more than a limited degree of clarity in legality. The features we have considered relate to what I called the "external identity" of a legal system. This has to do with its relation to its environment, its capacity to operate as a system of its own, distinct from other normative systems. To put it bluntly, to study its external identity is to ask whether a legal system has its own existence or identity. We have seen, for instance, that when a state of affairs obtains where the normative system relies heavily on (other) legal systems in order to be effective, its legality's clarity drops a few degrees to a level where its legal character is questionable. In other words, we have focused on legality qua structure.

But structure, although it is a necessary condition for a state of affairs where legality obtains, is not a sufficient condition. In addition, the normative content of the system must display certain properties that relate to the system's capacity to operate as law. Allow me to use a slogan here, for an approximation is sufficient to see enough, for the time being, of the point I want to make: to examine the internal identity of a legal system is to ask not whether it has its own existence, but what it is made of.

Why must we look at this internal identity of legal systems? For one, because we must contemplate the conditions under which a normative system deserves, in the proper sense of that word, the label of law. As we have seen in the first two chapters, the label of legality carries certain pre-understandings about the just character of the normative system so qualified. A legal system is a normative system that is usually considered, a priori, to achieve a higher degree of justice than an unqualified normative system. A normative system deserves to be called "law" only if it reaches a certain threshold of a certain form of justice. An understanding of the concept of law that disconnects it entirely from any consideration of justice is likely to be at odds with the historical, political, and cultural use of legality, with what is usually, socially, treated as law, and therefore with what individuals would understand when we call something law. Law, recall, is typically considered to be an achievements of mankind ("achievement" implying that it is something positive and valuable) and it is associated with justice in our collective conscience (as for instance demonstrated by the symbolism of law and in particular the scales of justice).

Then there is another, though related, reason to be insistent on justice, more precisely in the form of regulative quality. It is more specifically about arbitration. I need to take a step back to explain.

The last decades have been marked by a radical increase in the number of dispute resolution mechanisms in the international arena[1] and by a general liberalization of national arbitration laws,[2] leading to a decreasing control of national courts and national laws over arbitral procedures and awards, in what William Park views as a paradigm shift to "laissez-faire judicial review."[3] These movements were accompanied by a creeping expansion of private justice systems into new territories, such as foreign investment, sports, competition matters, internet-related disputes, and, to some extent, consumer disputes. Private justice mechanisms, and in particular arbitral systems have become more numerous and more autonomous, and have extended their realm. They have acquired a growing normative power, furthering the development of their own spheres of normativity, their own transnational regimes.

This development has triggered a political debate between the proponents of, on the one hand, economic efficacy and, on the other hand, state sovereignty—a debate where one of the main issues concerns the advisability and extent of state intervention.[4] One of the most straightforward parts of an answer to this question, which nevertheless has remained largely unaddressed so far, would appear to be the regulative quality of such transnational regimes. That is, we ought to ask ourselves how just the normativity is that is produced by arbitration.

Now, if the concept of law is to be explicitly connected to some just character of the normative system it characterizes, we need to use a global concept of justice, which is as culturally independent as possible. Such a concept more likely is formal rather than substantive. Procedural rather than substantive justice allows for a much narrower amplitude of reasonable disagreements, as the fundamental issue of the proper allocation of entitlements is left out of the debate. In a transnational context in particular, only procedural justice can serve as an acceptable common basis for community life. In other words, if the concept of law we use is to make sense of the just character of normative systems that qualify as legal, and if it is to be practicable on a global, transnational level and to be as objective as possible, then the essential features of law need to be formal in character and not

---

[1] Thomas Buergenthal, "The Proliferation of International Courts and Tribunals: Is It Good or Bad?" (2001) 14 *Leiden Journal of International Law* 267; Jenny S Martinez, "Towards an International Judicial System" (2003) 56 *Stanford Law Review* 429, 437–9 and Walid Ben Hamida, "L'arbitrage transnational face à un désordre procédural: la concurrence des procédures et les conflits de juridictions" in Ferhat Horchani (ed), *Où va le droit de l'investissement? Désordre normatif et recherche d'équilibre* (Pedone 2006).

[2] William W Park, *Arbitration of International Business Disputes* (2nd edn, Oxford University Press 2012) 118–19.

[3] Park, *Arbitration*, 124: "Under this paradigm, courts intervene *only* to monitor arbitration's basic procedural integrity."

[4] Emmanuel Gaillard, *Legal Theory of International Arbitration* (Martinus Nijhof 2010).

substantive. The understanding of law we want to hold on to needs to focus on the regulative quality of a normative system.

For such purposes, an important basis for the definition will be found in Lon Fuller's "inner morality of law,"[5] which offers certain minimal formal conditions, which may be inferred from the nature of human beings as moral agents,[6] that must be met for law to exist. A normative system that does not meet these conditions does not operate as a properly juristic phenomenon and therefore does not deserve the label of law, with all the consequences that attach to it, as we have seen in the first two chapters of this book.

Now, concretely, when referring to transnational arbitral regimes, a proper starting point for the discussion always seems to be found in the visions, purposes, and fate of the School of Dijon—the school of thought that was at the vanguard of a movement that labored hard to bring down legal statism, or classical legal positivism, first in the field of international commerce and later in other disciplines, such as sports. Accordingly, let us first review the central tenets of the School of Dijon. We will see that their identification of non-state arbitral legal systems, and the connected loosening of the bonds between law and government, actually opened an important path leading far beyond the mere battle on semantics that took place, for which the School of Dijon sometimes has been spurned. It is a path that, through the philosophical cruxes that the School of Dijon should not have eschewed, leads into the territories of the justice of systems of rules and the respect of the fundamental principles of the rule of law, which is the heart of our matter.

1. The School of Dijon's Eschewal of Analytic Jurisprudence

In France, it appears that not everything intellectual happens in Paris. Some of the most pregnant thoughts in the field of arbitration were actually thought in Dijon. It is there that was forged a great deal of what would initially be a counterculture in arbitration but later took control of the field's dogmas, in France. Scholars such as Berthold Goldman, Philippe Kahn, Philippe Fouchard, and Eric Loquin, who were or are at the University of Burgundy, in Dijon, launched some of the most effective missiles in the intellectual battles that shaped the French tradition in international arbitration. That tradition is worthy of attention, for it is marked by a few illuminating idiosyncrasies and a great multitude of academic virtuosities. And it helps understand some key omissions in many current claims about arbitral regimes being legal systems.

---

[5] Lon L Fuller, *The Morality of Law* (rev edn, Yale University Press 1969) 33–41.
[6] On the connections between Fuller's inner morality of law and the respect of the status of the law's addressees as moral agents—beings having moral autonomy—see Matthew H Kramer, *Objectivity and the Rule of Law* (Cambridge University Press 2007) Section 2.2 *passim*.

1.1 The School of Dijon and its detractors

Among the many contributions of the scholarship crafted in Dijon, the most lasting and characteristic, which forms the substance of the strand of thought that is designated by the School of Dijon, is the idea that there are transnational legal systems that cannot be reduced to any one public national legal system.[7] These transnational systems of legal rules, in the scholarship of the School of Dijon and its followers and kindred thinkers, typically manifest themselves and are partly produced by international arbitration.[8] Goldman and Fouchard, in particular the former, were among the strongest proponents of the theory of the "rebirth" of the lex mercatoria in its fullest sense: the development of non-state arbitral *legal* systems. It is the Latin formulation of the rebirth of the lex mercatoria, which we primarily owe to Goldman, that best captured and conveyed (and helped market) the central idea of these reflections. More recently, further successful Latin terminology was introduced, most notably the lex sportiva,[9] again in order to refer to the existence as law (that is, the legality) of non-state normative systems.

The School of Dijon and its kindred theories have come under criticism from a variety of fronts. The most massive onslaught came from the Kelsenian and Austinian camps. Not ready for a paradigm shift, many scholars exhibited various forms of fierce dogmatic determination to suppress any academic representation of non-state normativity. Such authors cling to the classical conception of legal positivism, which identifies law with the command of a sovereign, and thus ignores all manifestations of legality that are unconnected to the notion of government: it is the idea that there is no law outside of state law. Surely though, we should be aware that such an understanding of legal positivism has, outside the field of international commerce and arbitration, largely been abandoned in English-reading academic circles[10] since HLA Hart's 1958 article in the *Harvard Law Review*, which started the famous Hart-Fuller debate.[11] Hart's main point in this regard was to assert the undue restrictiveness and analytically unworkable character of Austin's proposal that

---

[7] For a lively account of the development of the School of Dijon, see Philippe Kahn's comments made during a colloquium held in Paris in 2001, in Habib Ghérari and Sandra Szurek (eds) *L'émergence de la société civile internationale* (Paris 2003) 266–8.

[8] See generally Philippe Fouchard, Philippe Kahn, and Antoine Lyon-Caen (ed), *Le droit des relations économiques internationales. Études offertes à Berthold Goldman* (Litec 1989); Antoine Kassis, *Théorie générale des usages du commerce* (LGDJ 1984); Filali Osman, *Les principes généraux de la Lex mercatoria* (LGDJ 1992); Fabrizio Marrella, *La nuova lex mercatoria* (CEDAM 2003); Klaus Peter Berger, *The Creeping Codification of the Lex Mercatoria* (Kluwer 1999); Pascale Deumier, *Le droit spontané* (Economica 2002).

[9] See for instance Franck Latty, *La lex sportiva* (Martinus Nijhoff 2007). I am guilty of that sort of Latin-based marketing myself: Thomas Schultz, "Online dispute resolution (ODR): résolution des litiges et ius numericum" (2002) 48 *Revue interdisciplinaire d'études juridiques* 153.

[10] It may be noted, en passant, that in order to get rid of the shackles of legal statism, the French world of arbitration had to wait for the translation in French, which occurred in 1975, of Santi Romano, *L'ordinamento giuridico* (first published 1917, Sansoni 1918), translated as Santi Romano, *L'ordre juridique* (Dalloz 1975). Hart's article in the Harvard Law Review, referred to in the following footnote, never was translated in French.

[11] H.L.A. Hart, "Positivism and Separation of Law and Morals" (1958) 71 *Harvard Law Review* 593.

we should understand law as a command backed up by the threat of a sanction, where the commander is someone "in receipt of habitual obedience from most of the society but [who] pays no such obedience to others," in other words a society's sovereign.[12]

But another and more important related argument remains in favor of the detractors of the School of Dijon: we ought not to, as a matter of principle, recognize law outside of state law, as such normative systems presumably fail to satisfy our aspirations to justice. Recall what we had seen near the outset of Chapter 3: Duguit and Kelsen's "resigned confidence" that non-state rule systems cannot live up to our standards of justice.[13] This cuts to the heart of this chapter.

Before we turn to the heart though, I want to flag another fierce attack that was made against the scholarship that originated in Dijon. It came from across the Channel. The English pragmatic approach to law spurned the doctrinal debate that in effect centered on the word "lex" in lex mercatoria for its lack of practical relevance. Surely, the pragmatists contended, all that matters is the question whether arbitral tribunals are allowed to apply the principles that the concept of lex mercatoria awkwardly seeks to designate, regardless of the latter's quality as a legal system. "Call it what you will," they seemed to say, "if we can apply it we can apply it, if not then not. Go think elsewhere."

And so the thinking about arbitration and law beyond the state, after a relatively short-lived success as the terrain for fashionable intellectual jousts, became a topic that led to "pulses abruptly ceas[ing] to race" and laments about "[yet] another published exposé of the 'New *lex mercatoria*'."[14] The question of the legality of non-state rule-sets was brushed aside on the grounds that scholars indulging in such studies merely were fiddling with verbal distinctions while dramatic practical socio-economic situations were urgently calling for legal solutions. As one author puts it in a more general discussion of legal pluralism: "It is... not clear what is gained, either analytically or instrumentally, by appending the label 'law' to [the intended normative manifestations]."[15] Legal scholars, in other words, should refrain from the intellectual joys of battling with concepts, and get back to real work, or at least let people who matter do their work.

Perhaps the charge of inconsequentiality is not entirely devoid of justification. But it is levelled too broadly. It is not the question that is inconsequential. The problem is in the way in which it is posed. Herein lies the issue: as long as the concept of law is not firmly anchored to some expressed and loaded tenor, engaging in semantics over the nature of the systems of rules that the School of Dijon identified may indeed be more confusing than illuminating. Chapter 1 told us as much.

---

[12] Hart, "Positivism," 602–3.
[13] See also Boaventura de Sousa Santos, *Toward a New Legal Common Sense: Law, Globalization, and Emancipation* (2nd edn, Butterworths 2004) 90: "the reduction of law to state law was, more than anything else, the result of a political fiat."
[14] Michael Mustill, "Lex Mercatoria and Arbitration (A Discussion of the New Law Merchant)" (1992) 8 *Arbitration International* 215.
[15] Brian Z Tamanaha, "A Non-Essentialist Version of Legal Pluralism" (2000) 27 *Journal of Law and Society* 296, 304.

And there is the rub: few, if any, of the scholars of the School of Dijon and its followers ever put more than scant reflective effort into the elucidation of the major premise—which ought to say what law is before arguing that the lex mercatoria is an instance of it. Whether this is the result of simple academic oversight or rather the mark of a purposeful enthymeme (a syllogism in which part of the argument is presented as so obvious that it is not worth including, making the argument difficult to challenge because questioning the obvious is a confession of ignorance) is not terribly important and hard to prove anyway. (Even though the mere reference by certain authors to the "traditional" concept of law, with no further explication, makes it tempting to believe the latter.[16])

In any event, this relatively unscientific practice led to the whole debate about the lex mercatoria being stigmatized as "woolly and unfocused."[17]

Some of the detractors of the School's ideas, however, had it better. They did read a meaning into the concept of law that gave the question some obvious relevance. But these detractors pertain to another class of critics than the one we have just come across (those who use a pre-1958 version of legal positivism and those who care mainly for practical relevance). These constructive detractors are shooting from a different angle. They sensed a further and more important defect than inconsequentiality in the doctrine of the School of Dijon.

Here is how Stephen Toope puts it: "It would appear that the so-called lex mercatoria is largely an effort to legitimise as 'law' the economic interests of Western corporations."[18] We should pause to consider these words: "an effort to legitimize as 'law'." Toope's statement appears to be the result of a rather immediate gut reaction (which is not necessarily bad: at least this is undoubtedly a more percipient basis for scholarship than the instrumentalist rationale prevalent in arbitration scholarship today). But it does point to an important aspect of the rhetoric of non-state legal systems, which I have sketched in Chapter 2: the pre-emptive character of legality, which is the idea that the label of law carries an opposition to legal intervention from outside and thus a claim for normative and political autonomy.

1.2 Legality and laissez-faireism

Let me recall that idea, and take the argument from Chapter 2 a bit further into arbitration territory. The pre-emptive character of legality expresses the frequent assumption that when law already rules a given social context, then there is no further need for law, and in particular there is no reason for state law to intervene.[19]

---

[16] Emmanuel Gaillard and John Savage (eds), *Fouchard Gaillard Goldman on International Commercial Arbitration* (Kluwer 1999) para 1450: "the criteria which *traditionally* defined the existence of a legal order" (emphasis is mine). See also Berthold Goldman, "Lex Mercatoria" (1983) 3 *Forum Internationale* 19, arguing that "it is manifest that the *lex mercatoria* has the status of law."

[17] Mustill, "Lex Mercatoria," 215.

[18] Stephen J Toope, *Mixed International Arbitration* (Cambridge University Press 1990) 96.

[19] See Tamanaha, "A Non-Essentialist Version," 304, who argues that one has "much greater rhetorical authority" when invoking the legitimacy of one's conduct on the basis of its accord with a

Let us cast our minds back to de Sousa Santos's argument of the "emancipatory potential of law": the legal character of non-state normative systems is in and of itself an enabling rhetorical factor in the opposition to state "interference."[20] This "potential" follows from the fact that the legal character of a rule system confers it some legitimate authority (think back to Chapter 1), and thus some pre-emptive power: what is legal in nature is presumed to be partaking of some regulative quality that is associated with some form of justice. Think again of Hart, for instance, when he states that there is "in the very notion of law consisting of general rules, something which prevents us from treating it as if morally it is utterly neutral, without any necessary contact with moral principles."[21]

Law partakes of the symbolism of justice, and vice versa. Legality is instrumental to the fulfillment of aspirations for justice. It is hardly inseparable from the pursuit, and a priori the presumed achievement, of a certain ideal of justice in a common-sense perspective on law. Such a perspective is relevant here for the understanding of the rhetorical dimensions of a doctrine, as analytic legal philosophers are not typically consulted when the question is pondered whether state regulation should extend to or be reinforced in a given social context.

Given as much, legality has a political dimension. There is, as Boaventura de Sousa Santos puts it, a "complex intertwining of analytical and political claims" in efforts to define law.[22] Hence Paul Lagarde's "suspicion [that the *lex mercatoria* is the vehicle for] a take-over of the transnational legal 'space' by private economic powers."[23] Likewise, Lord Mustill's argument that "[e]ssentially, the lex mercatoria is a doctrine of laissez-faire" clearly expresses the political argument carried by the seemingly innocuous statement that the lex mercatoria deserves the first part of its name.[24] Mustill thereby points to the proponents of arbitration who claim greater independence from states on the ground that certain transnational arbitration regimes form non-state legal systems.[25] These regimes, as Anna di Robilant puts it, are "normative orders claiming legal dignity."[26]

Perhaps you will remember that we have seen all of this in much greater detail in the opening chapters of this book: states were encouraged to refrain from intervening in the world of arbitration because, among a number of other reasons, the world of arbitration was represented as already having its own law. The rationale was that

---

body of law than when one invokes the mere fact that other people in the same situation happen to adopt the same course of action (social norms). This rhetorical effect, he suggests, does not change depending on the nature of the body of law (state or non-state).

[20] See de Sousa Santos, *Toward a New Legal Common Sense*, 90–5 and more generally chapter 9 entitled "Can Law Be Emancipatory?" See further Anna di Robilant, "Genealogies of Soft Law" (2006) 54 *American Journal of Comparative Law* 499, 545 in her reference to Gurvitch's concept of social law and legal pluralism: "social law and legal pluralism as critical instruments of emancipation."

[21] Hart, "Positivism and Separation," 624.

[22] See de Sousa Santos, *Toward a New Legal Common Sense*, 90.

[23] Paul Lagarde, "Approche critique de la lex mercatoria" in Philippe Fouchard, Philippe Kahn and Antoine Lyon-Caen (eds), *Le droit des relations économiques internationales—Études offertes à Berthold Goldman* (Litec 1982) 125–6.

[24] Michael Mustill, "The New Lex Mercatoria: The First Twenty-Five Years" (1988) 4 *Arbitration International* 86, 117.

[25] For example Gaillard, *Legal Theory*.   [26] di Robilant, "Genealogies," 542.

if there already is law, with the aforementioned presupposed implied regulative qualities, then there is less need, and even justification, for the state to interfere with this legal system. The use of the word "law" in the characterization of a normative order has in ordinary language strong normative valence. It is a desirable institution that evokes representations of justice; representations of justice yield assumptions of desirability; assumptions of desirability are strong arguments for laissez-faire.

Since this connection between law and justice can barely be removed from the collective mind, since law represents a certain ideal of justice, since it has rhetorical force on the political plane, we have to make this connection meaningful. Affixing the label of law to a normative system must, then, be subjected to certain expressed criteria of justice.[27]

The idea is thus to reintroduce in the debate about the autonomy of arbitral regimes an understanding of law that focuses on that which matters in the debate: the regulative quality of the normative system in question. Echoing Simon Roberts, we ought to offer a concept of law that helps "introduce, understand and justify processes" of private norm-making centered on dispute resolution mechanisms.[28] This is something that the School of Dijon eschewed, and should not have eschewed, focusing instead on various aspects of effectiveness and normative autonomy from the state.

1.3 Regulative quality

The assertion just made means that one meaningful factor in the determination of the intervention of states in arbitration is the overall quality of the work of arbitrators. (Recall: regulative quality "makes" legality—it is a necessary though not sufficient condition of legality—and legality leads to non-intervention, or more precisely less intervention.) An influential book adhering firmly to the French tradition in international arbitration is precisely based on the idea that the arbitration world needs just the right dose of collaboration of state courts.[29] Too much intervention would make the procedures too cumbersome and parochial, marked as they would be by each state's idiosyncrasies. Too little supervision and assistance of the courts, on the other hand, would diminish the effectiveness of arbitration and, as a Belgian experience showed (Belgium had for a time eliminated all rights to challenge the award in disputes between foreign parties), it would diminish its

---

[27] A dark parallel may be drawn here with the rhetorical use of the claim to adhere to the rule of law for the purposes of legitimizing an iniquitous political regime. Such arguments appear to have at least some political weight in a government's opposition to diplomatic interference by other states. The political operations of this argument are sometimes decried because of the emptiness of the regulative principles that are implied by a reference to the rule of law: see for instance Jan Paulsson, "Enclaves of Justice" (2007) 4 *Transnational Dispute Management* #5, who calls these political operations the "Fraudulent Consensus on the Rule of Law."

[28] Simon Roberts, "After Government? On Representing Law without the State" (2005) 68 *Modern Law Review* 1, 4.

[29] Christophe Seraglini, *Lois de police et justice arbitrale internationale* (Dalloz 2001).

credibility as a dispute resolution system that is reliable with regard to its procedural quality. In the Belgian experience, this "created more anxiety than comfort," as William Park put it. "There were no custodians to guard the custodians."[30]

In a section entitled "The quality of justice of international arbitration,"[31] the author of that book considers that, presumably because of the quality of the justice that arbitrators provide on average, arbitration is increasingly considered to be a system of justice of its own. Arbitration is consequently granted the "attributes that are necessary to accomplish this function,"[32] among which is the binding, even constraining character of arbitral awards, which is all the greater as opportunities to challenge them or oppose their enforcement are low. In other words, the author explains, "arbitration as an institution enjoys a systematic and lasting delegation of power ['habilitation']" in the field of justice.[33] In my words this time, arbitration would appear to be granted a high degree of effectiveness and autonomy by states because governments generally consider that it produces a normative system of comparatively high regulative quality.

Roughly put, governments believe that arbitrators produce a normative ordering that is more or less equivalent, in terms of its regulative quality, to the workings of other legal systems, and hence a laissez-faire policy is in order.

The issue with this rhetorical and often implicit argument—that states should refrain from intervening in a given social sphere because it already has its own law—is the following: the concept of law used by the majority of legal pluralists, and by many arbitration scholars in particular, is purely structural and contains no element relating to regulative quality. The concept of law and of a legal system used for instance by the School of Dijon is primarily based on Santi Romano's theory—the quite boring idea that every social body is a legal system if it has its own set of effective rules whose purpose is social ordering.[34] Being only structural, such a definition of the concept of law cannot be used as a yardstick for regulative quality, and therefore the presence of law under such conditions cannot legitimately be used as an argument, expressly or implicitly, against state intervention. Effectiveness is not a legitimate argument to call for laissez-faire.

However, the mere fact of characterizing a normative order as law, even if it is according to such strictly structural criteria, is likely to be intuitively associated with the idea that the normative order in question displays the virtues that our collective conscience associates with law. This is what one may describe as the unintended fallacious argument of the School of Dijon. Hence, if we want to deal with the question of the legality of non-state arbitral systems, now that we are aware of the consequences this question has, we seem forced to rely on a concept of law that contains express standards of regulative quality. One such concept, which

---

[30] Park, *Arbitration of International Business Disputes*, 130.   [31] Seraglini, *Lois de police*, 66–8.
[32] Seraglini, *Lois de police*, 67.   [33] Seraglini, *Lois de police*, 67.
[34] Romano, *L'ordinamento giuridico*. For a recent exposition of Santi Romano's theories, see Filippo Fontanelli, "Santi Romano and *L'ordinamento giuridico:* The Relevance of a Forgotten Masterpiece for Contemporary International, Transnational and Global Legal Relations" (2011) 2 *Transnational Legal Theory* 67.

represents a respected approach to the question in legal philosophy, is Lon Fuller's "inner morality of law."[35]

2. Legitimacy and Justice for Transnational Legality: A Laconically Selective Survey

So my argument, in what I have just said, was that if we want to make claims of laissez-faireism in the guise of claims of legality, we need, in order to be candid, to give the label of law some loaded tenor. We need to connect legality to some form of legitimacy or justice that could reasonably lead to laissez-faire. I have sketched the contention that regulative quality, in the form captured by Lon Fuller, is a sound reference for such purposes. That is to say, it would provide a valuable yardstick for gauging the qualities of a transnational stateless regime. Pro tanto, it would help assess in which respect and to what extent claims for autonomy, in the guise of claims for transnational legality, should be condoned.

Before we proceed with this argument, I want to very briefly review, and exclude, alternative candidates that would have offered themselves for the task of assessing the legitimacy and justice of transnational regimes aspiring to be stateless law. Why should we look to Lon Fuller? Can reference not be made to another yardstick, another way to ponder the legitimacy and justice of transnational regimes?

2.1 No democratic legitimacy

We have seen at various junctures of this book that the world of arbitration tends to become more independent from states. It tends to consolidate into a global arbitration culture which is increasingly self-regulated and thus gradually tends to form one or several global arbitration regimes. (Again, I am making a point in principle, and do not intend to provide particulars about the current state of play in arbitration setups: commercial vs investment vs sport, etc. I focus on the major premise, not the minor.)

Democracy, then, is a first port of call in our investigation about reasons to consider arbitration regimes to amount to legal regimes because of some form of justice or legitimacy: could the argument not be made that an arbitration regime is a particularly democratic form of regulation, and can therefore make claims for legality and autonomy? The answer is no. Let me explain why.

The private actors who create an important part of the rules of a global arbitration regime form a different group from those to whom the rules apply. Arbitration institutions, arbitrators, arbitration associations, counsel in arbitrations, to a certain extent authors of scholarly writings, make the rules that apply to the end users: the parties themselves, the companies, or individuals.[36] One way to call this

---

[35] Fuller, *Morality*, 33–41.
[36] William W Park, "The Procedural Soft Law of International Arbitration: Non-Governmental Instruments" in Loukas Mistelis and Julian DM Lew (eds), *Pervasive Problems in International Arbitration* (Kluwer 2006) 141–54.

issue is to call it an issue of "social reflexivity." The concept of social reflexivity expresses the ethical necessity, which underlies the very notion of democracy, that virtually all those to whom a given set of rules applies be allowed to participate in the creation of such set of rules.[37] As Jürgen Habermas puts it, "the modern legal order can draw its legitimacy only from the idea of self-determination: citizens should always be able to understand themselves as authors of the law to which they are subject as addressees."[38]

The companies and individuals appearing as parties in arbitration procedures do not form part of the epistemic community of arbitration, which creates and develops these rules. Those who will eventually receive the rough end of the rules forming the global arbitration regime do typically not participate in their making.

Admittedly, the parties to an arbitration could theoretically change the rules of the game, by instructing the arbitral tribunal to act precisely as they wish and thereby introducing near-perfect social reflexivity—arbitrators could be requested, for instance, not to "transnationalize" the applicable law and to disrobe of almost all the usual procedural guidelines. However, this would require that the two (or more) parties manage to agree on such exceptions to the usual rules, which is not something easily obtained from litigants in an antagonistic procedure. As William Park puts it, "[h]ere we see a disjunction between rhetoric and reality[:] specific norms inhabit the less elastic world where lawyers *do* care about the 'regular' way to do things."[39]

The weight of this sort of normative traditionalism seems real. The private proceduralization of arbitration has become such that certain leading arbitrators call it a creeping disease [40]—it has led to an almost overwhelming load of detailed procedural rules without reference to which it has become unusual to conduct an arbitration. To use Park's words again, "*Faute de mieux*, [procedural guidelines developed by the arbitration community] will be cited during the procedural debates that develop in most major arbitrations. Some guidelines may ultimately constitute a canon of authoritative writings cited during procedural battles."[41]

It remains an entirely marginal exception to see an arbitration conducted in splendid isolation of this wealth of procedural guidelines created by the arbitration epistemic community and in isolation of the social conventions that have developed within the community of international arbitrators. Social reflexivity, which obtains by degree and is thus a scalar notion, not an on/off feature, appears to be fulfilled only to a very limited degree with regard to the global private regime of international arbitration.

---

[37] Ulrich Beck, Anthony Giddens and Scott Lash, *Reflexive Modernization, Politics, Tradition and Aesthetics in the Modern Social Order* (Stanford University Press 1998); Jacques Lenoble and Marc Maesschalck, *The Action of Norms* (Kluwer 2002).

[38] Jürgen Habermas, *Between Facts and Norms* (MIT Press 1996) 449.

[39] Park, "Procedural Soft Law," 147 (emphasis in the original).

[40] See for instance Serge Lazareff, "Avant-propos: Le bloc-notes de Serge Lazareff" (2004) 124 *Gazette du Palais: Cahiers de l'arbitrage* 3 (No 338/339, December 3 and 4, 2004). Lazareff calls it a "regulatory pruritus" (prurit réglementaire), which is a fairly common metaphor in French to liken normative densification to an unpleasant sensation that elicits the desire to scratch.

[41] Park, *Arbitration of International Business Disputes*, 158.

Given as much, it is one of the important aims of the rule of law that fails to be achieved—under one of the theoretical formulations of the rule of law as a moral-political ideal[42] among its several alternatives.[43] As a prominent legal theorist puts it for that construal of the rule of law, democracy "may today be taken to be a central strand of the rule of law."[44] From a moral-political point of view and with regard to the legitimacy of arbitration's global governance effects (to wit, the effects of the global arbitration regime), this first, and relatively obvious, attempt to demonstrate the legitimacy or justice of the arbitration regime failed.

2.2 What else?

Let me now turn, with extreme brevity considering what would normally be the task, to the history of the concept of justice. Three main concepts of justice appear a priori relevant for the purposes of the current study: justice qua conformity to law, giving to each his own, and formal legality. I want to focus on the first two of these concepts here, and leave the third, which will lead us back to Fuller, for a separate discussion that follows immediately in the next sub-section.

The understanding of justice in the sense of conformity to law (often known in its German translation "*Gerechtigkeit als Rechtsmässigkeit*") probably corresponds to the dominant position of lawyers when dealing with questions of justice. Judith Shklar captured a great part of the idea with her notion of "legalism," which is "the ethical attitude that holds moral conduct to be a matter of rule following, and moral relationships to consist of duties and rights determined by rules."[45] The "rules," here, are the rules of the law.

The approach is based on the tenet that justice (*Gerechtigkeit*) can only be found in conformity to law (*Rechtsmässigkeit*); it conceives of justice qua justice according to law, where law stands for the utterances of the sovereign—the law of the state.[46] By force of circumstances, lawyers are occupied primarily with the achievement of practical justice, which is undertaken by focusing on the way in which legal decisions are rendered.[47] They typically may safely remain agnostic to the values

---

[42] On the distinction between the jurisprudential conception of the rule of law (the state of affairs that obtains when the necessary conditions for the existence of a regime of law are satisfied) and the moral-political conceptions of the rule of law (the constitutive elements of law as precepts of political morality), see Kramer, *Objectivity*.

[43] Brian Tamanaha distinguishes formal and substantive formulations of the rule of law. Among the formal formulations, he marks out three versions of the rule of law: "rule-by-law" ("law is the means by which the state conducts its affairs"), "formal legality" (a set of rules that is general, clear, prospective, certain, etc.) and "democracy + legality" ("consent determines content of law"). It is the last formulation that will be used here. See Brian Z Tamanaha, *On The Rule of Law* (Cambridge University Press 2004)

[44] Trevor RS Allan, *Law, Liberty, and Justice* (Clarendon Press 1993) 21–2; see also Tamanaha, *Rule of Law*, 99–101.

[45] Judith Shklar, *Legalism: Law, Morals, and Political Trials* (2nd edn, Harvard University Press 1986) 1.

[46] John Bell, "Justice and the Law" in Klaus R. Scherer (ed), *Justice: Interdisciplinary Perspectives* (Cambridge University Press 1992) 117.

[47] See generally Niklas Luhmann, "Gerechtigkeit in den Rechtssystemen der modernen Gesellschaft" (1973) 4 *Rechtstheorie* 131.

according to which legal rules are created: in the somewhat elliptical words of Roscoe Pound, "lawyers are not required to conduct a sit-down strike until philosophers agree" in order to achieve practical justice.[48]

Lawyers are usually neither required nor inclined to reflect on some transcendental ideal that may imbue their understanding of law and legal norms,[49] and essentially rely to achieve justice on interpretative proficiency and the science of legislation, rather than on reflections pertaining to the science of law.[50]

With regard to gauging the justice or regulative quality of arbitral regimes, with the already mentioned rhetorical consequences that attach to that sort of assessment, following such an approach would lead to one of two analytical frameworks for the assessment of the justice of arbitral regimes.

The first would focus on the applicable national laws and international conventions to determine the regulative quality of such regimes: the necessary and sufficient condition of justice would be the compliance by the regimes with the requirements that these legal instruments set for the validity of arbitration agreements and awards.

Such an approach would only achieve a total trivialization of the whole question, as all important international arbitration systems globally satisfy such requirements—arbitral awards would systematically be set aside were it not the case. To say that they all deserve, on the plane of justice, the autonomy that they have been granted by states is an entirely uninformative conclusion. To say that, because of this assessment of justice in the light of *Rechtsmässigkeit*, those systems deserve greater (or lesser) autonomy than they currently are granted because they ought to be recognized as independent legal systems would do violence to logics. Complying with current conditions of autonomy cannot be the grounds, through the artifices of legality as a flag sign of regulative quality, for a claim that these conditions should be lowered or heightened.

The second analytical framework that such a conception of justice may lead to would be built on the foundations of court decisions: if court decisions qualify or treat given non-state normative orders as legal systems, then these systems ought to be considered just and worthy of the label of law.[51]

The advantage of this analytical framework over the preceding one is that here the attribution of legality to the external normative system follows directly from a purposeful decision made by the recognizing legal system. The carriage of expectable rhetorical consequences of legality (using this attributed legality to claim

---

[48] Roscoe Pound, *Justice According to the Law* (Yale University Press 1951) 129.
[49] René Marcic, *Rechtsphilosophie: eine Einführung* (Rombach 1969).
[50] Wolfgang Friedmann, *Legal Theory* (3rd edn, Stevens & Sons 1953) 154, 294–5.
[51] It is a frequent argument among private international lawyers that the recognition by courts of the legal character of non-state rule systems ought to be the one decisive criterion for our scholarly determination on the nature of these systems. See for instance Thomas Clay, *L'arbitre* (Dalloz 2001) 217; Jean-Michel Jacquet, Michel Delebecque, and Sabine Corneloup, *Droit du commerce international* (2nd edn, Dalloz 2010) 60: speaking of stateless rules of law: "Leur reconnaissance à l'extérieur du milieu qui les a vu naître est cependant indispensable. Or celle-ci semble assez largement assurée en droit français par le biais de la consécration par la jurisprudence des sentences arbitrales internationales ayant appliqué la *lex mercatoria*."

further autonomy on the basis of the rhetoric discussed above) is then simply attached to this decision. It is no longer thrust upon a system that did not mean and barely could expect to open the door to claims of opposition to its intervention.

But this advantage at the same time calls for the demise of this analytical framework as a scientific one: because of the distinction, which we encountered in Chapter 5, between relative legality (the internal point of view of one specific legal system regarding the legality of another rule system) and absolute legality (the external point of view of the analyst studying the question whether a given system of rules instantiates the characteristic features of law), the decision of a court cannot prejudge any scholarly determination in the assessment of the nature of a normative system.

Whether we wish to scientifically endorse a given non-state normative system as law or not (which is the question here), with the rhetorical and political consequences that follow from such intellectual backing, is unrelated to what certain national legal systems provide. The reverse would run into the logical quagmire that manifests itself when one national legal system grants a non-state set of rules the label of law while another denies it. In sum, forget what courts say. (True, this is impiety in a lawyer's mouth, but there you are.)

So much for *Gerechtigkeit als Rechtsmässigkeit*. Let us move on to the second idea of justice I announced: giving to each his own.

In the third century AD, the revered Roman lawyer Ulpian, whom we recall most often for his legal and philosophical one-liners, wrote that "justice is the constant and perpetual will to give to each his own" ("*iustitia est constans et perpetua voluntas ius suum cuique tribuere*").[52] This definition of justice appears to have represented the most widely shared understanding of justice throughout history. According to John Bell, "[t]his notion of 'giving to each his own' brings forward the central elements of equal treatment and concern for how resources are allocated."[53]

The difference with the previously examined notion of justice, justice as conformity to law, is that the latter is merely concerned with "treating all according to their legal entitlements,"[54] whereas Ulpian's notion takes up the question "how the law ought to allocate entitlements in the first place."[55] *Suum cuique tribuere* thus represents the most basic understanding of substantive justice (as opposed to procedural justice).

The analytical framework that such a notion of justice would offer has certain advantages over the justice-according-to-law perspective. First, it would have greater analytical purchase, by allowing to draw consequences from the analysis that are truly meaningful as it would break the dogmatic frame that unavoidably is reflected in arbitration legislation. Second, it would steer clear of the logical meanders and inconsistencies that the *Rechtsmässigkeit* approach raises when applied to the question of non-state normative systems, which I have just sketched.

But on any scientific argument drawn from a purported misallocation of resources and thus on any battle led under the banner of substantive justice,

[52] Digest, 1.1.10; Inst 1.1. [53] Bell, "Justice," 115.
[54] Bell, "Justice," 115. [55] Bell, "Justice," 115.

Alf Ross, in a moment of polemical hyperbole, said this: "to invoke justice [in such a substantive sense] is the same thing as banging on the table: an emotional expression which turns one's demand into an absolute postulate."[56] Hans Kelsen expressed the same idea with more composure: "The problem of values is in the first place the problem of conflicts of values, and this problem cannot be solved by means of rational cognition. The answer to these questions is a judgment of value, determined by emotional factors, and, therefore, subjective in character—valid only for the judging subject, and therefore relative only."[57]

The issue is this: in the absence of ascertainable and agreed higher standards against which to judge the correct allocation of resources effected by a system of norms, any reference to "justice" in a discussion on the virtues and vices of a rule system necessarily would amount to a scientifically unsupportable expression of individual or collective preferences.[58] And the condition just exposed appears almost impossible to fulfill given the "fact of moral pluralism."[59] In short, it would be a purely subjective choice. Let us move on.

2.3 Predictability

Let us now consider another main construal of the rule of law, which relates not to law's democratic legitimacy but to its internal standards of merit, and more precisely to a standard of merit that is procedural, not substantive. This strand of the rule of law, called "formal legality,"[60] holds in substance that legality is a yardstick against which a normative system may be assessed because of certain formal virtues of legality, because of law's formal regulative quality.

Recall from Chapter 1: the qualification as "law" carries the expectation of certain formal qualities that we associate with that which is legal—the guarantees of the rule of law. In the words of Brian Tamanaha again: "The rule of law in this sense entails public, prospective laws, with the qualities of generality, equality of application, and certainty."[61] The rule of law is perceived as something good and valuable, here, because of its inherent formal virtues: it is a superior mode of regulation.

Such a claim, it must be pointed out, says nothing about the substantive qualities or substantive virtues of a specific instance of law. The contents of a specific law or even a given legal system in its entirety can be utterly bad, even evil. Law is fallible by nature, it may fail to promote the common good.[62] It is the way in which law operates that is perceived as valuable: as Neil McCormick puts it, "it is morally of value to people to have common [predictable] rules."[63]

---

[56] Alf Ross, *On Law and Justice* (Routledge 1958) 274.
[57] Hans Kelsen, "What is Justice?" in Hans Kelsen (ed), *What Is Justice: Justice, Law, and Politics in the Mirror of Science: Collected Essays* (essay first published 1957, Lawbook Exchange 2000) 4.
[58] Bell, "Justice," 116–17; Tamanaha, *Rule of Law*, 99–100.
[59] Tamanaha, *Rule of Law*, 100.   [60] Tamanaha, *Rule of Law*, 100.
[61] Tamanaha, *Rule of Law*, 119.
[62] David Lyons, *Ethics and the Rule of Law* (Cambridge University Press 1984) 63; H.L.A. Hart, *The Concept of Law* (2nd edn, Clarendon Press 1994) 185–6.
[63] Neil McCormick, *Rhetoric and the Rule of Law. A Theory of Legal Reasoning* (Oxford University Press 2005) 13.

Formal legality, then, provides a less ambitious analytical framework than the ones we have seen in the preceding sub-section, but one with greater use value.[64] It is a conception of the rule of law that subjects the attribution of the label of law to conditions of justice pertaining, for instance, to the way in which norms are promulgated, their clarity and their temporal dimension (prospectivity vs retroactivity, for instance).[65] It is a formal concept of justice, agnostic to the actual contents of the set of rules it characterizes.[66] As such, it would consider as law an iniquitous regime, one that under a substantive approach to justice would be flagged as "bad law," and would not discriminate it from a benign regime, provided both satisfy the applicable procedural conditions.[67] But at least law in this formal approach "enhances the dignity of citizens," as Brian Tamanaha puts it, "by allowing them to predict and plan."[68] This is why we have here a less ambitious approach than what is offered by an analytical framework based on a substantive version of justice. But as I said, it has greater use value.

The greater use value of formal legality lies in the fact that the amplitude of reasonable disagreements is incomparably smaller over ways in which to implement procedural justice than over the proper allocation of entitlements. This is what led Jürgen Habermas to consider that only "genesis, not a priori principles to which the *content* of norms would have to correspond, provides [a norm] with its justice" and, hence, the "legitimacy of positive law is conceived as procedural rationality."[69] The inherent variegatedness of conceptions of substantive justice requires that we dispense with arguments relating to the regulative quality of an arbitral regime on the basis of the contents of its rules or the way in which it redistributes resources and limit ourselves to procedural aspects of such a rules system. The question then simply is whether such a regime truly allows to "predict and plan."

As I have adumbrated, among the least objectionable yardsticks of procedural justice, precisely because it is based on deliberate efforts to expunge all elements of provincialism,[70] is Lon Fuller's account of the rule of law, which he calls the "inner morality of law."[71] Hence, in the third and last main section of this chapter, I maintain that this understanding of the concept of law is a device for expressing the necessary—though not per se sufficient—conditions of regulative quality that an arbitral regime must follow in order to be considered procedurally just, and thus to deserve the label of law, with all its attendant rhetorical consequences.

---

[64] On formal legality, see Tamanaha, *Rule of Law*, 91–101.
[65] Paul Craig, "Formal and Substantive Conceptions of the Rule of Law" (1997) *Public Law* 467.
[66] Robert S Summers, "A Formal Theory of the Rule of Law" (1993) 6 *Ratio Juris* 127, 135.
[67] Kramer, *Objectivity*, 102: "As a set of conditions that obtain whenever any legal system exists and operates, the rule of law is per se a morally neutral state of affairs. Especially in a sizable society, the rule of law is indispensable for the preservation of public order and the coordination of people's activities and the securing of individuals' liberties; but it is likewise indispensable for a government's effective perpetration of large-scale projects of evil over lengthy periods."
[68] Tamanaha, *Rule of Law*, 96.
[69] Jürgen Habermas, *Beyond Facts and Norms* (MIT Press 1996) 449, 453 (emphasis is mine).
[70] Kramer, *Objectivity*, 185.   [71] Fuller, *Morality*, 33–41.

3. The Inner Morality of Arbitration Regimes

So Lon Fuller's account of the rule of law, the "inner morality of law," is the concept of law I want to use as a yardstick to determine whether an arbitration regime—and any stateless normative regime for that matter—deserves the label of law. I want to use this particular yardstick because it is procedural. It is thus less exposed to disagreement. It is also the result of efforts to exclude local or cultural idiosyncrasies.

Now I need to enter an exposition of the regulatory desiderata for private justice regimes that may be inferred from Lon Fuller's concept of law. This section thus expounds the sundry bearings that seven of the eight cognate principles delineated by Fuller have on procedural questions in dispute resolution and, hence, on regulation through patterns of individual rule application and creation.

3.1 Fuller's principles of legality

Metaphors, and allegories, are often the best way to convey complex ideas. They are often the most enjoyable too. And so Lon Fuller told a story about what law is, and what it is not, in a way so simple, so enjoyable, that it became a central way in which we understand these questions. The story, with a few tweaks to make it more current, goes more or less like this.[72]

King Rex is a well-meaning monarch who has just come to the throne. He thinks that, as the new boss, he should change the rules of his kingdom. All the rules. So he repeals the existing law, all of it, and sets out to create a new legal order from scratch.

As he does not really know where to start, he considers it to be a clever idea to deal with legal questions as they come to him. He appoints himself the only judge of the kingdom. He hopes to progressively work out a system of rules over time. The idea is to infer general rules and principles out of his decisions in individual cases. But there is a hitch. As his accession to the throne did not exactly follow a meritocratic procedure, he finds himself unable to think in terms of generalization: no one can discern any pattern in the judgments he renders. His efforts leave his subjects confused. He is profoundly embarrassed. He steps down from his judgeship and withdraws to the highest tower of his castle.

Alone in his room, he tries to recall his law studies and what was written in all of these codes he was supposed to read. Based on these vague memories, he drafts one code after the other, intent on covering all aspects of his subjects' behavior. But as he is about to post the codes on the monarchy's official website, he starts brooding over the fact that he had spent more time in the classroom on Facebook than actually listening to what was being said. Unable to discard the idea that there

---

[72] Fuller, *Morality*, 33–8. I like telling this story. For a different version, see Thomas Schultz, "King Rex II" (2012) 3 *Journal of International Dispute Settlement* 1.

might be a link between his classroom activities and the quality of his new codes, he decides to keep them confidential. He would still decide cases in application of the codes. But the codes themselves he would not show to his subjects. The idea is not well received: his subjects, an unruly lot, threaten to mount a WikiLeaks campaign against him if he does not open the books.

After some quick musings, King Rex comes up with an offer for his subjects. He would show, at the end of each year, the rules he has used to decide the cases during that past year. But these rules would not count for future cases. The objective is to mobilize the power of hindsight. A great idea to be sure. All the same, the subjects remain unimpressed.

King Rex throws in the towel at this stage: he uploads the codes he has drafted to his website, and makes them publicly available. But very soon it becomes clear that the king was right in being insecure about his legal abilities: he has drafted the codes in extraordinarily convoluted language. While that was meant to sound learned and sophisticated, its effect is that no one, not even the lawyers in his kingdom, can understand the codes.

Completely at a loss about how to write clearly, King Rex calls his former PhD supervisor to ask for help. The benevolent old man takes over the task with a warm smile, while muttering something to the effect that Rex might need an editor not for his codes but for his life. He then painstakingly redrafts the codes in an intelligible way.

But a new problem emerges: now that the texts are understandable, it appears that they are full of contradictions and conflicts. The codes cannot but fail to orient the behavior of the subjects. King Rex ends up on the front page of the tabloids.

Outraged, he drafts a new code. It is simple, straightforward, and free of contradictions. In his rage however, he makes it a crime to sleep, to be taller than him, to have opinions, and to take decisions. The former PhD supervisor, at his home far away, sighs again and sends him a brief email: "Were you not trying to make law? Why make rules, then, that no one can obey?" Rex, grumpy but lucid, repeals the corresponding provisions.

Then something unexpected happens: his subjects like the new code. They start to use it as guideposts for their actions. The king becomes so enthusiastic about his newfound legislative virtuosities that, like an unstoppable painter, he drafts a new code every day, each new code replacing the previous one. Alas, the subjects have no choice but to ignore, again, the successive codes altogether.

Rex eventually sees the problem. Constantly changing rules are inefficacious in channelling people's conduct, and thus in carrying out any of his plans over a long period of time. So much he understands. So he freezes the law as it stands on the day of the anniversary of his accession to the throne, and reassumes his judicial functions. Very soon, however, he grows unhappy about the rules he has written. He starts to render judgments that bear only a faint relationship to the rules as set out in his codes. At this juncture, it is Rex's own wife who points out to him that he is back to square one. She suggests he rather sticks to making and spending money. He complies, with much greater success.

The point of the story is to describe what Fuller called "eight ways to fail to make law."[73] We can indeed discern, in King Rex's eight successive attempts to create law, eight aspects of a normative system that characterize it as non-legal. In Fuller's words, the failures to make law are the following: (1) "every issue [is] decided on an ad hoc basis"; (2) "failure to publicize"; (3) "abuse of retroactive legislation"; (4) "failure to make rules understandable"; (5) "enactment of contradictory rules"; (6) enactment of rules that "require conduct beyond the powers of the affected party"; (7) "introducing such frequent changes in the rules that the subject cannot orient his action by them"; and (8) "a failure of congruence between the rules as announced and their actual administration."[74] These failures, Fuller explains, "do not simply result in a bad system of law; [they] result[] in something that is not properly called a legal system at all."[75]

Fuller's idea is that we see, in the flip side of the story, in the inverted mirror image of the eight failures, eight positive principles of legality. They are procedural principles that a system of rules must satisfy in order to perform law's essential function and thus to count as law.[76] And law's essential function, Fuller wrote, is to "subject[...] people's conduct to the guidance of general rules by which they may themselves orient their behaviour."[77] The eight failures are, then, eight ways how not to allow the addressees of rules to orient themselves according to them, by failing to provide them with "dependable guideposts for self-directed action."[78] That makes the rules system unworthy of the label of law, because it cannot "perform [the] central guiding role" of law.[79]

Now we can see, as Hart puts it, that Fuller's principles are a list of conditions for an efficacious attainment of this end of guiding behavior.[80] Or in Matthew Kramer's words, the realization of each of these principles in a normative system "contributes indispensably to the attainment of the desiderata that can be secured through the existence and flourishing of law."[81] Why? Because in a normative system where the failures just described occur, the addressees of the norms are "unable to form any confident expectations on the basis of which they can interact with one another,"[82] and "no one [has] an informed sense of what anyone else is required or permitted or empowered to do."[83] Put yet differently, the idea of these principles is that people are ruled by laws, and not by men and women.[84]

---

[73] Fuller, *Morality*, 33. [74] Fuller, *Morality*, 38–9. [75] Fuller, *Morality*, 39.
[76] Fuller, *Morality*, 38–9, 42–3.
[77] Lon L Fuller, "A Reply to Professors Cohen and Dworkin" (1965) 10 *Villanova Law Review* 655, 657.
[78] Fuller, *Morality*, 229. [79] Kramer, *Objectivity*, 118.
[80] H.L.A. Hart, "Lon L. Fuller: The Morality of Law" in: *Essays in Jurisprudence and Philosophy* (Clarendon Press 1983) 350–1, 357.
[81] Kramer, *Objectivity*, 100. Note that Matthew Kramer means the rule of law in this quote as a moral-political ideal, not as a jurisprudential concept, because law may also contribute indispensably to the attainment of the objectives of a wicked regime.
[82] Kramer, *Objectivity*, 112. [83] Kramer, *Objectivity*, 112.
[84] Matthew H Kramer, *In Defense of Legal Positivism: Law Without Trimmings* (Oxford University Press 2003) 51: law has a general end, "which involves the control of human conduct by rules, rather than simply the control of human conduct." See also Tamanaha, *Rule of Law*, 122–6: "there is a vast difference between instructing persons... to follow or apply a relevant body of rules to a situation,

Fuller also called these eight conditions the "inner morality of law." The word "morality" is not to be taken in any analytical sense. A norms system that fails to satisfy one or several of these conditions is not morally deficient, or morally inferior to a norms system that does satisfy all of these conditions. It simply fails to effectively orient the behavior of its addressees. It fails to provide predictable and reliable signposts for action. And thus it fails to attain the intrinsic purpose of law:[85] it fails as law. The phrase "inner morality of law" is a catchy slogan, but analytically the word "morality" is misleading: Fuller's account of law is a positivist one.[86]

To best see the flip from failures to make law to positive conditions of legality, we should attend to Matthew Kramer's masterful exposition of Fuller's principle of legality. And so the eight constitutive elements of legality are, in Matthew Kramer's terminology:[87]

P1: governance by general norms, that is the generality of expression and application of the rules that are part of the system;

P2: public ascertainability, or the public promulgation of the rules of the system;

P3: prospectivity, meaning the non-retroactivity of the rules of the systems;

P4: perspicuity, that is the formulation of the mandates provided by the legal system in lucid language;

P5: non-contradictoriness and non-conflictingness, in other words the normative coherence of legal system;

P6: compliability, that is the near absence of unsatisfiable behests;

P7: steadiness over time, which calls for "limits in the pace and scale of the transformations of the sundry norms in a legal system";[88]

P8: congruence between formulation and implementation, in other words that the publicly promulgated rules are actually applied and are applied impartially.

(If that is too impenetrable a language, here is how John Gardner summarized it: "General, open, prospective, clear, consistent, stable, capable of being obeyed, and upheld by officials. So must the laws of a legal system be, according to Lon Fuller, if the system is to live up to the ideal known as the rule of law."[89])

---

versus instructing them to do as they please or to do what they consider right without regard to rules. This large difference is appropriately captured by the contrast between rule of law and rule of men." See Antonin Scalia, *A Matter of Interpretation: Federal Courts and the Law* (Princeton University Press 1997) 17: "Government of laws—of texts written down, not men."

[85] On the idea that Fuller's precepts embody an end that is intrinsic to law, Kramer, *In Defense*, 50–1.
[86] Matthew H Kramer, "On the Moral Status of the Rule of Law" (2004) 63 *Cambridge Law Journal* 65.
[87] Kramer, *Objectivity*, 103–86.   [88] Kramer, *Objectivity*, 132.
[89] John Gardner, *Law as a Leap of Faith* (Oxford University Press 2012) 195.

As mentioned above, only seven of these eight principles will enter the following discussion. The one that will not be dealt with is compliability (P6). This principle, which more precisely prohibits the presence of too many mandates requiring the impossible from the system's addressees, is not strictly speaking a formal condition of legality, but a substantial one, as it relates to both the precise contents of the rules and the concrete abilities of their addressees.[90] The fulfillment of this condition does not depend on procedural qualities of a regulatory system and hence it has no direct bearing on the matter at issue here. It does not translate into a principle that fittingly forms part of the setup of a dispute resolution system.

Now, let us return to the central question this section focuses on: can arbitration regimes display these features? Can they meet these requirements? First of all, it must be made clear that these features are scalar properties: they can be achieved to varying degrees of perfection. Accordingly, they represent an ideal that should be pursued and against which the regulative quality of a normative system can be assessed.[91] Second, if we focus on the normative effects of arbitral awards, we may recognize that the inner morality of law can be achieved through individual decisions. As opposed to Fuller, who considered that these criteria could only be fulfilled through direct promulgation of the general rules to the addressees, Matthew Kramer convincingly argues that "the regulation of behavior through the laying down of norms and the setting of standards... does not necessarily involve making those norms and standards known to [the addressees] by means other than the patterns of official approval and disapproval that implement the norms and the standards."[92] In other words, there is no need, with respect to the inner morality of law, for a publicly accessible code of general rules. These essential features of law may be attained through patterns of rule application by the system's officials, as the addressees of the rules could then "infer the content of the rules by studying the patterns of the decisions which authoritatively settle disputes."[93] However, in order for this inference of the content of the rules to effectively take place, the patterns of decisions must display certain qualities, as we will see below.

Let us now apply the principles of the inner morality of law to examine arbitral regimes: in light of these principles, do they deserve the label of stateless law?

---

[90] I think I have to acknowledge the fact that John Gardner considers none of the Fullerian principles to be formal, because they all "'pass judgment' on the content of the law." Accordingly, he maintains that the inner morality of law is not a question of formality or a formal understanding of the rule of law. See Gardner, *Law as a Leap of Faith*, 198–9. The debate is a matter of what you call "formal." What I call "formal" here is what can validly be expressed with undefined variables: for instance, if I tell you today to do X yesterday, the command is a violation of P3 regardless of what you want to replace the variable X with. P6 does not work with undefined variables. At any rate, the label of "form" has no impact on the argument I want to make here; its elucidation can thus remain at the level of the current approximation and its territory limited to this footnote.

[91] Fuller, *Morality*, 41–4; Kramer, *Objectivity*, 105.   [92] Kramer, *In Defense*, 46.
[93] Kramer, *In Defense*, 46.

3.2 A rule of precedent

At least four of Fuller's principles are cognate in a first challenge to arbitral regimes as rules systems with a tenable claim to legality. This first challenge revolves around the question of the role of prior arbitration cases, or precedents.

Governance by general norms (P1), public ascertainability (P2), prospectivity (P3), and steadiness over time (P7) all are principles that are not straightforwardly fulfilled by an outcome-centered mode of regulation. If arbitral awards are to collectively satisfy these principles, one element in the procedural setup of arbitral systems becomes crucial: the precedential force of the awards. The following paragraphs propound these connections, starting with a terse presentation of the aspects of these principles that are at stake.

As we have seen, Fuller presented his principle of governance by general norms (P1) in negative terms, as he did for all his principles of legality. Recall: if "every issue [is] decided on an ad hoc basis," then this constitutes an unwanted property of a normative system that would prevent it from being of a legal nature, from amounting to law.[94] Matthew Kramer presents this requirement in more sophisticated and nuanced terms: "situation-specific directives [must not be] the ... principal means of regulating people's conduct."[95] The generality of application and the generality of address of a system's rules are necessary for every addressee to form a confident idea about what she and the other addressees are "required and permitted and empowered to do."[96] Law cannot provide "dependable guideposts for self-directed action"[97] in the absence of a predominance of general norms.[98] By contrast, a casuistic approach could easily become a "higgledy-piggledy arrangement" that would be "antithetical to the rule of law."[99]

A normative system not primarily composed of general rules would not be functional as law. It would not deserve the label of law, neither for jurisprudential purposes nor, I maintain, for the rhetorical and political purposes of claims for a laissez-faire policy on the part of states.

The principle of public ascertainability (P2) formed the object of a rather elliptical though accurate evocation by Fuller: "it [is] very unpleasant to have one's case decided by rules when there [is] no way of knowing what those rules [are]."[100] Law, he contended, must be promulgated in order to count as law. Here again, Matthew Kramer clarifies the point: "a regime of law has to render its mandates and other norms ascertainable by the people to whose conduct they apply."[101] A rules system whose mandates and other norms are not ascertainable by their addressees, in other words when the addressees are kept in the dark about what the norms command, then the existence of the normative system would "make no difference to anyone's reasoning about appropriate courses of conduct."[102] It would be "thoroughly inefficacious in channelling people's behaviour."[103] It would fail as law.

---

[94] Fuller, *Morality*, 38.   [95] Kramer, *Objectivity*, 110.   [96] Kramer, *Objectivity*, 112.
[97] Fuller, *Morality*, 229.   [98] Hart, "Lon L. Fuller," 350–1, 357.
[99] Kramer, *Objectivity*, 111.   [100] Fuller, *Morality*, 35.   [101] Kramer, *Objectivity*, 113.
[102] Kramer, *Objectivity*, 113.   [103] Kramer, *Objectivity*, 113.

The purpose of this requirement matches the rationale of the principle of governance by general norms: allowing the addressees to appraise themselves of the "general norms under which the legal consequences of their conduct are assessed."[104] The addressees of norms must be allowed to enter dependable guideposts into their practical reasoning. Again, the consequences of a failure to meet this requirement is identical to any other failure of the Fullerian principles of legality: a rules system whose norms are not typically ascertainable by their addressees ought not to be considered law, neither for jurisprudential purposes nor for reasoning that partakes of the School of Dijon.

The principle of prospectivity (P3) requires that an overwhelming proportion of rules in a system are not retrospective, but prospective. The norms have to be created before the events occur to which they pertain. It is indeed a "brutal absurdity [to] command[] a man today to do something yesterday."[105] It is important to point out, however, that a total absence of retroactive norms is neither required nor possible. There will always be indeterminacies in a normative system. There will always be cases for which there are no determinately correct answers to be found in the body of the rules existing at the time of occurrence of the events.[106] At the other extreme, a normative system composed only of retrospective norms is, as Kramer puts it, "forbiddingly incoherent,"[107] and is not a legal system. In between, however, the exact threshold remains undefinable above which a normative system no longer qualifies as a legal system because of its overabundance of retrospective laws.

Echoing the raison d'être of the principles discussed earlier, the need for a rules system to be based on a great majority of prospective commands in order to be legal is that this is necessary to "impinge in any significant fashion on the choices and behaviour of the people who are subject to its sway."[108]

The principle of steadiness over time (P7) requires "limits on the pace and scale of the transformations of the sundry norms" that pertain to a system of rules.[109] These speed limits must be set so as to avoid "such frequent changes in the rules that the subject cannot orient his action by them."[110] This principle is based on the recognition that the creation of effective guideposts for self-directed action requires a degree of internalization on the part of the addressees.[111] The absorption of a rule into one's practical reasoning is barely possible if the rule merely befuddles its addressees as an ephemeral and "unreliable transitory" event in the normative landscape.[112] It seems unnecessary to provide evidence, for instance evidence

---

[104] Kramer, *Objectivity*, 114.   [105] Fuller, *Morality*, 59.
[106] Kramer, *Objectivity*, 119–20; Fuller, *Morality*, 53–4, 56–7.
[107] Kramer, *Objectivity*, 118.   [108] Kramer, *Objectivity*, 118.
[109] Kramer, *Objectivity*, 132.   [110] Fuller, *Morality*, 39.
[111] See for instance François Ost and Michel van de Kerchove, *De la pyramide au réseau? Pour une théorie dialectique du droit* (Publication des Facultés universitaires Saint-Louis 2002) 334–5 (referring to the *vis directiva* of canon law); Pierre Bourdieu, "Les rites comme actes d'institution" (1982) 43 *Actes de recherche en sciences sociales* 59 and Max Weber, *Wirtschaft und Gesellschaft: Grundriß der Verstehenden Soziologie* (first published 1922, Mohr Siebeck 1980) in Part II, Chapter VI §1 (on his concept of *Einverständnishandeln*).
[112] Kramer, *Objectivity*, 171.

taken from the field of psychology, to make that point credible enough to be considered valid.

The slowness required by the principle of steadiness over time does obviously never amount to full normative stagnancy over long periods of time (and thus obsolescence). It merely alerts us to the indispensable character of "a balance between constancy and adaptability," the "forging of a *via media* between destructive dislocation and preposterous ossification."[113] As is the case with the other Fullerian principles we have discussed heretofore, the purpose of the principle of steadiness is to enable the realization of law's chief function: to forge its addressees' actions "*qua* responses to the [rules system] rather than *qua* patterns of conduct that occur independently of the [rules system]."[114]

The requirements mandated by the principles adumbrated in the preceding paragraphs (governance by general norms (P1), public ascertainability (P2), prospectivity (P3), and steadiness over time (P7)) may make arbitral regimes stumble as legal systems. To understand why, the elucidation of a central feature of arbitral regimes is needed—a feature that has been assumed for most of the argument so far as an implicit postulate and as a definitional element of our object of study. The feature in question relates to the embodiment of rule expression and creation in such normative systems: it is assumed that arbitral awards constitute the primary normative source of arbitral regimes.

We can elide, without damages, the exact extent of the dominance of arbitral awards as a source of normativity in sundry arbitral regimes. I seek on purpose to proceed at a relatively high degree of abstraction. The idea is to make a generalization of arbitration to see appropriate theoretical frameworks for reflections. Generalizations do not have to be perfect to make a point. So in order to keep the argument manageable, I will radicalize the assumption that arbitral awards constitute the primary normative source of arbitral regimes. For the rest, consider that the applicability of the argument in practice obtains by degrees: the greater the normative strength of arbitral awards compared to other norms of each regime, the fuller the argument applies. In other words, the issues propounded in the following paragraphs also arise in arbitral regimes marked by more variegated and balanced normative sources, though simply less dramatically. Investigations into the intricacies and idiosyncrasies of normativity in specific arbitral regimes can be found elsewhere.[115]

So if we start from the postulate that arbitral regimes are, to a significant extent, normatively based on arbitral awards, the following issues arise with regard to the aforementioned Fullerian principles.

First, arbitral awards are in and of themselves individualized. Hence, a regulatory regime built on arbitral awards is exposed to the risk of being marked by

---

[113] Kramer, *Objectivity*, 170. [114] Kramer, *Objectivity*, 171.
[115] On investment arbitration, see for instance Florian Grisel, "Sources of Investment Law" in Zachary Douglas, Joost Pauwelyn and Jorge Viñuales (eds), *The Conceptual Foundations of International Investment Law: Bridging Theory into Practice* (Oxford University Press 2014, forthcoming). On commercial arbitration, see for instance Thomas Schultz, "Some Critical Comments on the Juridicity of the Lex Mercatoria" (2008) 10 *Yearbook of Private International Law* 667.

sweeping ad-hocness (P1), just as any other outcome-centered mode of normative production.

Second, every dispute-resolving decision is a mandate that is unascertainable (in advance) per se (P2). Thus, such a normative regime based on individualized decisions may be largely otiose as a *regulatory* order. The parties, and a fortiori the other addressees of such a regime, would perforce be left in the dark with regard to the norms that will be crafted or expressed by the awards.

Third, an inherent feature of outcomes of dispute resolution procedures is to be retrospective. Every decision rendered in a dispute resolution procedure is in fact an individualized norm commanding today to do something yesterday: it is a norm created at a time *t* but applying to a situation that occurred at a time *t-1* (P3). Such norms do not comport with the principle of prospectivity if they do not, en masse, overlap with thitherto existing norms that made the decisions predictable (remember that predictability obtains by degrees) and thus allowed the addressees to orient their behavior according to the norms existing at *t-1* and the projected norm of *t*.

Fourth, in a rules system composed preponderantly of scattered and inordinate individualized decisions, no *intrinsic* feature coordinates the decisions on a temporal dimension, and guarantees of normative constancy through time will therefore have fallen to the wayside (P7). Bewilderingly rapid changes over time do not necessarily ensue, but it is a greater possibility in outcome-centered regimes than in codified rule systems.

To recap: arbitral awards are individualized, unascertainable in advance, and retrospective directives that, by their *hic et nunc* nature, are hardly compatible with a requirement involving a temporal dimension. A regime built on arbitral awards would a priori seem to amount to governance by men and women (the arbitrators) and not by laws, thereby failing to constitute an instance of rule of law.

However, a set of individualized mandates does not perforce fail to achieve generality in address and application (P1), public ascertainability (P2), prospectivity (P3), and steadiness over time (P7). Here is how Matthew Kramer explains it: "Conflict-terminating judgments, as opposed to promulgation, can be the chief vehicle for the expression of legal requirements. So long as officials are provided with a matrix of norms that enable them to impose regularity and order on their society by resolving disputes methodically, and so long as they adhere quite firmly to those operative norms when gauging the merits of people's claims, their regime can aptly be classified as a regime of law."[116] This matrix of norms, he continues, must consist of "norms that transcend the respective contexts of... case-by-case proceedings."[117]

In other words, a system whose main vehicle for normative expression consists of individualized decisions may appropriately count as a legal system if its addressees are able to infer general and foreseeable rules from the decisions. Such rules are, then, applicable to other cases and are thus prospective. The possibility to infer

---

[116] Kramer, *In Defense*, 46.   [117] Kramer, *Objectivity*, 111.

general rules from decisions would also reduce the system's propensity to normative changingness.

The point is this: a normative regime based on arbitral awards, in order to count as law, must have certain mechanisms that ensure that the addressees can generalize the normative bearings of an award. These mechanisms enable the subjects to effectively grasp norms that transcend each individual case. They allow the subjects to apprise themselves of the rules under which the consequences of their present and future actions will be assessed. Thus are cognate situations made normatively relatable to one another, across cases and over time.

What, then, is a mechanism that relates the normative treatment of cognate situations to one another, hence turning decision-making into the setting of general, ascertainable, prospective rules that are unlikely to change chaotically? When we put the question like that, the answer is fairly obvious: a rule of precedent.

A brief recap is necessary at this juncture. True, normative orders based mainly on individualized directives made in dispute resolution procedures can be compatible with the Fullerian principles of governance by general norms (P1), public ascertainability (P2), prospectivity (P3) and steadiness over time (P7). This requires, as a necessary but not sufficient element, that the dispute resolution system includes a certain safeguard in its procedural setup, namely a rule of precedent. A rule of precedent creates patterns of interpretive practice. As Kramer puts it, "insofar as the officials' judgments and their rationales would have precedential force, those judgments and rationales themselves would constitute directly ascertainable legal norms."[118] Kramer focuses on public ascertainability but the other three Fullerian principles would equally be possibly satisfied.

The absence of a rule of precedent, combined with the absence or limited importance of other authoritative vehicles for the expression of the rules, makes it difficult to infer the norms' contents from their applications. What matters is that all decisions be expositions of the same contents of the law, that one decision does not suggest that the law is X while another implies that it is Y. If decision-makers do not follow prior cases, the risk that there be variations among the decisions is significant. Kramer explains the problem: "Because gaining knowledge of the contents of those norms is a far more difficult task when one's access to them is indirect rather than direct, the epistemically disruptive effects of any transformations of the norms will be greatly accentuated."[119] If the application of rules to the resolution of individual disputes is the only or main authoritative expression of the rules, then the slightest variation in these applications would be likely to frustrate efforts in inferring rules from their applications.

Let us briefly take one further step back and consider the question of precedents from a broader angle. In one of their books on the philosophical relationships between time and law, François Ost and Mark van Hoecke, who are rightfully metaphor enthusiasts in explaining legal questions, put the idea this way: giving decisions precedential force ensures that the regime is not "deprived of its 'memory'

[118] Kramer, *Objectivity*, 114.   [119] Kramer, *Objectivity*, 114–15.

and its 'planning'."[120] Carrie Menkel-Meadow, for her part, points to the anthropologically normal character of following precedents and assuming that precedents will be followed: it seems to be part of human nature that a decision in a case becomes a guidepost for future cases that are closely similar.[121]

One point is important to understand: for our purposes, it is nearly meaningless what form exactly the rule of precedent takes. It makes no difference whether the rule of precedent is an instance of stare decisis or of *jurisprudence constante* (with apologies for the horror to procedural lawyers). And it makes no difference either whether the precedential force of awards is best labelled as "juridical" (as in "de jure rule of precedent" or "de jure stare decisis," in other words when a formal doctrine of stare decisis is espoused) or as "factual" (as in "de facto rule of precedent" or "de facto stare decisis," in other words when not following a relevant precedent amounts to a failure of interpretative proficiency, since it sways from the rightfully anticipated interpretation, but does not formally give rise to a legally flawed decision). Such distinctions would merely muddle the argument by bringing it into the wrong intellectual terrain.[122]

Are arbitral awards, then, followed as precedents in practice? Does the way arbitrators decide cases make a difference to anyone's reasoning about appropriate rules of conduct? Or is the "law" rather "newly minted by the arbitrator on each occasion, with every [case] subject of its own individual proper law"?[123] Various studies have converged in their findings: the practice of following arbitral precedents is almost inexistent in the field of international commercial arbitration (including when the non-state lex mercatoria is applied), commonplace and increasingly frequent in investment arbitration (investment arbitrators do it "with rather excessive zeal," as Gilbert Guillaume, former President of the International Court of Justice, puts it[124]), and routine in sports arbitration.[125]

From the point of view of legality, or the rule of law, it is thus insufficient for decisions in dispute resolution procedures to be simply tailored to the case at hand with disregard for cognate cases, past or future. Do not misunderstand me: I do not mean to say that this is necessarily a bad thing. The freedom of the arbitrators with

---

[120] François Ost and Mark van Hoecke (eds), *Time and Law* (Bruylant 1998) on fourth cover.

[121] Carrie Menkel-Meadow, "Whose Dispute Is It Anyway?: A Philosophical and Democratic Defence of Settlement (in Some Cases)" (1995) 83 *Georgetown Law Journal* 2663, 2681.

[122] For an apposite study of some of these principles in action, see for instance Raj Bhala, "The Myth About Stare Decisis and International Trade Law (Part One of a Trilogy)" (1999) 14 *American University International Law Review* 845, 940–42.

[123] Mustill, "The New Lex Mercatoria," 94.

[124] Gilbert Guillaume, "The Use of Precedent by International Judges and Arbitrators" (2011) 2 *Journal of International Dispute Settlement* 5, 15.

[125] Guillaume, "The Use of Precedent," 15; also Jan Paulsson, "The Role of Precedent in Investment Arbitration" in Katia Yannaca-Small (ed), *Arbitration under International Investment Agreements* (Oxford University Press 2010); Christopher Seppëla, "The Development of Case Law in Construction Disputes Relating to FIDIC Contracts" in Emmanuel Gaillard and Yas Banifatemi (eds), *Precedent in Investment Arbitration* (Juris 2008); Christoph Schreuer and Matthew Weiniger, "Conversation Across Cases—Is There a Doctrine of Precedent in Investment Arbitration?" in Christoph Schreuer, Federico Ortino and Peter Muchlinksi (eds), *Oxford Handbook of International Investment Law* (Oxford University Press 2008); Jeffrey Commission, "Precedent in Investment Treaty Arbitration—A Citation Analysis of a Developing Jurisprudence" (2007) 24 *Journal of International Arbitration* 129.

regard to how they decide each case, and their quest for individually tailored solutions, may well be considered more beneficial than a stateless incarnation of the rule of law for international commerce. Tailoring applicable norms to the needs of the parties is often a sound way to resolve a dispute. But then we should not call it law. We should not call it a commercial transnational legal order.[126] As a mode of governance, it characterizes pre-legal communities. Per se such decisions do not collectively form a legal system.

3.3 Publication of arbitral awards

The Fullerian principle of public ascertainability (P2) has further, more obvious, procedural import: it requires a frequent and publicly accessible publication of arbitral awards. Two clarifications are in order.

First, recall that the principle calls for *public* ascertainability. It is a necessary but not sufficient condition that the *officials* of a rules systems—arbitrators for instance—are able to apprise themselves of the applicable norms. They certainly must be able to have access to what we called above, in the excerpt from Kramer, the "matrix of norms that enable[s] them to impose regularity and order [and to] resolv[e] disputes methodically."[127] But in addition to the decision-makers, it is the addressees of the arbitral regimes in question who must be easily able to acquaint themselves with the rules that the decisions reveal or create by having precedential force. Otherwise, if we think back to the rationale of this principle as it was sketched above, "those putative laws would not figure in anyone's reasoning about [his or her] appropriate courses of conduct."[128]

Consider, somewhat in passing: it is not unheard of in the community of international commercial arbitration, in those rare cases in which the precedential force of a prior award is invoked, that arbitrators refer to an arbitral precedent that almost no one has access to, including the vast majority of legal scholars. In such cases, reference is made to prior awards that cannot possibly orient the behavior of any subject. The reference to their precedential force is a simulacrum.

Second, I want to emphasize that the ease and practicality of public ascertainment is a requirement that must be satisfied to quite a substantial degree. The reason for it is that the general norms in an outcome-centered rules system are only indirectly discernable.[129] And indirect ascertainment is comparatively more prone to go astray. The required cognitive efforts, and the corresponding hazards, are substantial when seeking to infer clearly intelligible normative patterns from individual outcomes (decisions revealing norms) and when generalizing the normative contents of a decision (decisions creating norms). They are more substantial

---

[126] Mustill, "The New Lex Mercatoria," 116–17: "the purpose of a commercial legal order is to regulate transactions, not awards or judgments. What [the subject] requires is a legal framework, sufficient to inform him before any dispute has arisen what he can or must do next. If a dispute does arise he needs to be told whether he can insist or must yield, and how much room he has for maneuver."

[127] Kramer, *In Defense*, 46.   [128] Kramer, *Objectivity*, 111.

[129] Kramer, *Objectivity*, 111.

than the complications associated with the understanding, for purposes of self-direction, of authoritative written formulations in general terms. Hence, indirect ascertainment calls for particularly effective means for the addressees to apprise themselves of the decisions. Put simply, awards must be published in particularly accessible places. As international lawyers Christine Gray and Benedict Kingsbury put it, "[u]npublished awards have virtually no law-making effect; also those not easily accessible or not reported in full will have little impact."[130] Simple enough.

Public ascertainment may satisfactorily take the route of intermediate expositions through legal experts. In any modern national legal system, legal experts are "the vehicle through which the complicated norms of [a legal system] can become familiar to citizens and can thus become live factors in the citizens' practical reasoning."[131] Similarly, it is sufficient if only arbitration specialists are able to discern the rules that pertain to the arbitral regime in question. Hence, case commentaries in academic journals would in principle fulfill the publication requirement.

Not every award must be published of course. The proportion of published awards must simply be, in Kramer's words, sufficiently "plentiful and regularized to create clearly intelligible patterns"[132] from which a subject is "able to infer the content of the rules."[133] For if they are "few and far between," he continues, "they will not be adequately reliable and informative as conduits that provide indirect access to the norms that lie behind them."[134]

A cursory survey of arbitral practice reveals the following situation with regard to the publication of awards. In commercial arbitration, the proportion of published awards is very low. As Lord Mustill puts it, "the reported awards do not in all cases seem to sustain the wealth of commentary based upon them."[135] In investment arbitration, awards made under the rules of ICSID (about 60% of all investment arbitrations) are very often published, but a large number of other decisions, such as UNCITRAL ad hoc investment awards (about 30% of all investment arbitrations) remain in principle unpublished.[136] In sports arbitration, the awards of the Court of Arbitration for Sports (the highest instance in the worldwide pyramidal organization of dispute resolution in sports) are published, but the publication had for a long time been made in such fashion that even most academic lawyers had great difficulty in having access to the awards.[137]

---

[130] Christine Gray and Benedict Kingsbury, "Developments in Dispute Settlement: Inter-State Arbitration Since 1945" (1992) 63 *British Year Book of International Law* 97, 122.

[131] Kramer, *Objectivity*, 117.

[132] Kramer, *Objectivity*, 113–15. See also, more specifically in the context of arbitration, Philippe Fouchard, *L'arbitrage commercial international* (Dalloz 1965) 435, writing on "l'objet essentiel du droit, la prévisibilité."

[133] Kramer, *In Defense*, 46   [134] Kramer, *Objectivity*, 114.

[135] Mustill, "The New Lex Mercatoria," 114.

[136] On these percentages, see Thomas Schultz and Cédric Dupont, "Investment Arbitration: Promoting the Rule of Law or Over-Empowering Investors?," paper presented for ISA Annual Convention, San Francisco 3–6 April 2013.

[137] See for instance Antonio Rigozzi, *L'arbitrage international en matière de sport* (Helbing & Lichtenhahn 2005) 641.

From a jurisprudential perspective, it is squarely unmistakable that a normative regime whose dominant source of rules is constituted by individualized decisions that are largely kept confidential cannot count as a legal regime.

3.4 Reasoned decisions

Let us now shift our attention to another Fullerian principle of legality that can conveniently be used to gauge the legitimacy of the aspirations to legality of outcome-based normative orders: the principle of perspicuity (P4).

The idea of the principle is simply this, in Fuller's words: "How can anybody follow a rule that nobody can understand?"[138] Kramer puts it in a more analytical way: "Unless the mandates and other norms of a legal system are formulated in reasonably lucid language, the system will largely or completely fail to perform the basic function of law as a means of channelling people's behaviour along certain paths and away from other paths."[139]

The rules produced by an adjudicative system, in order for the system to count as law, must not only be susceptible of generalization, be ascertainable by their addressees, pertain to situations subsequent to their creation and be stable through time. They must also be understandable. With regard to the production of norms by dispute resolution mechanism, this requires that the reasoning of the decisions is supplied to the addressees.

Unreasoned decisions in individual situations may meet the principles of generality (P1) and public ascertainability (P2), provided they treat like situations alike and are publicly accessible. After a significant number of decisions have been handed down, a general rule is likely to become inferable from this patterned expression of a norm. In addition, such an inferred rule would apply prospectively (P3), provided similar situations continue to be treated similarly. The principle of steadiness over time (P7) may also be satisfied by unreasoned decisions, in the same circumstances.

But the principle of perspicuity (P4) cannot be fulfilled under such conditions: unreasoned decisions, or decisions accompanied by very succinct reasons do not form part of an informative exposition of a rule. Again, general rules may be inferable from such decisions, but they will be marked by great vagueness. Great vagueness does not stymie the rule's cardinal features of generality (P1), ascertainability by the addressees (P2), prospectivity (P3) and constancy through time (P7). But it is a credible possibility that it would stretch the rule's zones of penumbra, and shrink its hard core of standard cases, to a point where its imprecision barely permits any deductive reasoning. The rule, then, would in effect have a near-absence of meaning. To make it possible for anyone to infer from individual decisions a rule that has a perspicuous meaning (P4), the decisions forming the premises of such a *modus ponens* must be supplemented with sufficiently detailed reasons.

---

[138] Fuller, *Morality*, 36.   [139] Kramer, *Objectivity*, 120.

Even a cursory glimpse at arbitral practice reveals that unreasoned awards, or awards with only extremely succinct reasons, are no extraordinary occurrence. In international commercial arbitration, even those who have every reason to extol arbitration write that "the requirement of a reasoned award is particularly controversial."[140] A reasoned award is in fact required under most, though not all, national arbitration laws. And the requirement often does not apply if the parties agree to dispense the tribunal with it. It may seem surprising to people outside the field of arbitration that anyone would do such a thing, but it is in fact not too seldom an occurrence. The point is that the absence of reasons reduces the loser's ammunition to challenge the award. That increases the finality of the arbitration, which is often a central concern for the parties.[141] When reasons are required, they may be quite succinct, typically more concise than what is usually required from courts.[142] In investment arbitration, reasons are in principle both required and supplied with a great level of detail.[143]

3.5 Sundry devices to lessen conflicts and contradictions

Let us now consider the prohibition of conflicts and contradictions (P5). The principle expresses the want of one of the constitutive elements of legality that the positivist tradition in law most emphatically insists on: "the property of logical tidiness."[144]

A normative system plagued with inconsistent or incompatible rules provides at best muddled guidance. This is so whether such normative inconsistencies and incompatibilities are, analytically, conflicts (coexistent obligations to do X and –X) or contradictions (an obligation to do X contemporaneous with a liberty not to do X).[145] Pro tanto, such a normative system does not meet the regulative standards of the rule of law.

In a normative system primarily based on regulation through individual instances of adjudication, the principle of non-contradictoriness and non-conflictingness requires some procedural mechanism that prevents different arbitral

---

[140] Jean-François Poudret and Sébastien Besson, *Comparative Law of International Arbitration* (2nd edn, Sweet&Maxwell 2007) 901, see also 666–73.

[141] William W Park, "Finality and Fairness in Tax Arbitration" (1994) 11 *Journal of International Arbitration* 19, 24.

[142] Pierre Lalive, "On the Reasoning of International Arbitral Awards" (2010) 1 *Journal of International Dispute Settlement* 55; Thomas Bingham, "Reasons and Reasons and Reasons: Differences Between a Court Judgment and an Arbitral Award" (1988) 4 *Arbitration International* 1; Peter Gilles and Niloufer Selvadurai, "Reasoned Awards: How Extensive Must the Reasons be?" (2008) 7 *Arbitration* 125, 128ff.

[143] Article 48(3) of the ICSID Convention reads: "The award shall deal with every question submitted to the Tribunal, and shall state the reasons upon which it is based." Article 34(3) UNCITRAL Arbitration Rules 2010 reads: "The arbitral tribunal shall state the reasons upon which the award is based, unless the parties have agreed that no reasons are to be given."

[144] Kramer, *Objectivity*, 120. On the positivist tradition's insistence on this property, see for instance Hart, "Positivism and Separation," 602, 608–10.

[145] Matthew H Kramer, "Getting Rights Right" in Matthew H Kramer (ed), *Rights, Wrongs, and Responsibilities* (Palgrave Macmillan 2001) 73–4.

tribunals within the same arbitral regime from creating incompatible rules (in the sense of contradictory or conflicting). Let me qualify this assertion, in two ways.

First, consider time. The temporal dimension of the issue is primarily one of contemporaneousness. We are dealing primarily here with a matter of concurrent exercises of jurisdiction. If we take the question from a perspective integrated over time and consider incompatible rules created by arbitral tribunals at clearly distinct times, we would find ourselves in one of the two following situations.

Either awards have no precedential force and thus no general rules are created. In this case, the only required mechanism to avoid conflicts and contradictions between perforce individualized commands is the principle of res judicata, which is not really a problem in the field of arbitration.[146]

Or awards have some precedential force and the later decision must follow the precedent, meaning that the required procedural guarantee for the principle of non-contradictoriness and non-conflictingness is meant to be the rule of precedent itself: it must be strong enough to prevent the development of lines of cases that run in parallel. If that fails, the principal procedural device that helps is an appeals mechanism. I will return to that at the end of this sub-section.

We must also discern the hypothesis in which the precedent is distinguishable. This would imply that a new rule is needed that could not straightforwardly contradict or conflict with the prior existing rule. Of course, there is a logical possibility that it nevertheless does contradict or conflict with it. However, occasionally unfollowed precedents that are on point and occasional contradictions and conflicts do not jeopardize the rule of law. The Fullerian principles only have to be fulfilled up to a certain threshold. There is no requirement of perfect fulfillment of the principles of legality.[147]

More multifaceted, as I suggested at the outset, is the issue of commands and other norms created by contemporaneous decisions.

Here I need to enter the second qualification. We may distinguish two types of incompatible obligations and liberties. On the one hand, consider incompatible obligations, respectively liberties, for specific parties. On the other hand, consider the incompatible obligations, respectively liberties, for the addressees at large of the relevant arbitral regime.

The former—creating incompatible obligations or liberties for specific parties—call for the avoidance of concurrent assertions of jurisdiction by different tribunals, either over the same dispute, or over different but related disputes whose resolution has legal consequences for some of the same parties. (Typical examples would for instance be discrete claims brought against a company and its shareholders, or the main debtor and the guarantor.)

---

[146] See for instance Article III of the New York Convention on the Recognition and Enforcement of Foreign Arbitral Awards. See also Bernard Hanotiau, "L'autorité de la chose jugée des sentences arbitrales" (2003) Special Supplement to the *ICC Bulletin* 45.

[147] Kramer, *Objectivity*, 105–6.

In national legal systems, the mechanisms usually used to deal with such issues are the procedural principles of lis pendens and derived jurisdiction (which bundles or consolidates procedures on the basis of a *ratio connexitatis*).[148]

Arbitral tribunals tend to apply with very limited enthusiasm the principle of lis pendens to conflicts of jurisdiction between arbitral tribunals.[149] The consolidation of discrete but related arbitration procedures is problematic, and remains exceptional, because it typically requires the consent of the parties. This they are tempted not to give for reasons of confidentiality and due process (equal participation in the formation of a tribunal).[150]

In some rare cases, arbitration institutions have also relied on another strategy to avoid inconsistent results: the alignment of tribunals. The idea no longer is to prevent concurrent assertions of jurisdiction, but to pragmatically increase the chances that the different tribunals produce compatible awards. The idea is to appoint the same arbitrators to different arbitral tribunals for related cases. This solution, however, remains exceptional and raises concerns of due process, as a tribunal may rely on information acquired in one case for its resolution of another.[151]

The latter—creating incompatible obligations or liberties for the addressees at large of an arbitral regime—calls for the avoidance of a concurrent creation of incompatible general rules by different contemporaneous decisions that have precedential force. This would lead, to use fashionable terminology, to fragment the normative voice of the regime.

In national legal systems, the main mechanism to deal with such risks is appeal procedures, which serve to reduce the time during which incompatible court-made rules subsist. An appeal system does not currently exist in arbitration, but its desirability has recurrently given rise to debates.[152] Brutally simplified, the arguments of the two most interesting sides in the debate are the following. If you are in favor

---

[148] See for instance Article 8(1) of the Brussels I Regulation Recast (European Parliament and Council Regulation (EU) 1215/2012 of 12 December 2012 on jurisdiction and the recognition and enforcement of judgments in civil and commercial matters (recast) [2012] OJ L351/1): "A person domiciled in a Member State may also be sued (1) where he is one of a number of defendants, in the courts for the place where any one of them is domiciled, provided the claims are so closely connected that it is expedient to hear and determine them together to avoid the risk of irreconcilable judgments resulting from separate proceedings." Article 28(3) of the same regulation similarly provides: "For the purposes of this Article, actions are deemed to be related where they are so closely connected that it is expedient to hear and determine them together to avoid the risk of irreconcilable judgments resulting from separate proceedings." In the *Tatry Ship* case (*The Tatry v. Maciej Rataj*, Case C-406/92, Judgment of 12 December 1994, §§54, 57), the CJEU held that the objective of the equivalent provision in the Lugano Convention is "to avoid conflicting and contradictory decisions."

[149] See for instance Campbell McLachlan, *Lis Pendens in International Litigation* (Martinus Nijhoff 2009) 189ff; Frank Spoorenberg and Jorge Viñuales, "Conflicting Decisions in International Arbitration" (2009) 8 *The Law & Practice of International Courts and Tribunals* 91, 98.

[150] See for instance Hanno Wehland, *The Coordination of Multiple Proceedings in Investment Treaty Arbitration* (Oxford University Press 2013).

[151] VV Veeder, "Report on England" in J Paulsson (ed), *International Handbook on Commercial Arbitration*, supp. 23 1997, fn 34.

[152] See for example Donald McRae, "The WTO Appellate Body: A Model for an ICSID Appeals Facility?" (2010) 1 *Journal of International Dispute Settlement* 375; D Brian King, "Consistency of Awards in Cases of Parallel Proceedings Concerning Related Subject-Matters" in Emmanuel Gaillard (ed), *Towards a Uniform International Arbitration Law* (Juris 2005).

of arbitration promoting the rule of law, you would tend to support an appeals mechanism. If you believe arbitration should provide another type of services than providing law, then you would tend to think that an appeals mechanism merely stands in the way of an efficient removal of the dispute from the table.

3.6 Settlements: nothing too much

The last of Fuller's principles to be considered, congruence between formulation and implementation P8), actually contributes to identifying arbitral regimes both as legal systems and as arbitral regimes.

Generally speaking, the principle requires a cognitively reliable effectuation of the norms of the system. The effectuation must achieve a correspondence in normative contents between the publicly ascertainable general norms and the administered individual decisions.[153]

Rule of law scholarship typically accents cognitive reliability. In this context, cognitive reliability is understood as the interpretation and application of the rules according to the expectations of a dispassionate observer who has been apprised of publicly ascertainable general norms and the rules of interpretation prevailing in the system.[154] Cognitive reliability, then, requires from the legal system's officials the virtues of impartiality and proficiency in interpretative construal of the norms.[155]

Applied more specifically to questions pertaining to the procedural setup of dispute resolution regimes, the principle of congruence between formulation and implementation may displace the core of the issue to effectuation tout court. The principle of congruence in such an analytical setting sets a limit to the recourse that can be made to conciliatory or settlement techniques.

The reasoning is the following: impartial and competent adjudication is cognitively reliable, while conciliation is by its very nature devoid of guarantees that the authoritatively applicable norms are applied at all to determine the outcome of a case. This is actually one of the grounds that fuelled the anti-ADR movement. Notice how the use of conciliatory dispute resolution mechanisms is at odds with the rule of law: used too massively, it incapacitates all other guarantees that partake of the rule of law, because of the non-application of "official law."[156]

There seems to be no reliable far-reaching empirical study on the rise or fall of practicing conciliation within arbitral procedures. We seem to be safe, however, in assuming that the arbitral process, taken as a generality, has not been denatured into a dominantly conciliatory process. A dominance of non-adjudicative dispute settlement nevertheless remains a theoretical possibility, and a reality in other dispute resolution contexts. It may in any event be analytically discerned and thus contributes to erecting guideposts for the assessment of dispute resolution systems against the regulatory standards of the rule of law.

---

[153] Kramer, *Objectivity*, 134ff.   [154] Kramer, *Objectivity*, 139.
[155] Kramer, *Objectivity*, 134–5.
[156] Owen Fiss, "Against Settlement" (1984) 93 *Yale Law Journal* 1073; Owen Fiss, "The History of an Idea" (2009) 78 *Fordham Law Review* 1273, 1277. See also Thomas Schultz, "The Three Pursuits of Dispute Settlement" (2011) 1 *Czech & Central European Yearbook of Arbitration* 227.

References

Abernethy, Steve "Building Large-Scale Online Dispute Resolution and Trustmark Systems" in Proceedings of the UNECE Forum on ODR 2003, <http://www.odr.info/unece2003>
Abi-Saab, Georges "Cours général de droit international public" (1987) 207 *Hague Lectures* 1
Akehurst, Michael "Jurisdiction in International Law" (1974) 46 *British Year Book of International Law* 145
Allan, Trevor RS *Law, Liberty, and Justice* (Oxford: Clarendon Press 1993)
Allott, Philip "Self-Determination—Absolute Right or Social Poetry?" in Christian Tomuschat (ed), *Modern Law of Self-Determination* (Leiden: Martinus Nijhoff 1993)
Andenas, Mads and Fairgrieve, Duncan "Finding a Common Language for Open Legal Systems" in Guy Canivet, Mads Andenas, and Duncan Fairgrieve (eds), *Comparative Law Before the Courts* (London: British Institute of International and Comparative Law 2004)
Anderson, Benedict *Imagined Communities: Reflections on the Origin and Spread of Nationalism* (first published 1983, London: Verso 2006)
Arendt, Hannah *The Origins of Totalitarianism* (New York: Harcourt, Brace and Co 1951)
d'Aspremont, Jean "Softness in International Law: A Self-Serving Quest for New Legal Materials" (2008) 19 *European Journal of International Law* 1075
Auerbach, Jerold S *Justice Without Law?* (New York: Oxford University Press 1983)
Austin, John *The Province of Jurisprudence Determined and the Uses of the Study of Jurisprudence* (first published 1832, London: Weidenfeld & Nicolson 1954)
von Bar, Christian and Mankowski, Peter *Internationales Privatrecht* (2nd edn, Munich: Beck 2003)
Baron, David P "Private Ordering on the Internet: The eBay Community of Traders" (2002) 4 *Business and Politics* 245
Beaulac, Stéphane "The Westphalian Legal Orthodoxy—Myth or Reality?" (2000) 2 *Journal of the History of International Law* 148
Beck, Ulrich, Giddens, Anthony, and Lash, Scott *Reflexive Modernization, Politics, Tradition and Aesthetics in the Modern Social Order* (Stanford, CA: Stanford University Press 1998)
Bell, John "Justice and the Law" in Klaus R Scherer (ed), *Justice: Interdisciplinary Perspectives* (Cambridge: Cambridge University Press 1992)
Ben Hamida, Walid "L'arbitrage transnational face à un désordre procédural: la concurrence des procédures et les conflits de juridictions" in Ferhat Horchani (ed), *Où va le droit de l'investissement? Désordre normatif et recherche d'équilibre* (Paris: Pedone 2006)
van den Berg, Albert Jan "Enforcement of Annulled Awards?" (1998) 9/2 *ICC Bulletin* 15
Berger, Klaus Peter *International Economic Arbitration* (Deventer: Kluwer 1993)
—— *The Creeping Codification of the Lex Mercatoria* (The Hague: Kluwer 1999)
Berman, Harold J *Law and Revolution: The Formation of the Western Legal Tradition* (Cambridge, MA: Harvard University Press 1983)
Berman, Harold J and Dasser, Felix "The 'New' Law Merchant and the 'Old': Sources, Content, and Legitimacy" in Thomas Carbonneau (ed), *Lex Mercatoria and Arbitration: A Discussion of the New Law Merchant* (rev edn, Dordrecht: Juris and Kluwer 1998)
Berman, Paul S *Global Legal Pluralism. A Jurisprudence of Law Beyond Borders* (Cambridge: Cambridge University Press 2012)

Besson, Sébastien and Pittet, Luc "La reconnaissance à l'étranger d'une sentence annulée dans son Etat d'origine" (1998) 16 *ASA Bulletin* 498

Beyleveld, Deryck and Brownsword, Roger "Normative Positivism: The Mirage of the Middle Way" (1989) 9 *Oxford Journal of Legal Studies* 462

Bhala, Raj "The Myth About Stare Decisis and International Trade Law" (1999) 14 *American University International Law Review* 845

Bianchi, Andrea "Reflexive Butterfly Catching: Insights from a Situated Catcher" in Joost Pauwelyn, Ramses Wessel, and Jan Wouters (eds), *Informal International Lawmaking* (Oxford: Oxford University Press 2012)

Bingham, Thomas "Reasons and Reasons and Reasons: Differences Between a Court Judgment and an Arbitral Award" (1988) 4 *Arbitration International* 1

Blackaby, Nigel, Partasides, Constantine, with Redfern, Alan and Hunter, Martin *Redfern and Hunter on International Arbitration* (Oxford: Oxford University Press 2009)

Blackman, Keith "The Uniform Domain Name Dispute Resolution Policy: A Cheaper Way to Hijack Domain Names and Suppress Critics" (2001) 15 *Harvard Journal of Law & Technology* 211

Bobbio, Norberto "Ancora sulle norme primarie e norme secondarie" (1968) 1 *Rivista di filosofia* 35

—— *Giusnaturalismo e positivismo giuridico* (Milan: Edizioni di Comunita 1965)

—— *Il positivismo giuridico* (Turin: Giappichelli 1961)

—— *Teoria dell'ordinamento giuridico* (Turin: Giappichelli 1960)

—— "Teoria e ideologia nella dottrina di Santi Romano" in Paolo Biscaretti di Ruffia (ed), *Le dottrine giuridiche di oggi e l'insegnamento di Santi Romano* (Milan: Giuffrè 1977)

Bohannan, Paul "The Differing Realms of the Law" (1965) 67 *American Anthropologist* 33

Boucher, David *Political Theories of International Relations* (Oxford: Oxford University Press 1998)

Bourdieu, Pierre "Les rites comme actes d'institution" (1982) 43 *Actes de recherche en sciences sociales* 59

Bowden, Paul "L'interdiction de se contredire au détriment d'autrui (estoppel) as a Substantive Transnational Rule in International Commercial Arbitration" in Emmanuel Gaillard (ed), *Transnational Rules in International Commercial Arbitration* (Paris: International Chamber of Commerce 1993)

Brabandère, Eric de "Arbitral Decisions as a Source of International Investment Law" in Tarcisio Gazzini and Eric de Brabandère (eds), *International Investment Law. The Sources of Rights and Obligations* (Leiden: Martinus Nijhoff 2012)

Brecht, Arnold *Political Theory: The Foundations of Twentieth-Century Political Thought* (Princeton, NJ: Princeton University Press 1959)

Bredin, Jean-Denis "La loi du juge" in Philippe Fouchard, Philippe Kahn, and Antoine Lyon-Caen (eds), *Le droit des relations économiques internationales—Études offertes à Berthold Goldman* (Paris: Litec 1982)

Briggs, Adrian "The Principle of Comity in Private International Law" (2011) 354 *Hague Lectures* 65

Buchanan, Scott M *Rediscovering Natural Law* (Santa Barbara, CA: Center for the Study of Democratic Institutions 1962)

Bucher, Andreas "La dimension sociale du droit international privé" (2009) 341 *Hague Lectures* 9, 144

Bucher, Andreas and Tschanz, Pierre-Yves *International Arbitration in Switzerland* (Basel: Helbing & Lichtenhahn 1988)

Buergenthal, Thomas "The Proliferation of International Courts and Tribunals: Is It Good or Bad?" (2001) 14 *Leiden Journal of International Law* 267

Bush, George W State of the Union Address of 28 January 2002, available at <http://www.johnstonsarchive.net/policy/bush-speeches.html>
Calliess, Gralf-Peter "Online Dispute Resolution: Consumer Redress in a Global Marketplace" (2006) 7 *German Law Journal* 647
—— "Transnational Consumer Law: Co-Regulation of B2C E-Commerce" in Olaf Dilling, Martin Herberg, and Gerd Winter (eds), *Responsible Business: Self-Governance and Law in Transnational Economic Transactions* (Oxford: Hart 2008)
Calliess, Gralf-Peter and Zumbansen, Peer *Rough Consensus and Running Code. A Theory of Transnational Private Law* (Oxford: Hart 2010)
Carbonneau, Thomas "A Definition of And Perspective Upon The Lex Mercatoria Debate" in Thomas Carbonneau (ed), *Lex Mercatoria and Arbitration: A Discussion of the New Law Merchant* (rev edn, Dordrecht: Juris and Kluwer 1998)
—— "Arbitral Law-Making" (2004) 25 *Michigan Journal of International Law* 1183
—— "Debating the Proper Role of National Law under the New York Arbitration Convention" (1998) 6 *Tulane Journal of International & Comparative Law* 277
Carbonnier, Jean *Sociologie juridique* (Paris: A Colin 1972)
Casarosa, Federica "Transnational Private Regulation of the Internet: Different Models of Enforcement" in Fabrizio Cafaggi (ed), *Enforcement of Transnational Regulation. Ensuring Compliance in a Global World* (Cheltenham: Elgar 2012)
Cassese, Antonio *International Law* (Oxford: Oxford University Press 2001)
Castells, Manuel *The Internet Galaxy: Reflections on the Internet, Business, and Society* (New York: Oxford University Press 2001)
Charmont, Joseph *La renaissance du droit naturel* (2nd edn, Paris: Librairie de jurisprudence ancienne et moderne 1927)
Chevallier, Jacques "L'ordre juridique" in Jacques Chevallier and Danièle Loschak (eds), *Le droit en procès* (Paris: Presses universitaires de France 1983)
Clark, George *Early Modern Europe from about 1450 to about 1720* (Oxford: Oxford University Press 1957)
Clay, Thomas *L'arbitre* (Paris: Dalloz 2001)
—— "Qui sont les arbitres internationaux? Approche sociologique" in José Rodell (ed), *Les arbitres internationaux* (Paris: Éditions de la société de législation comparée 2005)
Coleman, Jules L "Negative and Positive Positivism" (1982) 11 *Journal of Legal Studies* 139
—— *The Practice of Principle* (New York: Oxford University Press 2001)
Comaroff, John L *Rules and Processes* (Chicago: University of Chicago Press 1981)
Commission, Jeffrey "Precedent in Investment Treaty Arbitration—A Citation Analysis of a Developing Jurisprudence" (2007) 24 *Journal of International Arbitration* 129
Cooter, Robert, Marks, Stephen, and Mnookin, Robert "Bargaining in the Shadow of the Law: A Testable Model of Strategic Behavior" (1982) 11 *Journal of Legal Studies* 225
Cordy, Robert "Gulags Give Way to the Rule of Law," *Boston Herald*, November 18, 2002, A25
Cotterrell, Roger "What is Transnational Law?" (2012) 37 *Law & Social Inquiry* 500
Cover, Robert M "The Folktales of Justice: Tales of Jurisdiction" (1985) 14 *Capital University Law Review* 179
Craig, Paul "Formal and Substantive Conceptions of the Rule of Law" (1997) 16 *Public Law* 467
Craig, W Laurence, Park, William W, and Paulsson, Jan *International Chamber of Commerce Arbitration* (3rd edn, Dobbs Ferry, NY: Oceana 2000)
Crawford, James *The Creation of States in International Law* (2nd edn, Oxford: Oxford University Press 2007)
Cruquenaire, Alexandre *Le règlement extrajudiciaire des litiges relatifs aux noms de domaine* (Brussels: Bruylant 2002)

Cuniberti, Gilles "Three Theories of Lex Mercatoria" (2013) 52 *Columbia Journal of Transnational Law*
von Daniels, Detlef *The Concept of Law from a Transnational Perspective* (Aldershot: Ashgate 2010)
Delmas-Marty, Mireille *Global Law: A Triple Challenge* (Leiden: Martinus Nijhoff 2003)
Deumier, Pascale *Le droit spontané* (Paris: Economica 2002)
Dezalay, Yves and Garth, Bryant G *Dealing in Virtue: International Commercial Arbitration and the Construction of a Transnational Legal Order* (Chicago: University of Chicago Press 1996)
Duerr, Hans-Peter *Nacktheit und Scham. Der Mythos vom Zivilisationsprozess* (Frankfurt am Main: Suhrkamp 1988)
Duguit, Léon and Kelsen, Hans "Avant-propos" (1926–1927) 1 *Revue internationale de la théorie du droit* 1
Dworkin, Ronald *Law's Empire* (Cambridge, MA: Harvard University Press 1986)
—— "Philosophy, Morality, and Law—Observations Prompted by Professor Fuller's Novel Claim" (1965) 113 *University of Pennsylvania Law Review* 668
Ehrlich, Eugen *Fundamental Principles of the Sociology of Law* (first published 1913, New Brunswick: Transaction Publishers 2002)
Elias, Norbert *Der Prozess der Zivilisation* (Frankfurt am Main: Suhrkamp 1976)
Ewald, François "The Law of Law" in Gunter Teubner (ed), *Autopoietic Law: A New Approach to Law and Society* (Berlin: de Gruyter 1988)
Fadlallah, Ibrahim "Le projet de convention sur la vente de marchandises" (1979) 106 *Journal du droit international* 764
Finnis, John *Philosophy of Law Collected Essays Volume IV* (New York: Oxford University Press 2011)
Fioravanti, Maurizio "Per l'interpretazione dell'opera giuridica di Santi Romano: Nuove prospettive della ricerca" (1981) 10 *Quaderni fiorentini per la storia del pensiero giuridico moderno* 169
Fischer, Markus "Feudal Europe, 800–1300: Communal Discourse and Conflictual Practice" (1992) 46 *International Organization* 427
Fiss, Owen "Against Settlement" (1984) 93 *Yale Law Journal* 1073
—— "The History of an Idea" (2009) 78 *Fordham Law Review* 1273
Fontanelli, Filippo "Santi Romano and *L'ordinamento giuridico*: The Relevance of a Forgotten Masterpiece for Contemporary International, Transnational and Global Legal Relations" (2011) 2 *Transnational Legal Theory* 67
Fortier, Yves "The New, New Lex Mercatoria, or Back to the Future" (2001) 17 *Arbitration International* 121
Foucault, Michel *L'ordre du discours* (Paris: Gallimard 1971)
Fouchard, Philippe "Alternative dispute resolution et arbitrage" in Charles Leben, Eric Loquin, and Mahmoud Salem (eds), *Souveraineté étatique et marchés internationaux à la fin du 20e siècle: à propos de 30 ans de recherche du CREDIMI: Mélanges en l'honneur de Philippe Kahn* (Paris: Litec 2000)
—— "La portée internationale de l'annulation de la sentence arbitrale dans son pays d'origine" (1997) *Revue de l'arbitrage* 329
—— *L'arbitrage commercial international* (Paris: Dalloz 1965)
—— "Où va l'arbitrage international?" (1989) 34 *McGill Law Journal* 435
Fouchard, Philippe, Kahn, Philippe, and Lyon-Caen, Antoine (eds) *Le droit des relations économiques internationales. Études offertes à Berthold Goldman* (Paris: Litec 1989)
Friedman, Lawrence M "One World: Notes on the Emerging Legal Order" in Michael Likosky (ed), *Transnational Legal Processes. Globalisation and Power Disparities* (London: Butterworths 2002)

Friedman, Thomas L *The Lexus and the Olive Tree* (New York: Anchor Books 2000)
Friedmann, Wolfgang *Legal Theory* (3rd edn, London: Stevens & Sons 1953)
—— *The Changing Structure of International Law* (New York: Columbia University Press 1964)
Froomkin, A Michael "Wrong Turn in Cyberspace: Using ICANN to Route Around the APA and the Constitution" (2000) 50 *Duke Law Journal* 17
Fuller, Lon L "A Reply to Professors Cohen and Dworkin" (1965) 10 *Villanova Law Review* 655
—— *The Law in Quest of Itself* (Chicago: Foundation Press 1940)
—— *The Morality of Law* (rev edn, New Haven: Yale University Press 1969)
Gaillard, Emmanuel "Anti-Suit injunctions et reconnaissance des sentences annulées au siège: une évolution remarquable de la jurisprudence" (2003) 130 *Journal du droit international* 1105
—— *Aspects philosophiques du droit de l'arbitrage international* (Leiden: Martinus Nijhoff 2008)
—— comment on the *Hilmarton* case, French *Cour de Cassation*, (1994) *Revue de l'arbitrage* 327 and (1994) 121 *Journal du droit international* 701
—— "La distinction des principes généraux du droit et des usages du commerce international" in *Études offertes à Pierre Bellet*, (Paris: Litec 1991)
—— *Legal Theory of International Arbitration* (Leiden: Martinus Nijhoff 2010)
—— "L'exécution des sentences annulées dans leur pays d'origine" (1998) 125 *Journal du droit international* 645
—— "L'ordre juridique arbitral: réalité, utilité et spécificité" (2010) 55 *McGill Law Journal* 891
—— "Souveraineté et autonomie: réflexions sur les représentations de l'arbitrage international" (2007) 134 *Journal du droit international* 1163
—— "The Representations of International Arbitration" (2010) 1 *Journal of International Dispute Settlement* 271
—— "Thirty Years of Lex Mercatoria: Towards the Selective Application of Transnational Rules" (1995) 10 *ICSID Review* 208
—— "Transnational Law: A Legal System of a Method of Decision Making?" (2001) 17 *Arbitration International* 59
Gaillard, Emmanuel and Banifatemi, Yas (eds) *Precedent in International Arbitration* (Huntington, NY: Juris 2008)
Gaillard, Emmanuel and Savage, John (eds) *Fouchard, Gaillard, Goldman on International Commercial Arbitration* (The Hague: Kluwer 1999)
Galanter, Marc "The Legal Malaise: Or, Justice Observed" (1985) 19 *Law & Society Review* 537
Gardner, John *Law as a Leap of Faith* (Oxford: Oxford University Press 2012)
—— "Legal Positivism: 5½ Myths" (2001) 46 *American Journal of Jurisprudence* 199
—— "What is Legal Pluralism?," paper delivered at Osgoode Hall Law School, May 8, 2013, available at <http://www.youtube.com/watch?v=q-aTJgTTOA8>
Gellner, Ernest *Nations and Nationalism* (Ithaca: Cornell University Press 1983)
Gharavi, Hamid G "Chromalloy: Another View" (1997) 12 *Mealeys's International Arbitration Report* 21
—— *The International Effectiveness of the Annulment of an Award* (The Hague: Kluwer 2002)
Ghérari, Habib and Szurek, Sandra (eds) *L'émergence de la société civile internationale* (Paris: Pedone 2003)

Giddens, Anthony *The Nation-State and Violence* (Cambridge: Polity 1985)
Gilles, Peter and Selvadurai, Niloufer "Reasoned Awards: How Extensive Must the Reasons be?" (2008) 7 *Arbitration* 125
Gillroy, John M "Justice-as-Sovereignty: David Hume and the Origins of International Law" (2007) 78 *British Year Book of International Law* 429
Goldman, Berthold "Frontières du droit et lex mercatoria" (1964) 9 *Archives de philosophie du droit* 17
—— "Instance judiciaire et instance arbitrale internationale" in *Etudes offertes à Pierre Bellet* (Paris: Litec 1991)
—— "La Lex Mercatoria dans les contrats et l'arbitrage internationaux: réalité et perspectives" (1979) 106 *Journal du droit international* 475
—— "Lex Mercatoria" (1983) 3 *Forum Internationale* 19
—— "Nouvelles réflexions sur la lex mercatoria" in Christian Dominicé (ed), *Études de droit international en l'honneur de Pierre Lalive* (Basel: Helbing & Lichtenhahn 1993)
Goldsmith, Jack L and Wu, Tim *Who Controls the Internet? Illusions of a Borderless World* (New York: Oxford University Press 2006)
Gray, Christine and Kingsbury, Benedict "Developments in Dispute Settlement: Inter-State Arbitration Since 1945" (1992) 63 *British Year Book of International Law* 97
Green, Leslie "Legal Positivism" in Edward N Zalta (ed), *Stanford Encyclopedia of Philosophy* (Stanford: Stanford University Fall 2009 edn)
—— "Positivism and Conventionalism" (1999) 12 *Canadian Journal of Law and Jurisprudence* 35
—— "The Concept of Law Revisited" (1994) 94 *Michigan Law Review* 1687
Greenawalt, Kent "The Rule of Recognition and the Constitution" (1986) 85 *Michigan Law Review* 621
Griffiths, John "What is Legal Pluralism?" (1986) 24 *Journal of Legal Pluralism* 1
Grisel, Florian "Sources of Foreign Investment Law" in Zachary Douglas, Joost Pauwelyn, and Jorge Viñuales (eds), *The Conceptual Foundations of International Investment Law: Bridging Theory into Practice* (Oxford: Oxford University Press 2014, forthcoming)
Guillaume, Gilbert "The Use of Precedent by International Judges and Arbitrators" (2011) 2 *Journal of International Dispute Settlement* 5
Guinchard, Serge "L'évitement du juge civil" in Jean Clam and Gilles Martin (eds), *Les transformations de la régulation juridique* (Paris: LGDJ 1998)
Gurvitch, Georges *L'idée du droit social: notion et système du Droit Social; histoire doctrinale depuis le XVIIe siècle jusqu'à la fin du XIXe siècle* (Paris: Sirey 1932)
—— *Sociology of Law* (first published 1940 in French and 1942 in English, New Brunswick: Transaction publishers 2001)
Haas, Peter M "Epistemic Communities and International Policy Coordination" (1992) 46 *International Organization* 1
Habermas, Jürgen *Between Facts and Norms: Contributions to a Discourse Theory of Law and Democracy* (Cambridge, MA: MIT Press 1996)
—— *Between Naturalism and Religion* (Cambridge: Polity 2008)
—— *Justification and Application* (Cambridge, MA: MIT Press 1993)
—— *The Postnational Constellation: Political Essays* (Cambridge, MA: MIT Press 2001)
—— *The Theory of Communicative Action* (Boston: Beacon 1987)
—— "Wahrheitstheorien" in Helmut Fahrenbach (ed), *Wirklichkeit und Reflexion* (Pfullingen: Neske 1973)
—— in Peter Dews (ed), *Autonomy and Solidarity: Interviews with Jürgen Habermas* (London: Verso 1986)
Haines, Charles G *The Revival of Natural Law in America* (Cambridge, MA: Harvard University Press 1930)

Hanotiau, Bernard "L'autorité de la chose jugée des sentences arbitrales" (2003) Special Supplement to the *ICC Bulletin* 45

Hart, HLA "Lon L. Fuller: The Morality of Law" in *Essays in Jurisprudence and Philosophy* (Oxford: Clarendon Press 1983)

—— "Positivism and the Separation of Law and Morals" (1958) 71 *Harvard Law Review* 593

—— *The Concept of Law* (2nd edn, Oxford: Clarendon Press 1994)

Hartkamp, Arthur "The UNIDROIT Principles For International Commercial Contracts and the United Nations Convention on Contracts for the International Sale of Goods" in Katharina Boele-Woelki and Dimitra Kokkini-Iatridou (eds), *Comparability and Evaluation: Essays on Comparative Law, Private International Law, And International Commercial Arbitration, in Honour of Dimitra Kokkini-Iatridou* (Leiden: Martinus Nijhoff 1994)

Heidegger, Martin *The Question Concerning Technology and Other Essays* (transl W Lovitt, New York: Harper & Row 1977)

Helfer, Laurence R and Slaughter, Anne-Marie "Toward a Theory of Effective Supranational Adjudication" (2003) 107 *Yale Law Journal* 273

Hodgen, Margaret T *Early Anthropology in the Sixteenth and the Seventeenth Centuries* (Philadelphia: University of Pennsylvania Press 1964)

Holmes, Oliver W "The Path of the Law" (1897) 10 *Harvard Law Review* 457

Horn, Norbert "Uniformity and Diversity in the Law of International Commercial Contracts" in Nobert Horn and Clive M Schmitthoff (eds), *The Transnational Law of International Commercial Transactions* (Deventer: Kluwer 1982)

Jacquet, Jean-Michel, Delebecque, Philippe, and Corneloup, Sabine *Droit du commerce international* (2nd edn, Paris: Dalloz 2010)

Jellinek, Georg *Allgemeine Rechtslehre* (2nd edn, Berlin: O Häring 1905)

Jennings, Robert and Watts, Arthur (eds) *Oppenheim's International Law*, vol 1 (9th edn, New York: Longman 1992)

Jessup, Philip C *Transnational Law* (New Haven: Yale University Press 1956)

Jhering, Rudolf von *Law as a Means to an End* (first published 1877–83, Boston: Boston Books 1913)

Kahn, Philippe "Les principes généraux du droit devant les arbitres du commerce international" (1989) 116 *Journal du droit international* 305

Kant, Immanuel *The Metaphysics of Morals* (first published 1797, Cambridge: Cambridge University Press 1996)

Kassis, Antoine *Théorie générale des usages du commerce* (Paris: LGDJ 1984)

Katsh, Ethan "Adding Trust Systems to Transaction Systems: The Role of Online Dispute Resolution" in Proceedings of the UNECE Forum on ODR 2002, <http://www.ombuds.org/un/unece_june2002.doc>

—— "Online Dispute Resolution: Some Implications for the Emergence of Law in Cyberspace" (2006) 10 *Lex Electronica*, available at <http://www.lex-electronica.org/docs/articles_65.pdf>

Katsh, Ethan, Rifkin, Janet, and Gaitenby, Alan "E-Commerce, E-Dispute, and E-Dispute Resolution: In the Shadow of 'eBay Law'" (2000) 15 *Ohio State Journal on Dispute Resolution* 705

Kaufmann-Kohler, Gabrielle "Arbitral Precedent: Dream, Necessity, or Excuse?" (2007) 23 *Arbitration International* 357

—— "Le contrat et son droit devant l'arbitre international" in François Bellanger, Christine Chappuis, and Anne Héritier Lachat (eds), *Le contrat dans tous ses états* (Bern: Stämpfli 2004)

Kaufmann-Kohler, Gabrielle and Schultz, Thomas *Online Resolution: Challenges for Contempory Justice* (Kulwer 2004)

Kelly, John M *A Short History of Western Legal Theory* (Oxford: Clarendon Press 1992)
Kelsen, Hans *General Theory of Law and State* (first published 1945, Cambridge, MA: Harvard University Press 1949)
—— *Pure Theory of Law* (Berkeley: University of California Press 1967)
—— "The Function of a Constitution" in Richard Tur and William L. Twining, *Essays on Kelsen* (Oxford: Clarendon Press 1986)
—— "What is Justice?" in Hans Kelsen (ed), *What Is Justice: Justice, Law, and Politics in the Mirror of Science: Collected Essays* (essay first published 1957, Union: Lawbook Exchange 2000)
Kerchove, Michel van de and Ost, François *Le droit ou les paradoxes du jeu* (Paris: Presses universitaires de France 1992)
—— *The Legal System between Order and Disorder* (Oxford: Clarendon Press 1993)
King, D Brian "Consistency of Awards in Cases of Parallel Proceedings Concerning Related Subject-Matters" in Emmanuel Gaillard (ed), *Towards a Uniform International Arbitration Law* (Huntington, NY: Juris 2005)
Klabbers, Jan "The Undesirability of Soft Law" (1998) 67 *Nordic Journal of International Law* 381
Klabbers, Jan and Piiparinen, Touko (eds), *Normative Pluralism and International Law: Exploring Global Governance* (Cambridge: Cambridge University Press 2013)
Kramer, Matthew H "For the Record: A Final Reply to N.E. Simmonds" (2011) 56 *American Journal of Jurisprudence* 115
—— "Getting Rights Right" in Matthew H Kramer (ed), *Rights, Wrongs, and Responsibilities* (New York: Palgrave Macmillan 2001)
—— *In Defense of Legal Positivism: Law Without Trimmings* (Oxford: Oxford University Press 2003)
—— *Objectivity and the Rule of Law* (Cambridge: Cambridge University Press 2007)
—— "Of Final Things: Morality as One of The Ultimate Determinants of Legal Validity" (2005) 24 *Law and Philosophy* 47
—— "On the Moral Status of the Rule of Law" (2003) 63 *Cambridge Law Journal* 65
—— *Where Law and Morality Meet* (Oxford: Oxford University Press 2008)
Kuhn, Thomas S *The Structure of Scientific Revolutions* (2nd edn, Chicago: University of Chicago Press 1970)
Lagarde, Paul "Approche critique de la lex mercatoria" in *Le droit des relations économiques internationales: Études offertes à Berthold Goldman* (Paris: Litec 1982)
Lalive, Pierre "Arbitration—The Civilized Solution?" (1998) 16 *ASA Bulletin* 483
—— "Avantages et inconvénients de l'arbitrage 'ad hoc'" in *Etudes offertes à Pierre Bellet* (Paris: Litec 1991)
—— "Nouveaux regards sur le droit international privé, aujourd'hui et demain" (1994) 1 *Revue suisse de droit international et européen* 3
—— "On the Reasoning of International Arbitral Awards" (2010) 1 *Journal of International Dispute Settlement* 55
Lando, Ole "The Lex Mercatoria in International Commercial Arbitration" (1985) 34 *International and Comparative Law Quarterly* 747
Latty, Franck *La lex sportiva* (Leiden: Martinus Nijhoff 2007)
Lazareff, Serge "Avant-propos: Le bloc-notes de Serge Lazareff" (2004) 124 *Gazette du Palais: Cahiers de l'arbitrage* 3 (No 338/339, December 3 and 4, 2004)
Lenoble, Jacques and Maesschalck, Marc *The Action of Norms* (The Hague: Kluwer 2002)
Lessig, Lawrence *Code: Version 2.0* (2nd edn, New York: Basic Books 2006)
—— "The New Chicago School" (1998) 27 *Journal of Legal Studies* 661

Lew, Julian DM and Shore, Laurence "International Commercial Arbitration: Harmonizing Cultural Differences" in *AAA/ICDR Handbook on International Arbitration and ADR* (2nd edn, Huntington, NY: Juris 2010)

Linné, Carl von *A General System of Nature* (London: Lackington, Allen & Co 1806)

Locke, John *Second Treatise of Civil Government* (first published 1690, Amherst, NY: Prometheus 1986)

Loquin, Eric "L'application des règles anationales dans l'arbitrage commercial international" in *L'apport de la jurisprudence arbitrale: l'arbitrage commercial international* (Paris: ICC 1986)

—— "Où en est la lex mercatoria?" in Charles Leben, Eric Loquin, and Mahmoud Salem (eds), *Souveraineté étatique et marchés internationaux à la fin du 20e siècle—Mélanges en l'honneur de Philippe Kahn* (Paris: Litec 2000)

Lowenfeld, Andreas F "Lex Mercatoria: An Arbitrator's View" (1990) 6 *Arbitration International* 133

Luban, David "The Rule of Law and Human Dignity: Re-examining Fuller's Canons" (2010) 2 *Hague Journal on the Rule of Law* 29

Luhmann, Niklas "Gerechtigkeit in den Rechtssystemen der modernen Gesellschaft" (1973) 4 *Rechtstheorie* 131

Ly, Filip JM de "Emerging New Perspectives Regarding Lex Mercatoria in an Era of Increasing Globalization" in Klaus Peter Berger, Werner F Ebke, Siegfried Elsing, Bernhard Großfeld, and Gunther Kühne (eds), *Festschrift für Otto Sandrock* (Heidelberg: Recht und Wirtschaft 2000)

Lynch, Katherine *The Forces of Economic Globalization* (The Hague: Kluwer 2003)

Lyons, David *Ethics and the Rule of Law* (Cambridge: Cambridge University Press 1984)

Malanczuk, Peter *Akehurst's Modern Introduction to International Law* (7th edn, London: Routledge 1997)

Malinowksi, Bronislaw *Crime and Custom in Savage Society* (first published 1926, Patterson, NJ: Littlefield Adams 1985)

Mann, FA "Lex Facit Arbitrum" in *Liber Amicorum for Martin Domke* (Leiden: Martinus Nijhoff 1967)

Marcic, René *Rechtsphilosophie: eine Einführung* (Freiburg: Rombach 1969)

Marmor, Andrei *Law in the Age of Pluralism* (New York: Oxford University Press 2007)

—— *Positive Law & Objective Values* (New York: Oxford University Press 2001)

Marrella, Fabrizio *La nuova lex mercatoria* (Padova: CEDAM 2003)

Martinez, Jenny S "Toward an International Judicial System" (2003) 56 *Stanford Law Review* 429

McCormick, Neil *Rhetoric and the Rule of Law. A Theory of Legal Reasoning* (Oxford: Oxford University Press 2005)

McLachlan, Campbell *Lis Pendens in International Litigation* (Leiden: Martinus Nijhoff 2009)

McRae, Donald "The WTO Appellate Body: A Model for an ICSID Appeals Facility?" (2010) 1 *Journal of International Dispute Settlement* 375

Meinecke, Friedrich *Weltbürgertum and Nationalstaat: Studien zur Genesis des deutschen Nationalstaates* (first published 1908, Munich: Oldenbourg 1915)

Melissaris, Emmanuel "The More the Merrier? A New Take on Legal Pluralism" (2004) 13 *Social & Legal Studies* 57

—— *Ubiquitous Law: Legal Theory and The Space for Legal Pluralism* (Farnham: Ashgate 2009)

Menkel-Meadow, Carrie "Whose Dispute Is It Anyway?: A Philosophical and Democratic Defence of Settlement (in Some Cases)" (1995) 83 *Georgetown Law Journal* 2663

Merry, Sally E *Colonizing Hawai'i: The Cultural Power of Law* (Princeton, NJ: Princeton University Press 2000)

—— "Legal Pluralism" (1988) 22 *Law and Society Review* 869

Mertens, Hans-Joachim "Das lex mercatoria-Problem" in Reinhard Böttcher, Götz Hueck, and Burkhard Jähnke (eds), *Festschrift für Walter Odersky* (Berlin: de Gruyter 1996)

Michaels, Ralf "A Fuller Concept of Law Beyond the State? Thoughts on Lon Fuller's Contributions to the Jurisprudence of Transnational Dispute Resolution—A Reply to Thomas Schultz" (2011) 2 *Journal of International Dispute Settlement* 417

—— "Rollen und Rollenverständnisse im transnationalen Privatrecht" in *Paradigmen im internationalen Recht: Implikationen der Weltfinanzkrise für das internationale Recht* (Heidelberg: Müller 2012)

—— "The Re-State-ment of Non-State Law: The State, Choice of Law, and the Challenge from Global Legal Pluralism" (2005) 51 *Wayne Law Review* 1209

Mnookin, Robert H *Bargaining with the Devil. When to Negotiate, When to Fight* (New York: Simon & Schuster 2010)

Mnookin, Robert H and Kornhauser, Lewis "Bargaining in the Shadow of the Law: The Case of Divorce" (1979) 88 *Yale Law Journal* 950

Moore, Sally Falk *Law as Process. An Anthropological Approach* (first published 1970, Hamburg: LIT 2000)

Mueller, Milton *Ruling the Root: Internet Governance and the Taming of Cyberspace* (Cambridge, MA: MIT Press 2004)

Muir Watt, Horatia "Private International Law Beyond the Schism" (2011) 2 *Transnational Legal Theory* 347

Mustill, Michael "Lex Mercatoria and Arbitration (A Discussion of the New Law Merchant)" (1992) 8 *Arbitration International* 215

—— "The History of International Commercial Arbitration—A Sketch" in Lawrence W Newman and Richard D Hill (eds), *The Leading Arbitrators' Guide to International Arbitration* (Huntington: Juris 2004)

—— "The New Lex Mercatoria: The First Twenty-Five Years" (1988) 4 *Arbitration International* 86

Neff, Stephen "A Short History of International Law" in Malcolm D Evans (ed), *International Law* (Oxford: Oxford University Press 2003)

Oppetit, Bruno "Le droit international privé, droit savant" (1992) 234 *Hague Lectures* 331

—— *Théorie de l'arbitrage* (Paris: Presses universitaires de France 1998)

Osiander, Andreas *Before the State: Systemic Political Change from the Greeks to the French Revolution* (Oxford: Oxford University Press 2007)

Osman, Filali *Les principes généraux de la Lex mercatoria* (Paris: LGDJ 1992)

Ost, François "Essai de définition et de caractérisation de la validité juridique" in François Rigaux, Guy Haarscher and Patrick Vassard (eds), *Droit et pouvoir:* vol 1: *La validité* (Ghent: Story-Scientia 1987)

—— "Le rôle du juge. Vers de nouvelles loyautés?" in *Le rôle du juge dans la cité* (Brussels : Bruylant 2002)

—— *Shakespeare, la comédie de la loi* (Paris: Michalon 2012)

—— "Validité" in André-Jean Arnaud (ed), *Dictionnaire encyclopédique de théorie et de sociologie juridique* (Paris: LGDJ and Ghent: Story-Scientia 1988)

Ost, François and Hoecke, Mark van (eds) *Time and Law* (Brussels: Bruylant 1998)

Ost, François and Kerchove, Michel van de *De la pyramide au réseau? Pour une théorie dialectique du droit* (Brussels: Publication des Facultés universitaires Saint-Louis 2002)

—— *Jalons pour une théorie critique du droit* (Brussels: Publication des Facultés universitaires Saint-Louis 1987)

—— "Finality and Fairness in Tax Arbitration" (1994) 11 *Journal of International Arbitration* 19

—— "The Procedural Soft Law of International Arbitration: Non-Governmental Instruments" in Loukas Mistelis and Julian DM Lew (eds), *Pervasive Problems in International Arbitration* (Alphen aan den Rijn: Kluwer 2006)
Park, William W *Arbitration of International Business Disputes* (2nd edn, Oxford: Oxford University Press 2012)
Pashukanis, Evgeny *Law and Marxism: A General Theory* (first published 1929, London: Ink Links 1978)
Paulsson, Jan "Enclaves of Justice" (2007) 4 *Transnational Dispute Management* <http://www.transnational-dispute-management.com/article.asp?key=1034>
—— "Enforcing Arbitral Awards Notwithstanding a Local Standard Annulment" (1998) 9/1 *ICC Bulletin* 14
—— "La Lex Mercatoria dans l'arbitrage CCI" (1990) *Revue de l'arbitrage* 55
—— "May or Must under the New York Convention: An Exercise in Syntax and Linguistics" (1998) 14 *Arbitration International* 227
—— "The Case for Disregarding LSAS (Local Standard Annulments) under the New York Convention" (1996) 7 *American Review of International Arbitration* 99
Pauwelyn, Joost *Conflict of Norms in Public International Law* (Cambridge: Cambridge University Press 2003)
—— "Is It International Law Or Not and Does It Even Matter?" in Joost Pauwelyn, Ramses Wessel, and Jan Wouters (eds), *Informal International Lawmaking* (Oxford: Oxford University Press 2012)
Pellet, Alain Foreword to Frank Latty, *La lex sportiva* (Leiden: Martinus Nijhoff 2007)
Perrin, Jean-François *Sociologie empirique du droit* (Basel: Helbing & Lichtenhahn 1997)
Petrochilos, Georgios C "Enforcing Awards Annulled in Their State of Origin under the New York Convention" (1999) 48 *International and Comparative Law Quarterly* 856
Pospisil, Leopold J *Anthropology of Law: A Comparative Theory* (New York: Harper and Row 1971)
Poudret, Jean-François "Quelle solution pour en finir avec l'affaire Hilmarton?" (1998) *Revue de l'arbitrage* 7
Poudret, Jean-François and Besson, Sébastien *Comparative Law of International Arbitration* (2nd edn, London: Sweet & Maxwell 2007)
Pound, Roscoe *Justice According to the Law* (New Haven: Yale University Press 1951)
Pradelle, Géraud de la "La justice privée" in Habib Gherari and Sandra Szurek (eds), *L'émergence de la société civile internationale: vers la privatisation du droit international?* (Paris: Pedone 2003)
Prost, Mario "All Shouting the Same Slogans: International Law's Unities and the Politics of Fragmentation" (2006) 17 *Finnish Yearbook of International Law* 1
Provost, René "Judging in Splendid Isolation" (2008) 56 *American Journal of Comparative Law* 125
Ramsay, Hayden "The Revival of Natural Law Theories" (1994) 35 *Analytic Philosophy* 153
Rau, Alan S "Contracting Out of the Arbitration Act" (1997) 8 *American Review of International Arbitration* 225
Rawls, John *A Theory of Justice* (Cambridge, MA: Harvard University Press 1971)
—— "Two Concepts of Rules" (1955) 64 *Philosophical Review* 5
Raz, Joseph *Practical Reason and Norms* (Oxford: Oxford University Press 1999)
—— *The Authority of Law* (2nd edn, Oxford: Oxford University Press 2009)
—— *The Concept of a Legal System: An Introduction to the Theory of Legal System* (2nd edn, Oxford: Clarendon Press 1980)
—— "The Institutional Nature of Law" (1975) 38 *Modern Law Review* 489
Reisman, W Michael "A Hard Look at Soft Law: Remarks" (1988) 82 *American Society of International Law Proceedings* 371

—— "Soft Law and Law Jobs" (2011) 2 *Journal of International Dispute Settlement* 25

Rheingold, Howard *The Virtual Community: Homesteading on the Electronic Frontier* (Reading, MA: Addison-Wesley 1993)

Rigaux, François *La loi des juges* (Paris: Odile Jacob 1997)

—— "La relativité générale des ordres juridiques" in Eric Wyler and Alain Papaux (eds), *L'extranéité ou le dépassement de l'ordre juridique étatique* (Paris: Pedone 1999)

—— "Le droit au singulier et au pluriel" (1982) 9 *Revue interdisciplinaire d'études juridiques* 45

—— "Les situations juridiques individuelles dans un système de relativité générale" (1989) 213 *Hague Lectures* 1

—— "Souveraineté des États et arbitrage transnational" in Philippe Fouchard, Philippe Kahn, and Antoine Lyon-Caen (eds), *Le droit des relations économiques internationales—Études offertes à Berthold Goldman* (Paris: Litec 1982)

Rigozzi, Antonio *L'arbitrage international en matière de sport* (Basel: Helbing & Lichtenhahn 2005)

Roberts, Simon "After Government? On Representing Law Without the State" (2005) 68 *Modern Law Review* 1

Robilant, Anna di "Genealogies of Soft Law" (2006) 54 *American Journal of Comparative Law* 499

Rogers, Catherine "The Vocation of the International Arbitrator" (2005) 20 *American University International Law Review* 957

Romano, Cesare PR "A Taxonomy of International Rule of Law Institutions" (2011) 2 *Journal of International Dispute Settlement* 241

Romano, Santi *L'ordinamento giuridico* (first published 1917, Florence: Sansoni 1918)

Rommen, Heinrich A *Die ewige Wiederkehr des Naturrechts* (Leipzig: J Hegner 1936)

Ross, Alf *On Law and Justice* (London: Routledge 1958)

Rousseau, Charles *Droit international public* (Paris: Sirey 1970)

Sacco, Rodolfo "Mute Law" (1995) 43 *American Journal of Comparative Law* 455

Said, Edward W *Orientalism* (rev edn, London: Penguin 1978)

Sampliner, Gary H "Enforcement of Nullified Foreign Arbitral Awards—Chromalloy Revisited" (1997) 14 *Journal of International Arbitration* 141

Sanders, Pieter "New York Convention on the Recognition and Enforcement of Foreign Arbitral Awards" (1959) 6 *Netherlands International Law Review* 43

Scalia, Antonin *A Matter of Interpretation: Federal Courts and the Law* (Princeton, NJ: Princeton University Press 1997)

Scherer, Maxi "Effects of Foreign Judgments Relating to International Arbitral Awards: Is the 'Judgment Route' the Wrong Road?" (2013) 4 *Journal of International Dispute Settlement* 587

Schmitthoff, Clive M "Das neue Recht des Welthandels" (1964) 28 *Rabel Journal of Comparative and International Private Law* 47

—— "International Business Law: A New Law Merchant" (1961) 2 *Current Law and Social Problems* 129

Schreuer, Christoph and Weiniger, Matthew "Conversation Across Cases—Is There a Doctrine of Precedent in Investment Arbitration?" in Christoph Schreuer, Federico Ortino, and Peter Muchlinksi (eds), *Oxford Handbook of International Investment Law* (Oxford: Oxford University Press 2008)

Schrijver, Nico "The Changing Nature of State Sovereignty" (1999) 70 *British Year Book of International Law* 65

Schultz, Thomas "King Rex II" (2012) 3 *Journal of International Dispute Settlement* 1
—— "Online dispute resolution (ODR): résolution des litiges et ius numericum" (2002) 48 *Revue interdisciplinaire d'études juridiques* 153
—— *Réguler le commerce électronique par la résolution des litiges en ligne. Une approche critique* (Brussels: Bruylant 2005)
—— "Secondary Rules of Recognition and Relative Legality in Transnational Regimes" (2011) 56 *American Journal of Jurisprudence* 59
—— "Some Critical Comments on the Juridicity of Lex Mercatoria" (2008) 10 *Yearbook of Private International Law* 667
—— "The Concept of Law in Transnational Arbitral Legal Orders and some of its Consequences" (2011) 2 *Journal of International Dispute Settlement* 59
—— "The Three Pursuits of Dispute Settlement" (2011) 1 *Czech & Central European Yearbook of Arbitration* 227
Schultz, Thomas and Dupont, Cédric "Investment Arbitration: Promoting the Rule of Law or Over-Empowering Investors?," paper presented for ISA Annual Convention, San Francisco April 3–6, 2013
Schultz, Thomas and Holloway, David "Retour sur la comity I—Les origines de la comity au carrefour du droit international privé et du droit international public" (2011) 138 *Journal du droit international* 864
Schultz, Thomas and Holloway, David "Retour sur la comity II: La comity dans l'histoire du droit international privé" (2012) 138 *Journal du droit international* 571
Schütz, Alfred and Luckman, Thomas *The Structures of the Life-World* (Evanston, IL: Northwestern University Press 1973)
Searle, John *The Construction of Social Reality* (London: Penguin Press 1995)
Seppëla, Christopher "The Development of Case Law in Construction Disputes Relating to FIDIC Contracts" in Emmanuel Gaillard and Yas Banifatemi (eds), *Precedent in Investment Arbitration* (Huntington, NY: Juris 2008)
Seraglini, Christophe *Lois de police et justice arbitrale internationale* (Paris: Dalloz 2001)
Shapiro, Scott J *Legality* (Cambridge, MA: Belknap Press 2011)
Shaw, Malcolm N *International Law* (5th edn, Cambridge: Cambridge University Press 2003)
Shiner, Roger A *Norm and Nature: The Movement of Legal Thought* (New York: Oxford University Press 1992)
Shklar, Judith N *Legalism* (Cambridge, MA: Harvard University Press 1964)
Simma, Bruno and Pulkowski, Dirk "Of Planets and the Universe: Self-contained Regimes in International Law" (2006) 17 *European Journal of International Law* 483
Simmonds, Nigel "Straightforwardly False: The Collapse of Kramer's Legal Positivism" (2004) 63 *Cambridge Law Journal* 98
Slaughter, Anne-Marie "A Global Community of Courts" (2003) 44 *Harvard International Law Journal* 191
—— *A New World Order* (Princeton, NJ: Princeton University Press 2004)
—— "International Law in a World of Liberal States" (1995) 6 *European Journal of International Law* 503
Snyder, Francis G "Economic Globalisation and the Law in the Twenty-First Century" in Austin Sarat (ed), *Blackwell Companion to Law and Society* (Malden, MA: Blackwell 2004)
—— "Governing Economic Globalization: Global Legal Pluralism and European Law" (1999) 5 *European Law Journal* 334
Sousa Santos, Boaventura de *Toward a New Legal Common Sense: Law, Globalization, and Emancipation* (2nd edn, London: Butterworths 2002)

Spoorenberg, Frank and Viñuales, Jorge "Conflicting Decisions in International Arbitration" (2009) 8 *The Law & Practice of International Courts and Tribunals* 91
Stone, Julius *Social Dimensions of Law and Justice* (Stanford, CA: Stanford University Press 1966)
Stone Sweet, Alec and Grisel, Florian "L'arbitrage international: du contrat dyadique au système normatif" 2009 (52) *Archives de philosophie du droit* 75
Strayer, Joseph R *On the Medieval Origins of the Modern State* (Princeton, NJ: Princeton University Press 1970)
Strong, Stacie I "Why is Harmonization of Common Law and Civil Law Procedures Possible in Arbitration but Not Litigation?" in Mónica María Bustamante Rúa (ed), *Cultura y Proceso* (Medellín: Universidad de Medellín 2013)
Summers, Robert S "A Formal Theory of the Rule of Law" (1993) 6 *Ratio Juris* 127
Tamanaha, Brian Z "A Non-Essentialist Version of Legal Pluralism" (2000) 27 *Journal of Law and Society* 296
—— *On the Rule of Law: History, Politics, Theory* (Cambridge: Cambridge University Press 2004)
—— "The Folly of the 'Social Scientific' Concept of Legal Pluralism" (1993) 20 *Journal of Law and Society* 192
Tarello, Giovanni "La dottrina dell'ordinamento e la figura pubblica di Santi Romano" in Paolo Biscaretti di Ruffia (ed), *Le dottrine giuridiche di oggi e l'insegnamento di Santi Romano* (Milan: Giuffrè 1977)
Terris, Daniel, Romano, Cesare PR, and Swigart, Leigh "Toward a Community of International Judges" (2008) 30 *Loyola of Los Angeles International and Comparative Law Review* 419
Teubner, Gunther "Breaking Frames: The Global Interplay of Legal and Social Systems" (1997) 45 *American Journal of Comparative Law* 149
—— *Law as an Autopoietic System* (Oxford: Blackwell 1993)
Thompson, Edward Palmer *Whigs and Hunters: The Origin of the Black Act* (London: Allen Lane 1975)
Thornburg, Elizabeth G "Going Private: Technology, Due Process, and Internet Dispute Resolution" (2000) 34 *University of California at Davis Law Review* 151
Toope, Stephen J *Mixed International Arbitration* (Cambridge: Cambridge University Press 1990)
Troper, Michel "Système juridique et Etat" (1986) 30 *Archives de philosophie du droit* 2
Vecchio, Giorgio del "On the Statuality of Law" (1937) 19 *Journal of Comparative Legislation and International Law* 1
—— "Sulla statualita del diritto" (1929) 9 *Rivista internazionale di filosofia del diritto* 1
Veeder, VV "Report on England" in J Paulsson (ed), *International Handbook on Commercial Arbitration*, supp 23 1997
Villey, Michel "Law in Things" in Paul Amselek and Neil McCormick (eds), *Controversies About Law's Ontology* (Edinburgh: Edinburgh University Press 1991)
Virally, Michel *La pensée juridique* (Paris: LGDJ 1960)
Virilio, Paul *The Information Bomb* (London: Verso 2000)
Waldron, Jeremy "Normative (or Ethical) Positivism" in Jules Coleman (ed), *Hart's Postscript: Essays on the Postscript to The Concept of Law* (New York: Oxford University Press 2001)
—— "The Concept and the Rule of Law" (2008) 43 *Georgia Law Review* 1
Waluchow, Wilfrid J *Inclusive Legal Positivism* (Oxford: Clarendon Press 1994)
Weber, Max *Economy and Society: An Outline of Interpretive Sociology*, vol 1 (first published 1925, Berkley: University of California Press 1978)
—— *Wirtschaft und Gesellschaft: Grundriß der Verstehenden Soziologie* (first published 1922, Tübingen: Mohr Siebeck 1980)

Webster, Thomas H "Domain Name Proceedings and International Dispute Resolution" (2001) 2 *Business Law International* 215

Wehland, Hanno *The Coordination of Multiple Proceedings in Investment Treaty Arbitration* (Oxford: Oxford University Press 2013)

Wittgenstein, Ludwig *Philosophical Investigations* (first published 1953, Oxford: Blackwell 1974)

Wolfers, Arnold *Discord and Collaboration: Essays on International Politics* (Baltimore: Johns Hopkins University Press 1962)

Wolff, Robert P *In Defense of Anarchism* (New York: Harper & Row 1970)

—— "The Conflict Between Authority and Autonomy" in William Atkins Edmundson (ed), *The Duty to Obey the Law: Selected Philosophical Readings* (Lanham, MD: Rowman & Littlefield 1999)

Woodman, Gordon R "Legal Pluralism and the Search for Justice" (1996) 40 *Journal of African Law* 152

Woolf, Marie "Mugabe Told He Has Lost Moral Right to Govern," *The Independent*, August 1, 2002, A8

Xiangwei, Wang and Cheung, Gary "Keeping Economic Drive on Track Will Require Huge Effort, Warns Hu," *South China Morning Post*, March 8, 2003

Zumbansen, Peer "Debating Autonomy and Procedural Justice: The Lex Mercatoria in the Context of Global Governance Debates—A Reply to Thomas Schultz" (2011) 2 *Journal of International Dispute Settlement* 427

—— "Defining the Space of Transnational Law: Legal Theory, Global Governance, and Legal Pluralism" (2012) 21 *Transnational Law & Contemporary Problems* 305

—— "Law and Legal Pluralism: Hybridity in Transnational Governance" in Poul Kjaer, Paulius Jurcys, and Ren Yatsunami (eds), *Regulatory Hybridization in the Transnational Sphere* (Leiden: Brill 2013)

Index

1984 (book) 37
Addressees (of law) 56
Administration 56
ADR, *see* Mediation
Advocacy 45, 48
Agenda 35, 46–9
Algerian decolonization 55
Analytic purchase, *see* Explanatory power
Anarchy 41
Anglo-American law 53
Annulment of arbitral awards 137, 152
   see also Enforcement of annulled arbitral awards
Anomalies (scientific), *see* Kuhn, Thomas
Anthropology, of law 15, 53–4, 120, 127, 130–2
Arbitral jurisprudence, *see* Arbitration (precedents)
Arbitration
   autonomy 89, 92, 98, 126, 152, 157, 159, 160, 163–4
   award 89–99, 136, 146, 174–84
   community 14, 46–7, 120, 123–7, 160–1
   conduct of proceedings 123–4
   culture 123, 126
   dependents 3
   future of 4
   precedents in 125–6, 172–8
   representations of 5, 98
   seat of 5, 89–99
Arbitrators 121–3, 159
   appointment 1–3, 125
   authority 47
   glorification 47
   reputation 46
Architecture (built) 41, 148
Argumentative discourses 38
Aspremont, Jean d' 16
Auerbach, Jerold 25
Austin, John 27, 39, 101, 104, 136, 154–5
Authority of law 13–14, 25, 28–31, 42, 56, 67, 74–5
Autonomy 43–4, 57, 68, 89, 126, 134–8, 159
Autopoiesis 131
Award, *see* Arbitration

Babylonian law 8
Bad citizen 28
Belgium 158
Belief 31, 51, 63, 66–7, 123–4
   see also Justice beliefs
Bentham, Jeremy 39, 51, 101, 103
Berger, Klaus Peter 113
Berman, Harold 113

Bianchi, Andrea 5, 62–6
Biblical law 8
Billiard balls 44, 63
Bindingness 3, 27–8
Bobbio, Norberto 59–60, 126, 128–30
Bodin, Jean 76
Bohannan, Paul 16–17, 70, 128–32
Bolsheviks 55
Bredin, Jean-Denis 47
Bucher, Andreas 82, 108
Bush, George W 25

Calliess, Gralf-Peter 58, 143
Cambridge 148
Capitalism 53
Carbonnier, Jean 39, 74, 81, 114–15
Carroll, Lewis 33
Certification (law as) 39
Chagall, Marc 54–5
Chevallier, Jacques 104
China 26
Christianity 53
Church 76
Churchill College 148
Citizenry (control of) 37
Civilization 53
Clay, Thomas 120
Coercive power 28, 39, 136–7, 146–50
Coexistence (law of) 44
Coherence, *see* Predictability
Collective imagination 37, 45
   see also Ordinariness (in law)
Colonization 53–4
Comity 95
Commercial law 5, 46, 114–15
   see also Lex mercatoria
Commonsense (in understanding law) 38
Communities 120–3, 126, 131, 150
   as boundaries of legal systems 78–9
   epistemic 122, 161
   in arbitration, *see* Arbitration (communities)
   in scientific disciplines, *see* Kuhn, Thomas
Comparative law 53
Completeness (of a legal system) 113–14, 146
Comprehensiveness 39, 73–80, 114
Conflicts of law 43, 85
   see also International law (private)
   mandatory rules 58, 143
Consistency, *see* Predictability
Constitution 27–8
Contracts 26, 124–6, 137, 143
   model contracts 58

Control (through law) 37, 147
  see also Coercive powers
Copyright law 1–3
Cotterrell, Roger 68
Court of Arbitration for Sport 179
Courthouses 26, 53
Cultural diversity 53–4
Cultural understanding of law 37
Cuniberti, Gilles 58

Daniels, Detlef von 62
Dasser, Felix 113
Definitions
  as beliefs 66–7
  as political projects 54–62, 68, 77, 156–8
  implications 35–6, 51, 65–8
  importance 4
  purposes 48, 50, 59, 65–6, 157
  see also Explanatory power; Paradigms
Delegation of power 46, 159
Democracy 21, 25, 30–1, 140, 160–2
Dictionary 9
Dignity 44
Discipline 53
Domain names, see ICANN
Dreyfuss Affair 55
Duguit, Léon 49–51, 62, 65
Dutch Revolt 44
Dworkin, Ronald 21, 68–71

East Germany 24
eBay 140–50
Effectiveness, see Legal realism
Emancipation 44, 157
Encyclopedia 9
Enforcement of annulled arbitral award 88–99
Epistemology 9, 126
Ex aequo et bono 19
Exclusiveness of law 73–80
Expert systems 142
Explanatory power 35, 45, 47, 65, 157–8, 164
  see also Paradigms
External point of view 40–1, 43, 56
EU law 62
Evil systems 18, 24, 26, 37, 115, 165–6,
Ewald, François 104

Falsifiability 36–8
Fascism 60, 66
Federal legal systems 75–6
Feudal lords 76
Financial markets 14
Finnis, John 31
Fontanelli, Filippo 60
Formalism, see International law; Rules (pedigree of)
Forum shopping 121
Foucault, Michel 59
Fragmentation 59, 61–2, 121, 183

French Revolution 13
French school of arbitration 46–7, 60–2, 153–8
Friedmann, Wolfgang 44
Fuller, Lon 16, 20, 33–4, 37, 69, 76, 97, 153–4, 160, 166–84

Gaillard, Emmanuel 5, 60, 88–99, 105
Galanter, Marc 145
Gardner, John 27, 51, 170
General principles of law 105, 108, 117, 124
Goldman, Berthold 46, 111, 146, 153–4
Government (heinous) 37, 115
Gray, Christine 179
Green, Leslie 85, 94, 97, 122
Grundnorm 27
Guideposts 2, 20, 47, 168–9, 172–3
  see also Self-directed action
Guillaume, Gilbert 177
Gurvitch, Georges 55, 59, 65

Habermas, Jürgen 30–1, 77, 161, 166
Hart, HLA 25, 40, 42, 101–2, 110, 116, 122, 126, 128–9, 132, 154, 157, 169
Hawaii 53–4
Heidegger, Martin 38
Hierarchies
  of norms 63
  tangled 8–9, 86
Hobbes, Thomas 51, 75–6, 103
Hoecke, Mark van 176
Holmes, Oliver Wendell 135
Humpty Dumpty 33

ICANN 143–50
ICSID
  Arbitration 179
    see also Investment arbitration
  Convention 113
Indigenous law 53–4
Indonesia 26
Information technology 78, 148
  see also Internet; ICANN
Intellectual property law 1–3
Internal point of view 10, 41, 43
International commerce 57, 112, 114–15, 124–5
International courts and tribunals 10
International criminal law 62
International law 16, 62–3, 66, 125
  as law 22–3
  the Establishment in 13
  formalism 14, 22, 64
  fragmentation of 61–2
  private 46, 81–2
  public 4–5, 20–3, 10–14, 46, 61–2, 114, 121–2
International Monetary Fund 25
International public policy 19
Internet 15, 138–50

Interpretation 114, 121–6, 163
Investment arbitration vii, 19, 113, 125–6, 152, 160, 174, 177, 179, 181, 183

Jellinek, Georg 66
Jewish culture 55
Jhering, Rudolf von 136
Judges 56, 121, 130–1, 133–5
Judicial function 121
Jurisdiction 136–7
Jurisprudence
  analytic 8–9, 26–8, 30, 34, 37, 45, 62, 87, 95, 157
  normative 8–9
Jurisprudence constante, *see* Arbitration (precedents)
Justice 160–6
  as an element of legality 102, 151–2
  see also Separability of law and morality
  expectations of 3, 14, 19, 38, 40, 45–7, 49, 56, 61, 67, 157–8, 165
  see also Symbolism of law
  pursuits of law and 8, 25, 51–2, 151–3, 157–8
  beliefs in 49–51, 73, 155
Juxtaposition 44

Kafka, Franz 20
Kant, Immanuel 30, 136
Kelsen, Hans 27, 49–51, 63, 65, 74–5, 84–6, 94, 96, 104, 135, 137, 154, 165
Kerchove, Michel van de 64, 77, 86–8, 130, 133, 135
King Rex 167–9
Kingsbury, Benedict 179
Klabbers, Jan 10
Kramer, Matthew 24, 40, 42, 70–1, 74, 110, 120, 132, 147, 148, 169–73, 175–6, 178–80
Kuhn, Thomas 63–4, 123

Label (of law) 3, 8, 19, 27, 29–30, 38, 45, 47–9, 51
Lady Justice 38
Lagarde, Paul 157
Laissez-faire 44, 47–9, 57–9, 127, 152, 156–8, 160, 172
Lando, Ole 106, 108
Law
  and rhetoric 33–48, 53–4, 57–9, 68, 95–6, 156–9, 163–4, 166
  as a hurdle 38
  as a noetic unity 16–17
  as a political project, *see* Definitions (as political projects)
  as a qualified social normative system 39, 128–32, 134
  as beliefs 66–7
  as empowerment 38, 55

  as system 101–17, 128–32
  function of 104, 172, 174
    see also Orienting behavior; Self-directed action
  instrumentalizing other regulators 41, 147–8
  perceptions of 36–38
  preference for 40, 151–2
  scalability 18, 68–71, 171
  teaching 4, 48
  threshold, *see* Threshold of legality
  trivialization 49
  violence in characterization 14, 42
  vs a law 109–10
Law books 26
Law schools 48
Legal dignity 44
Legal intervention 43, 156–9
Legal materials 16
Legal monism 54, 79, 81, 147
Legal pluralism 43–4, 51–2, 54, 56, 58–9, 61, 81
  within international law 62
Legal positivism, *see* Positivism
Legal realism 115–16
  see also Holmes, Oliver Wendell
Legal reforms 53
Legal statism, *see* Positivism: classical
Legal systems 42, 101–17
  officials of 10, 24, 81, 84–7, 95–7, 110, 116, 122, 132–3, 170–1, 175–6, 178, 184
  see also Recognition (rule of)
Legitimacy 3, 13–14, 20–6, 30–1, 56, 62, 115, 140, 156, 160–6, 180
Lessig, Lessig 15, 147
Leviathan 75–6
Lex mercatoria 12, 19, 46, 82, 84, 96, 105–17, 125, 146, 154–5, 157, 177
Lex sportiva 154
Lexicography 35, 53
Liberal arbitration laws 47, 127, 152
Liberal democratic tradition 8
Libertarians 37
Linné, Carl von 53–4
Locke, John 25, 134
Logophobia 59
Lowenfeld, Andreas 106

Mafia 11, 28
Malinowksi, Bronislaw 103
Mann, FA 92
Market forces 41, 142–3, 147–8, 150
Market needs 58
Marmor, Andrei 75–6, 122
Marriage 53
McCormick, Neil 17, 165
Mediation 2, 142, 184
Menkel-Meadow, Carrie 177
Merry, Sally Engle 53
Metaphorical effect (of law) 41
Metaphysics 25, 30

Index

Meta-theory 5, 62
Michaels, Ralf 33, 52–4
Midas Principle 84–6, 94–6
Money 66
Monism, *see* Legal monism
Moral pluralism 164–6
Moral value of law 18, 20–1, 24–5, 29, 31, 37, 96, 165–6, 170
Morality
  and law, *see* Separability of law and morality
  inner morality of law, *see* Fuller, Lon
  morality of inner morality of law 170
Mnookin, Robert 1–3, 142
  see also Shadow of the law
Mugabe, Robert 26
Mussolini, Benito 60
Mustill, Michael 106, 108, 123, 157, 179

Nations 44, 50, 63, 76–7
Natural law 40, 114–15
  minimal contents of 102
Nazi law 40, 97
New York Convention of 1958 89–91, 93
Non-interference 43–4, 47–8, 50–1, 157
Non liquet 113
Normative autonomy 43–4, 126, 134–7, 152, 158

Obeying the law, *see* Authority of law; Orienting behavior
Oppetit, Bruno 123
Ordinariness (in law) 34, 36, 37, 45, 48
Organization 42
Orienting behavior 41–2, 46, 172, 180
  see also Law (function of); Self-directed action
Orwell, George 37
Ost, François 64, 77, 86–8, 130, 133, 135, 176
Overlaps 43, 50, 52
Oxford University Press 16

Pacta sunt servanda 2, 115
Paradigms 16, 154
  battle of candidates 4–5, 62–8
  definition of 63
Park, William 123, 126, 152, 159, 161
Parliament 26, 130–1
Pauwelyn, Joost 9–14, 20–3
Peace 38
  of Westphalia 44, 76
Pellet, Alain 44
Perrin, Jean-François 103
Persuasion (of legality) 34
Petrochilos, Georgios 93
Planning 42
Pluralism, *see* Legal pluralism; Moral pluralism
Poiesis 38
Police 26
Political doctrines 49–50
Political power 12–13, 54–6

Positivism (legal) 40, 73–80, 101–4, 116, 122
  classical 15, 46, 51, 116, 147, 153–4, 156
  normative 102–3
Pound, Roscoe 163
Precedents, *see* Arbitration (precedents)
Predictability 2, 17–20, 23, 46, 49, 127, 129, 165–84
  scalability of 17
Prisons 53
Private economic actors 46, 116, 157
Private international law, *see* International law (private)
Prost, Mario 61, 64, 66
Psychosocial approach 37
Putin, Vladimir 25
Pyramid, law as a 8, 63

Rawls, John 137, 147
Raz, Joseph 13, 15, 39, 43, 68, 74, 85–6, 132, 147
Reasons-for-action 26–30, 67, 147–8
  prudential 66
  moral 9, 31, 49, 65
Rechtsstaat 134
Recognition
  of arbitral awards, *see* Arbitration
  of stateless law by states 81–99
  rule of 10, 83–7, 94–7, 102, 105–11, 116, 120–50
  see also Reinstitutionalization
Regulatory backlash 48
Regulatory dominance 39
Regulatory reasonings 41
Reinstitutionalization 116, 129–37
Reisman, Michael 12–13, 18–19
Reliability, *see* Predictability
Retroactive lawmaking 19–20
Rex, *see* King Rex
Rhetoric, *see* Law (and rhetoric)
Rigaux, François 86–7, 135
Roberts, Simon 79, 146, 158
Robilant, Anna di 57–8, 157
Roman law 8
Romano, Cesare 121
Romano, Santi 60–2, 66, 86–8, 159
Ross, Alf 165
Rousseau, Charles 135
Rule of law 17, 24–6, 29, 37, 42, 134, 158, 162, 165–71, 178, 182, 184
Rules
  pedigree of 11, 103–4, 109–10
  of recognition, *see* Recognition
Russian Revolution 55–6

Sale of goods 115
Sanctions, *see* Coercive powers
Sanders, Pieter 91–2
Scepter of legality 42, 55, 57
Schütz, Alfred 77

Scientific disciplines, *see* Kuhn, Thomas
Searle, John 66
Secondary rules 8, 10, 42, 83–6, 94–7, 105–11, 116, 119, 120–50
  see also Recognition (rule of)
Self-directed action 2, 20, 47, 58, 169, 171–3
  see also Predictability; Law (function of)
Self-regulation 58, 127
Semantics 35, 155
Separability of law and morality 40, 51, 101–3, 115, 157–8
Sexuality 53
Shadow of the law 142, 145–6
Shakespeare 8, 38
Shapiro, Scott 8–9, 23, 26–8, 35, 41, 67
Shklar, Judith 25, 162
Slaughter, Anne-Marie 121
Smoking 133–4
Sociability 78
Social autonomy 43–4
Social class 55–7
Social control 37, 42, 55–7, 59
Social field 43
Social normative system 39–40, 120, 128, 132, 134
Social norms 41, 53, 65, 103–4, 116, 120–6, 132, 140–2
Socialism 57
Sociality 55–7
  see also Gurvitch, Georges
Sociology, of law 15, 55–7
Soft law 18–19, 68
Sousa Santos, Boaventura de 43–4, 157
Sovereignty 44, 50–1, 79, 152
Spontaneous law, see Gurvitch, Georges
Sports arbitration vii, 44, 126, 152–4, 160, 177, 179
Stare decisis, *see* Arbitration (precedents)
State
  collapse 59
  state law as paradigmatic instance of law 41, 44, 49, 71, 76, 79
  system 50
Statelessness 41
Statism, *see* Positivism: classical
Stewart, Leigh 121
Students 48, 66
Superiority of law 13–14, 39, 41, 43
Supremacy of law 43, 73–80

Symbolism of law 38, 44, 157–8
Symbols 25, 41, 48, 56

Tamanaha, Brian 25, 40, 103, 165–6
Tarello, Giovanni 61
Terris, Daniel 121
Territory 43, 50, 62, 73, 75–9
Teubner, Gunther 127
Thirty Years' War 44, 49–50
Threshold of legality 71
Thompson, EP 25
Time 70
Toope, Stephen 156
Trademarks, *see* ICANN
Tschanz, Pierre-Yves 108
Tyranny 40

Ubi societas, ibi ius 120, 131
UDRP, *see* ICANN
UNCITRAL
  ad hoc arbitration 179
  Model Law on Arbitration 112, 123
Unequivocalness 59, 66
UNIDROIT Principles 116–17, 124
Unity 59, 68

Validity of theories 36–7
Vengeance 38
Virilio, Paul 78

Waldron, James 82–3, 102–3
Weber, Max 122, 136
Western political tradition 25
Westphalian
  order 43
  Treaties 44, 49–50
Wittgenstein, Ludwig 68
Wolfers, Arnold 44
Wolff, Robert Paul 28–9
Women 53
Working class 55–7
World Bank 25
World Wars 50, 55, 60, 97
Worldviews 53
WTO law 62

Zimbabwe 26
Zola, Emile 55
Zumbansen, Peer 5, 58, 65, 143